T.L.S.

ESSAYS AND REVIEWS FROM
The Times Literary Supplement · 1968

7

T.L.S.

ESSAYS AND REVIEWS FROM

The Times Literary Supplement · 1968

7

London
OXFORD UNIVERSITY PRESS
NEW YORK   TORONTO
1969

Oxford University Press, Ely House, London W.1

GLASGOW NEW YORK TORONTO MELBOURNE WELLINGTON
CAPE TOWN SALISBURY IBADAN NAIROBI LUSAKA ADDIS ABABA
BOMBAY CALCUTTA MADRAS KARACHI LAHORE DACCA
KUALA LUMPUR SINGAPORE HONG KONG TOKYO

Printed in Great Britain by
Alden & Mowbray Ltd
at the Alden Press, Oxford

CONTENTS

NOTE

T.L.S. 7 is a selection of some of the most interesting contributions to last year's *Times Literary Supplement*. We hope that it provides not just an accurate and useful reflection of the journal's general character but also an informative account of the year's most stimulating publications. 1968 was a good year for memoirs—V. S. Pritchett, Harold Nicolson, Norman Podhoretz, André Malraux—and for novels, with new work from Iris Murdoch, Lawrence Durrell, Norman Mailer, and John Updike. It was also the year in which Marianne Moore and Theodore Roethke had collected English editions of their poems; in which George Orwell had a near-definitive collection of his letters and his journalism and Oswald Mosley had a kind welcome (though not from the *T.L.S.*) for his autobiography. These are just a few of the topics discussed in the following pages. There is also a section on 'The Little Magazine' taken from one of the many special issues published by the *T.L.S.* during 1968.

I

THE ABC OF X

GEORGE F. KENNAN'S FOREIGN POLICY

IN JULY, 1947, an article appeared in that admirable American periodical *Foreign Affairs*, entitled 'The Sources of Soviet Conduct'. It was signed simply 'X'. But its doctrine, understood or misunderstood, was cogently stated and appeared highly relevant to a nation discovering, with bewilderment and increasing anger, that not only does complete victory not solve all problems, but that victory does not keep. And immediately the hunt was up. Who was X? It was the astute Mr. Arthur Krock of *The New York Times* who remembered another version of the article which had been shown to him by Mr. James Forrestal, the first Secretary of Defence of the United States, and so identified X. He was George Kennan, a highly esteemed second echelon member of the Foreign Service of the United States, an expert on Russia and a pioneer in what is now believed to be the science of Kremlinology.

*   *   *

From the moment of the publication of the article, Mr. Kennan moved out of the shadow into the limelight, a good deal to the annoyance of the Secretary of State, General George Marshall. But when it was explained to General Marshall that the article had been passed by the appropriate censoring committee of the Department of State the General, with characteristic justice, withheld all marks of disapproval.

Like other men who have awoken to find themselves famous, Mr. Kennan had soon to reflect on the dangers of fame and how soon it becomes mere notoriety. The article preached the famous doctrine of 'containment' but, by that potent word, Mr. Kennan did not mean an automatic military confrontation of Soviet power wherever it seemed to be pushing against what was now being called 'the free

---

GEORGE F. KENNAN: *Memoirs, 1925–1950*. 583 pp. Hutchinson £3 5s.

world'. He did not think that military confrontation was likely, much less necessary. He had no doubt that, basically, the Soviet power was hostile to the policy of the United States and he had no patience with the day-dreamers who thought that the real and permanent problems of power, given by history, geography, doctrine, could be charmed away by invoking the power of the infant United Nations or by evoking memories of the victorious partnership in arms in the 'anti-Fascist War'. For the United States, as for Russia, the war that had just ended was a 'great patriotic war' fought, no doubt, in favour of ethical principles which, even on the Russian side, were far superior to the pathological ideology of the Third Reich. In spite of a great economy of truth in reporting about Russia and such boldly mendacious propaganda as the film *Mission to Moscow* (which had, for its hero, Mr. Joseph Davies whom F. D. R. had, to the horror of the professionals in the Moscow embassy, sent as ambassador to Stalin), Mr. Kennan had long made up his mind that the Soviet Union was not (one could say *could* not be) 'a fit ally, actual or potential, for this country'. This opinion, formed in 1933, Mr. Kennan had seen no reason to change after years of service in war-time Moscow, and the new 'hard' doctrine was launched at a moment when the American public, with characteristic versatility, was turning from toasting 'Joe for President' to the fevered state which another Joe, Senator McCarthy—and other formally more respectable American leaders—were soon to rouse to dangerous hysteria.

Mr. Kennan tells us that he was one of the comparatively few experts on Russia who had never swallowed the Marxist line or drug. He had never believed that a new birth of freedom had taken place in Russia, and, consequently, he had not to repent his own credulity and make of that past credulity a new credential on the principle that 'Only those who brave its perils comprehend its mystery'. As X he was not preaching a crusade, not even 'killing Stalin with his mouth', as so many Americans a little later, above all John Foster Dulles, were to do. There *were* Russian interests that, in the traditional politics of power, were legitimate and which the United States would be foolish to thwart. There were many wrongs that could not be undone. There were marginal areas where the two superpowers clashed or, at any rate, encountered each other. That was the frontier where cool-headed diplomacy was likely to be useful.

It should be assumed that the basic principle of the rulers in the Kremlin was the maintenance and, if possible, the extension of the power of the Russian state. An ideological weapon of some potency, the international Communist movement was useful to the Soviet government (strong Communist parties in France and Italy were more useful to the Soviet Government than a Russian occupation on the model of the German occupation would have been). But, basically, the power of the Soviet Government was the power of Russia and the aims of Soviet Russia had more in common with the traditional aims of Tsarist policy than with the Utopia of Lenin's *State and Revolution*.

*   *   *

The lesson was not learnt. One of Mr. Kennan's objects had been to undo, as far as possible, the *bourrage de crâne* which had been inflicted on the American (and British) peoples during the war, and in that work of confusion the honest and not so honest fellow-travellers were far more effective agents than the open Communists. But the lesson taught by X was very imperfectly learnt. Mr. Walter Lippmann misunderstood the article as a cry for general and unlimited resistance to Soviet aggression everywhere. In the language of today, Mr. Kennan had provided, so they thought, the Hawks with a most effective propaganda tool and the reputation of being a fanatical crusader was not lost till it was replaced, in the mind of John Foster Dulles, long before he was Secretary of State, with the belief that Mr. Kennan was 'soft on Communism', representative of those doctrinaires who had 'lost' China and a great part of Europe. To other less sophisticated alarmists, Mr. Kennan, like so many other agents of American foreign policy, was a semi-traitor till the final madness of the John Birch society was to make all such charges meaningless; the United States was asserted to be as full of conscious traitors in its ruling establishment as the Soviet Union had been proven to be in the great prewar purges.

What manner of man could evoke such different responses so quickly? George Kennan is a kinsman and namesake of the George Kennan who wrote an exposure of the Siberian convict system which had (though the younger George Kennan does not mention this) the effect of producing reforms, an achievement inconceivable a generation later when enlightened foreign commentators were stressing the educational effects of working on the White Sea Canal.

Coming from a prosperous, cultivated, deeply-rooted Middle-Western family, young George Kennan went to Princeton (not long after Scott Fitzgerald) and entered the American Foreign Service when it was being professionalized and reorganized under the Rogers Act, and under the pressure of a public opinion that was, it thought, tired of 'cookie-pushers' in striped pants, but not yet impatient enough of ambassadors like Mr. Davies whose main qualification was having made an extremely rich marriage into soup; the equivalent in English politics and society is marrying into beer, like 'Chips' Channon.

The new recruits to what had been mainly a combination of rich playboys, climbing snobs, more or less competent politicians and a large number of 'deserving Democrats' or 'Republicans' are admirably recounted here. The young men like Mr. Kennan and 'Chip' Bohlen took their training as seriously as did the soldier pupils of George Marshall. And although his first service was in Germany, the younger George Kennan began to study not only Russian but Russia—and not only Soviet Russia.

That he studied Russian and Russia with great profit his whole career testifies. His deep admiration not only for the Russian language but for the Russian people shines out and invests his discussion of Russian government and institutions with a tragic interest. Was there in Russian history a built-in tragedy? Mr. Kennan saw and admired many of the good qualities of the Germans but he seems (he is not explicit) to see Hitler as a diabolical aberration, while Stalin may well have been the heir of Ivan the Terrible and Peter the Great. (It must also be said that despite the citation of brave and even heroic German enemies of the regime, Mr. Kennan does not seem to have absorbed so much of the German spirit or to be so committed in his interest in Germany as he was committed to Russia. Birth in Milwaukee, the most German of American cities, had perhaps bred too much familiarity?)

*　　　*　　　*

And here we come to a possible effect of so profound an immersion in foreign cultures. (Mr. Kennan married a Norwegian girl.) The 1920s in America was, for some, the 'era of beautiful nonsense'; the 1930s was the grim age when the bills came in. Scott Fitzgerald's Princeton had vanished; no one saw that better than Scott Fitzgerald; his fellow-Princetonian and Middle-Westerner, whose family had suffered near ruin in the traumatic 'Depression', did not much like what survived in his native land any more than he had liked the world of *The Great Gatsby* by experience or reading. The account of how Mr. Kennan saw his own country when he came back from his long pilgrimage abroad (pilgrimage rather than exile) recalls, and is perhaps meant to recall, the disillusionment of Henry Adams when he returned to America after the Civil War. This was a world that neither Adams nor Mr. Kennan had made or liked. And each looked back to a happier American past, to the Quincy of the early chapters of *The Education*, to the idyllic Wisconsin countryside recollected in profoundly foreign lands. Reading the brilliantly evocative passages (fully worthy of comparison with the corresponding parts of *The Education*), one has the impression that Mr. Kennan was becoming, like Adams, what the French used to call an 'émigré à l'intérieur'. He sees the empty country roads, with the little animals killed by the careless and pointlessly fleeing motorists. There is no tolerable life in the small towns (many of which were in fact dying).

He notes the lack of life, the young men and girls shooting off in cars probably to petting parties or to drive-in movies, if they can be distinguished (a development of his argument that one may dare to supply). He notes that there is no life even in the saloons. The slip is revealing. The promise of 1933 had been kept, there had been no return to the old-fashioned saloon; there were cafés, pubs, lounges, but no saloons. Then going off *à la recherche du temps perdu*, Mr. Kennan surely idealizes his Combray? There was Ed Howe's *Country Town*; there had recently been Sinclair Lewis's *Main Street*. Ruth Suckow's Iowa was a little too much like Goldsmith's Sweet Auburn. And Willa Cather was getting ready to leave her Nebraska for the stabler and more archaic societies of New Mexico and New France. And some of the troubles that befell Mr. Kennan in his official career may have come from his distance from normal American reactions, though he also owed to this distance a great deal of that sad lucidity that was too often little appreciated, but which made him sometimes unjust to men who were more deeply involved in the dust that goes with the palm in America. It was and is salutary to have a farm in Pennsylvania and to spend the weekends there away from the noise, fumes and follies of Washington. But officials and politicians who have to act sometimes without enough reflection know that great events happen at weekends (as Mr.

Kennan discovered on one occasion), and that few active politicians can assume the role of Goethe's Pope:

> Der hohe Sinn des Papsts,
> Ersieht das Kleine klein, das Grosse gross.

That this view from the mountain has great advantages is most certainly true. Some American reviews of Mr. Kennan's fascinating and important *Memoirs* have given the impression of its saying repeatedly: 'I told you so'. This is most unjust. Mr. Kennan is generous to men like Mr. Dean Acheson. He is grateful to the senior diplomatic servants of the United States like Alexander Kirk who taught him so much and to outsiders like Mr. Harriman, who were admirable and effective chiefs even if they did not take the claims of the Foreign Service as highly as Mr. Kennan does or did.

*　　*　　*

For Mr. Kennan has an ideal of diplomacy that is almost too pure and good for human nature's daily food. This not only makes him exaggerate the importance of what diplomacy or even foreign policy can do, but also ignore the real world in which diplomats, even great diplomats, have to work. Even if professional diplomats have a razor, they have to cut stones with it. It is part of Mr. Kennan's overestimation of what diplomacy can do and underestimation of the hardness of the material that diplomacy and diplomats have to work with, or of the world in which they have to work, that he should be both astonished and unjust to Secretaries of State like General Marshall and Mr. Dean Acheson who tried to conciliate or disarm politicians like Senator Vandenberg. Mr. Kennan notes that Senator Vandenberg was not an agent of a foreign power but a servant of the United States like Mr. Acheson and Mr. Kennan. Maybe, but the senior Republican member of the Foreign Relations Committee was an independent power in the service of the United States who, in the real world of Washington, *had* to be negotiated with.

The Senate was intended to be a 'censorial' body, intended to deny any transfer to the infant nation of 'le secret du roi'. If anyone was to blame for this state of affairs, it was James Madison. But even in bodies not blessed with the American constitutional system this separation of foreign from domestic policy is seldom achieved. It has been noted that French Foreign Ministers have suffered from delusions when they found themselves behind 'le bureau de Monsieur de Vergennes'. We may assume that M. Couve de Murville does not see himself as a new Vergennes, still less a new Richelieu. But we can also be sure that the President of the French Republic does not control the actions of M. Couve de Murville with no regard to internal politics. And even the most highly professionalized government departments, freest from mere democratic temptations, do not always work like the most finely adjusted machinery. Professor Norman Rich has shown how far from frictionless was Bismarck's Foreign Office and, to quote a more prestigious institution, the most brilliant officer of the Great General Staff in the First World War, General Max Hoffmann, wrote that when any colleague promised him 'Nibelungtroth', he knew he was going to be stabbed in the back.

The same unwillingness to accept the facts of life in this far from perfect world is shown in Mr. Kennan's resentment at the Treasury butting into negotiations that, he thinks, should have been left to the Department of State. But then negotiations involving great sums of money (and so involving close congressional supervision) necessarily involve the Treasury, as they do and did in England. That the Secretary of the Treasury of the United States of the time, Mr. John Snyder, was not one of the most worthy successors of Alexander Hamilton or Albert Gallatin is true. But Mr. Kennan is wrong in thinking that President Truman had to conciliate Mr. Snyder for political reasons. Mr. Snyder had no more political 'clout', to use the current Washington phrase, than has Mr. Patrick Gordon Walker; indeed, if it can be believed, he had less. But he was a close friend of Mr. Truman, and in the Court of the White House that is what matters. Obviously, Mr. Kennan needs no reminder of Chancellor Oxienstierna's advice to his son to notice with how little wisdom the world is ruled. But whereas the Chancellor thought that this would remain true under any regime, Mr. Kennan seems to think that by education, research, planning, 'pure' policy can be distilled. All these things help; they are indispensable for the working of any satisfactory foreign policy, but they are not the one thing necessary, which is wisdom, and wisdom has to be timely as well as wise. The 'tact des choses possibles' was what the greatest modern diplomatic technician wanted of his servants, but Cavour knew that inside a narrow field of free action there was need for flair, *doigté*, daring— and luck. Mr. Kennan is perhaps most American in thinking that these sad truths can be abolished or reduced to minor obstacles. He is in voluntary exile at Princeton but will there ever be a diplomatic

'Guardian' class even if the lessons of the sad present are learnt?
There may be, but at the risk of being unjust one may have some
suspicion that Mr. Kennan is not immune to the great American
heresy, that what must be learnt can necessarily be taught.
What Mr. Kennan learnt (and it was a great deal) he learnt himself.
This made him an admirable reporter and often a sagacious coun-
sellor (although he candidly admits how much of his past advice he
thinks was wrong). And he equally candidly tells us how little
enamoured of the modern world he was and is.

For Mr. Kennan is not only an 'émigré à l'intérieur' of his country,
but also an émigré from his century. His tone recalls the famous
Russian story of the resident of Leningrad who had to fill up a census
form after the last war. 'Where were you born?' 'Petersburg.'
'Where were you educated?' 'Petrograd.' 'Where do you live?'
'Leningrad.' 'Where do you want to live?' 'Petersburg.' With Mr.
Kennan, one may guess, it would be Goethe's Weimar or Mr.
Jefferson's Virginia. Nice work if you can get it, if one reflects all the
time how unrepresentative a minister in the Saxon duchies Herr von
Goethe was and how much a sport Mr. Jefferson was in Mr. Jeffer-
son's Virginia.

*   *   *

Of course, Mr. Kennan is not naively nostalgic like a modern
Jacobite (or disillusioned Fabian). He looks back on political
structures that have got a bad name or a bad press and often not
only assesses them more kindly than do orthodox 'liberal' critics,
but surveys some admired examples of progress with a very sceptical
eye. Noting a great many imperfections in Masaryk's Czechoslovakia
and comparing it, not totally to its advantage, with the Habsburg
Kingdom of Bohemia, he is puzzled at the ease with which the
fable of the only real democracy among the Succession States was
sold. That there was a great deal to be said for the Bohemia of
Franz-Josef is true. It was not economically exploited and its
industrial development was actually forced on by imperial policy
(something of the same might be said of the forced draft development
of cities like Lodz in Russian Poland). The great baroque city of
Prague was, like Dublin, a conqueror's capital. The greatest name
associated with Prague is that of a Salzburger, Wolfgang Amadeus
Chrysostomos Mozart, who owed more to Prague than to Vienna.
Why was the destruction of this political achievement welcomed by

enlightened opinion? Here Mr. Kennan reveals, so one may think, the limitations even of a sophisticated 'Wasp' upbringing. He does not remember or perhaps never knew how effectively the Protestant (and Slovak) Masaryk played on Anglo-Saxon dislike of Giant Pope. The Protestant Czechs and many of the Catholic Czechs wanted to undo the Battle of the White Mountain, as Irish Catholics wanted to undo the Battle of the Boyne. But English-speaking Protestants wanted to renew the work of John Hus; many assumed that Bohemia could be redeemed from Rome. There was, after all, a brief period when American Methodists wanted to build a vast ecclesiastical complex on the Janiculum overshadowing the palaces and temples of the Pope who was believed to be on the way out.

Mr. Kennan, of course, had some of the illusions of American Methodists and of *The Daily News*. He was born in Milwaukee, a city whose 'ethnic' composition has moved from being mainly German (Protestant and Catholic) to being largely Polish and so Catholic. But this does not seem to have inspired him with much curiosity. He believes that Islam was and is an apparently unbreakable barrier to Soviet policies and ideology. But what of Rome? When spending years in Riga, Mr. Kennan seems never to have visited the one Catholic Baltic state, Lithuania. He seems to have paid comparatively little attention to Poland at that time. Indeed, his view of Poland was odd. In an ambiguous phrase, he seems to regret that Poland reappeared in 1919. But how could this have been prevented (except by a Soviet conquest) after the German and Austrian governments had launched a 'Kingdom of Poland' in 1916 when they ruled most of 'Congress Poland'? In what way could the Dual Monarchy have been preserved when Germany was defeated? And is there not evidence that the Magyar rulers of the Crown Lands of St. Stephen, even in the last months of 1918, outdid the Bourbons in learning nothing? In the spirit of the General of the Jesuits who in the eighteenth century said the Order would be as it had been or would not be, the rulers of the Kingdom of St. Stephen committed suicide. Of course, if the Germans had been wiser in 1917, if they had not brought in the New World to undo the balance of the Old, there could have been peace and any peace then would have meant a German victory. One can argue that a German victory would have been better than the collapse of the new order in 1939 (or 1936). But Mr. A. J. P. Taylor has argued, very powerfully, that no government could have accepted a peace of compromise or a

B

'peace without victory'. Too much had been promised, too much had been suffered. Only a great internal revolution (as in Russia) or a total defeat (as among the Central Powers) could stop the war. The Imperial and Royal garrison of Tirana, parading on New Year's Day in 1919, in the name of the Emperor-King, already in exile, was a truly Austrian requiem march for the death 'of the imperial eagle of the House of Austria' as Gibbon put it.

Mr. Kennan is more interesting and more impressive when he argues later might-have-beens. Starting from his premise that the Soviet government was not in any real sense an ally (not even a strange ally as General Deane called it), Mr. Kennan would have had the western powers, that is the United States and, in a weaker role, the wiser but less powerful Britain, pursue their own interests, would have accepted the truth that no appeal to gratitude, to common suffering, to the comradeship of arms would have any effect on Russian policy. Attempts by Roosevelt to cajole Stalin, as he had cajoled so many Senators and Governors, was worse than wasted effort. It was throwing dust in one's own eyes. That American (or Rooseveltian) credulity about Russia was in its political effects disastrous is hardly to be doubted. But Mr. Kennan underestimates the political difficulties both of Roosevelt and Churchill—especially Churchill. True, the Russians fought and won at Stalingrad entirely for their own aims, but Stalingrad was seen, in Britain at any rate, as the first real break in the clouds. Popular instinct was right and it had to be allowed for. Not in the high moralistic fashion of Romain Rolland, Mr. Kennan is yet curiously 'above the battle'. A *guerre en dentelles* was no longer possible. Carnot had seen to that. At the best, the era of Oxienstierna had returned. (Many would argue that this is being unjust to the age of the Thirty Years' War.) Would it have been possible for Churchill or Roosevelt to have adopted the policy that Mr. Kennan seems to recommend, not to aid Russia in the invasion of Germany, to take for their own benefit the advice that Kutuzov gave Alexander I when the French had fled from Russian soil? Would the people of London, tense under the rain of V1 and V2, have accepted such a cold-blooded policy that might have suited the Prussia of Frederick (or, as a Prussian might have said, of the England of George III)? It is highly doubtful.

That the political direction of the war under F. D. R. was increasingly muddled is true. That the pushing of the new Polish frontiers so far west would (as a Pole deeply involved in the negotiations noted in despair) make real peace between Poland and Germany impossible, and that this was one of Stalin's motives, is at least highly probable. That East Prussia was raped, as if it had been a German state in the early seventeenth century or like Munster in the early years of the reign of Queen Elizabeth I (these examples are not Mr. Kennan's), is true: modern war has become hell beyond the dreams of General Sherman.

One last example of Mr. Kennan's obviously most deeply-rooted horror of war is his criticisms of the Nuremberg trials. There was and is something obscene at the sight of a tribunal making new international law when that law condemned some members of the Court as much as it condemned Göring or Ribbentrop. But what alternative was there? An eminent American scholar, at the time an important American official, opposed in private the trials and recommended in true American fashion six months of sanctioned lynching bees. Can anyone seriously believe that the leaders and agents of a government which, far more than the feeble Bourbons of Naples, was 'the negation of God erected into a system of government' would have been allowed to sink quietly into the background? No one who has studied or saw the *épuration* in France in 1944–45 can doubt that a spontaneous *Vehmgericht* would have sprung up, with rough justice on a scale that would have quite avoided problems like those presented by the Eichmann trial many years later. Perhaps a sanctioned series of St. Bartholomew's Nights might have been the best answer. But Mr. Kennan does not suggest any solution. In what was nominally a Christian continent no doubt the text that asserts that 'vengeance is mine' should have been acted on, but a more probable slogan, if no legal action had been taken, would have been that of the Scottish Covenanters of Kilsyth: 'Jesus and No Quarter'.

If this book is open to criticism it is yet one of the most remarkable contributions to the history of the last war—and the 'entre deux-guerres'—that has been published. Mr. Kennan is not intimidated by any of Bacon's Idols. (Has he not very recently defied enlightened opinion by denouncing demonstrating and politically-minded American students in terms that might seem excessive to Mr. Muggeridge?) His account of the outrageous meanness of the State Department will not be welcomed in Foggy Bottom. And few commentators have been less moved by naive or even sophisticated American nationalism. The limitations on American power are great and should be great. The American people has no mission, no duty, no capacity to save the world. Officially, the most important part of Mr. Kennan's career will be dealt with in the next volume, but at a time when the American people are angry, bewildered, fearful, these reflections and the often brilliant narrative, if only by asking questions about the moralistic premises of American policy, fully justify the existence of the Institute for Advanced Study, Princeton, where this book was written.

2

RIGHT AND LEFT

(a) OSWALD MOSLEY

NO TWENTIETH-CENTURY British politician has been hated as much as Sir Oswald Mosley. Leader of a blackshirted 'army' in the 1930s, he brought Fascism to our own doorsteps. Those who lived through that wretched period, without falling under his spell, can never forget the squalid beastliness of the movement he created and sustained. How dangerous his British version of Fascism really was will continue to be debated by historians. The Communists, for reasons of their own, chose to exaggerate its significance; but, whatever Mosley's own intentions may have been, there can be little doubt that his followers constituted a potential menace to Britain's security when the war with Germany broke out in 1939, and that the government of that time, although a poor thing, did well to put both them and their leader behind bars or barbed wire. Since then, the reconstituted Fascist movement has been more of a nuisance than a menace, but, currently engaged as it is in exacerbating an already serious racial situation, it still cannot be safely disregarded.

The leader himself, seventy-one years of age, has now chosen to publish a lengthy and turgid apologia. In the approved manner of the 'radical right', he presents himself as a super-patriot whose whole career has been devoted to rescuing Britain from the clutches of the incompetent and supine politicians who have ruined the two major political parties and brought the country itself to the verge of

---

(a) OSWALD MOSLEY: *My Life*. 521 pp. Nelson. £3 10s.

(b) ERNESTO 'CHE' GUEVARA: *Bolivian Diary*. Translated by Carlos P. Hanson and Andrew Sinclair. Introduction by Fidel Castro. 160 pp. Cape/Lorrimer. 25s. (Paperback, 12s. 6d.).

DANIEL JAMES: *The Complete Bolivian Diaries of Ché Guevara and other Captured Documents*. 330 pp. Allen and Unwin. £2 2s.

LEO HUBERMAN and PAUL M. SWEEZY (Editors): *Régis Debray and the Latin American Revolution*. 138 pp. Monthly Review Press. £2 5s.

RAMÓN EDUARDO RUÍZ: *Cuba. The Making of a Revolution*. 189 pp. University of Massachusetts Press. $6.00.

disaster. He has never, he assures us, been either an anti-semite or a racialist. He has always loved peace and consistently pursued it, regardless of the unpopularity his pacificatory efforts have brought him. As a good 'European' patriot as well as a British one, his aim has been to defend a beloved civilization against the menace of Bolshevism and to prevent its more subtle subversion by transatlantic influences. Whatever one may think of this story, one must admit that he has chosen just the right time to tell it.

No well-informed person who has followed his career, however, can accept this version of the Mosley Mission. The special pleading is all too obvious, the rhetoric synthetic, the complaint of persistent 'misunderstanding' pathetically unconvincing. Those who have formed, and still form, the hard core of his movement are not likely to read, still less to understand, this high-flown stuff; the politically sophisticated will find it not only difficult to stomach but unnecessary to refute; for refutation can be directed only to 'believers' beyond the reach of rational argument.

Strangely enough, one begins to feel some degree of pity for this extraordinary demagogue whose career now lies in such irretrievable ruin. The old man, whose personal contribution to the various causes he has espoused is now almost certainly at an end, has taken refuge in fighting his battles all over again, on paper. 'I withdrew from party warfare when I began to write this book', he says, 'and the Union Movement has since been conducted by a Directory of five members. . . . I detached myself from party politics in order to advocate a policy and action which is beyond party.' He then produces a lot of familiar froth about 'a temporary union of the whole people for national action as in time of war' which he himself can hardly find convincing.

There is an element of tragedy as well as farce in a career which ends thus; for one must never forget that the man who now writes an autobiography to remind us of his continued existence was once the brightest of stars in the Labour Party's galaxy of young talent. Commentators as various as Mr. Malcolm Muggeridge, Lord Boothby, and Mr. R. H. S. Crossman have said, with truth, that he could easily have become Prime Minister. This tempting opportunity, which he knew to be within his grasp, he deliberately threw away when he resigned his ministerial office in the Labour Government of 1929–1931, first to form the so-called 'New Party', which never got off the ground, then to present himself to a sceptical and

predominantly hostile public as the British version of Benito Mussolini. Why on earth did he do it? The answer lies partly in character
and partly in circumstance.

His resignation from the Labour Government was certainly the
most honourable political act he has ever performed. Given the task
of assisting the grotesquely ignorant J. H. Thomas in the search for a
cure for unemployment, Mosley came up with proposals which Mr.
A. J. P. Taylor has described, with only slight exaggeration, as
offering 'a blue-print for most of the constructive advances in economic thinking to the present day'. Keynesian in inspiration, these
shocked the orthodox and enthused the rebellious in all the parties.
Thomas, however, did not even make the effort to understand them;
Snowden, the Chancellor of the Exchequer, had become the apostle
of a rigid financial 'rectitude'; and the leader of the Labour triumvirate,
James Ramsay MacDonald, had reached the stage where social
ambition combined with mental woolliness to disable him from
taking any initiative that appeared to be even remotely inspired by
distinctively socialist thinking. Quite rightly, Mosley resigned. Had
he bided his time, he could have made a tremendous come-back, as
the only minister to emerge from the 1931 debacle with a not only
untarnished but actually enhanced reputation. He received a mighty
ovation from the 1930 Labour Party Conference, which defeated his
proposals by only the narrowest of card votes. This was his finest
hour. Never again did he enjoy a popular following remotely comparable in size and enthusiasm.

That he threw it all away was partly due to a miscalculation which
he was persistently to repeat in the later stages of his career. Convinced that only mass unemployment would move the British people
to decisive political action, he believed that his hour as a charismatic
leader had arrived. He underestimated both the patience of his
compatriots and the skill of those older and more experienced politicians whose pusillanimity and opportunism seemed to him so con-
temptible. Throughout the economic crisis, the power of the party
machines remained intact. The lone wolf, for all the sharpness of his
tongue and ferocity of his bite, was ostracized and driven out of the
fold.

First his respectable friends abandoned him, by resigning from the
'New Party' as its leader's Fascist inclinations became more overt and
pronounced; then, left almost on his own, he turned for support to
wolves indeed—the blackshirted toughs whom he still praises as

vigorous, clean-living young patriots. Thus the irrevocable step was taken. Once he had declared himself a Fascist there was no way back. Like the cruder kind of Marxist revolutionary, he had to place his faith in the 'inevitability' of another—and presumably even worse—economic crisis, as a means of teaching the British people the stern lesson they had failed to learn the first time. Yet so flimsy was his organization, behind its façade of disciplined violence, that the mere banning of political uniforms by the Public Order Act of 1936 was sufficient to arrest its progress. This, of course, he denies; but he nevertheless admits that the British Union of Fascists became faced with serious financial difficulties in the later 1930s and displays a remarkable coyness about giving information about the number of its paid-up members, during this or any other period.

So much for circumstances. That he reacted to them as he did is to be explained by certain personal characteristics which, recessive in the 1920s, become dominant in the subsequent period. During the heyday of his popularity as Labour's most brilliant recruit from the Tories (via a period of service in the House of Commons as an Independent), Beatrice Webb, with that positively feline intuition she sometimes displayed, wrote of him: 'So much perfection argues rottenness somewhere.' Mr. Kingsley Martin, with the advantage of hindsight, describes him at that time as 'clever, arrogant, handsome, impatient, rich, endlessly ambitious and, above all, wilful'. His cleverness enabled him to compose the Mosley Manifesto. His arrogance, which he continues to display on almost every page of *My Life*, led him to believe, like the elder Pitt, although with far less justification, that he could save England and no one else could. Impatience and wilfulness made it essential to him that Operation Salvation should be undertaken immediately, as a military-type exercise under his own unchallenged personal leadership. To it he could bring his considerable wealth, his social connexions (about which *My Life* is fully informative), his spellbinding oratory and his organizational ability. Self-consciously donning the mantle of Julius Caesar, he confidently set foot on the path that was to lead first to prison and finally to self-imposed semi-exile in the absurdly-named Temple de la Gloire at Orsay. Ambition had overreached itself.

His psychological conditioning for such a career is well illustrated in the earlier chapters of this book, in which he tells the story of his youth and early manhood. This narrative, inconveniently but sometimes revealingly punctuated with embarrassingly jejune reflections of a 'philosophical' sort, shows us a young lord of the earth, much given to 'manly' sports of the more individualist kind, such as boxing and fencing, impatient of restraint, and occasionally insensitively crude and violent in behaviour. During the First World War he served with gallantry and distinction in the Royal Flying Corps, a service suited to his temperament.

These not unfamiliar traits, of course, are by no means characteristic of the potential Fascist leader. Indeed, an aristocratic manner, particularly when combined with inherited wealth, may well be a disability, since it tends to inhibit the successful adoption of 'man of the people' poses of the kind that were the stock-in-trade of the lowly-born Hitler or Mussolini. Top-drawer attitudes lend themselves more readily to the 'boiled-shirted' than to the black-shirted type of Fascism, and the former could have claimed Sir Oswald, but for two additional qualities he discovered in himself: a mind that was far above the average in originality, and a capacity for oratory that put him well in the class of Lloyd George or Aneurin Bevan. Such talents, combined with arrogance and impatience, proved his undoing.

Once he had made the disreputable 'ideology' of Fascism his own, the keen intelligence that had made him such an asset to the Labour movement inevitably became blunted. Apparently convinced by his own demagogic utterances, he ceased to be capable of conducting any public discourse in normal rational terms—although everyone who knew him conceded that in private conversation his famous 'charm' remained unimpaired. The vulgarity that was never far below the surface of his character received corresponding accentuation. *My Life* shows that, despite a certain mellowing of outlook, it is still there. He tells stories of Hitler (who attended his second, Berlin-located wedding) and Mussolini (whom he visited frequently up to 1936) to show what good-humoured fellows they really were. One of the quoted quips from Mussolini's repertoire of barrack-room 'humour' is so nasty that only a reader as 'manly' as Sir Oswald himself could possibly appreciate its side-splitting qualities.

To his credit, he deplores Hitler's massacre of the Jews; but even this most atrocious of all the Nazi dictator's crimes, which he condemns as 'a breach of the supreme moral law', cannot be mentioned without reference to mitigating circumstances,

the agony of defeat, his [Hitler's] fixed belief that the Jews were responsible for the war, the fact that Germans were dying and starving and that the Jews suspected of relentless enmity to the state had to be guarded and fed.

About Hitler's leading accomplices there is not one word of condemnation. Goebbels, 'distinguished in public by his qualities as an orator and master of mass propaganda', is said to have had 'in private life an almost exaggerated sense of humour'; Göring, we are told, 'would have been far more at home than most foreigners in all the varied social and sporting occasions of English life, the ex-service clubs and institutions above all, but also the horse show, the football final, the pub, and even the drawing room'. Indeed, this droll and earthy character 'would laugh at himself in a way which would make particular appeal to the English people if translated into our national terms by sensitive intelligence'. The impression is given that these two monsters of iniquity would have adjusted themselves quite easily not only to the atmosphere of a British blackshirt 'barracks' but to that of some of the more exalted social milieux in which Sir Oswald moved with such confidence and grace. A man who can write such lines does not need to be abused by his opponents. From his own mouth he condemns himself, utterly and irrevocably.

Today, Sir Oswald claims that his mental and physical powers remain unimpaired, in spite of the advances of old age. On the subject of his physical powers one can only accept his own assurances; as for his continued mental prowess, those who read his book may judge for themselves. Can a 'European' who not only approves of apartheid but recommends its extension throughout Africa expect to be taken seriously as a thinker?

My Life should be read, nevertheless, despite the weariness induced by the pomposity of its style and the poverty-stricken quality of its thought. Apart from serving as a cautionary tale for potential megalomaniacs, it contains information about men and events—most of which has already been serialized in *The Times*—of interest to the historian of the interwar and postwar periods. Everything this would-be Caesar says needs to be checked and rechecked against other and more reliable narratives; but if the account of the 'Olympia' meeting of June, 1934 is an obvious travesty, that of the decline and fall of the Labour Government of 1929–1931 gives some real information about the people responsible for this tragic farce.

In the end, the sentiment that prevails is sorrow for a man who might have achieved so much and who achieved so little, and who, in his old age, must inevitably be gnawed by horrifying doubts which he dare not express, even to himself.

(b) CHE GUEVARA

EARLY IN THE AFTERNOON of October 8, 1967, at Quebrada del Yuro, in the remote south-east corner of Bolivia, a small guerrilla force, led by Ernesto 'Che' Guevara, found itself surrounded by units of the Bolivian Army's 2nd Ranger Battalion and suffered a decisive defeat. Six guerrillas were killed and Che himself was wounded and captured. Twenty-four hours later, on October 9, he was executed. Two diaries were found among his papers: the first, a spiral notebook, covered the period from November 7, 1966 (the day he arrived— heavily disguised—from Havana, via Prague, São Paulo and La Paz, at the guerrilla base of Nancahuazú), to the the end of the year; the second, an appointments book bearing the name of a German pharmaceutical company, ran from January 1, 1967, to October 7, the day before the final battle.

*   *   *

Clearly the Guevara diaries were documents of the greatest political and historical interest and importance. However, neither the Bolivians nor the Americans—American counter-insurgency specialists had been training the Bolivian anti-guerrilla forces and the C.I.A. agents were apparently in at the kill—were at first prepared to authorize their publication. Photocopies of the diaries did nevertheless reach Havana, where, in June of this year, after their authenticity had been satisfactorily established, they were published, together with a 'Necessary Introduction' by Dr. Fidel Castro, in which he honoured the memory of Che, declared his solidarity with the Latin-American revolutionary movement, and argued strongly that although recent events in Bolivia constituted a setback for the Revolution they were not a defeat. The Cuban Government has consistently refused to reveal the source of the photocopies, but it is now known that they were handed over by Sr. Antonio Arguedas, the Bolivian Minister of the Interior, no less, whose defection in July triggered off a major political crisis in Bolivia. The Cape/Lorrimer edition of Che Guevara's Bolivian diaries is a translation of the Cuban edition complete with Dr. Castro's introduction and a translation of the July Proclamation by the Bolivian guerrilla, Inti Peredo, which begins with the stirring declaration, 'Guerrilla warfare in Bolivia is not dead! It has just begun.'

It has been widely assumed that besides being incomplete—in his introduction Dr. Castro admitted that a few pages were not yet in his possession—the Cuban edition of the Guevara diaries had been heavily edited in order to suppress or 'soften' passages damaging to the Castro regime. However, the publication in this country by Allen and Unwin of the American edition of the diaries, which their American publishers, Stein and Day, claim to be the 'only authentic, uncensored and complete version', makes it quite clear that this is not the case. Certainly the American edition is *complete*: it includes entries for January 4, 5, 8 and 9, February 8 and 9, March 14, April 4 and 5, June 9 and 10, July 4 and 5, which do not appear in the Cuban edition. Interesting as they are, however, Dr. Castro was quite correct when he wrote, 'they are entries for dates when nothing important happened and they in no way alter the diary's overall contents'. So far as the remaining 300 or so entries are concerned, there are minor variations in translation but no significant differences between the two editions. The very fact that both sides had the diaries (or photocopies of them)—and that each knew this to be the case—ensured that neither could tamper with the text and hope to get away with it.

Besides the thirteen entries missing from the Cuban version of the Guevara diaries, the American edition offers as an additional bonus, the captured diaries of three of Che's closest lieutenants, all, like himself, veterans of the Sierra Maestra and officers of the Cuban Revolutionary Army: first, *Pombo* (Captain Harry Villegas Tamayo), a 27-year-old Negro and one of the few survivors of the campaign, whose diary begins on July 14, 1966, and ends on May 29, 1967, and is therefore particularly valuable for the information it gives about the establishment of the guerrilla base before Che's arrival; secondly, *Rolando* (Captain Eliseo Reyes Rodríguez), a member of the central committee of the Cuban Communist Party, killed in action at the age of twenty-four, whose diary runs from August 11, 1966, to April 20, 1967: and, thirdly, *Braulio* (Lieutenant Israel Reyes Zayas), whose diary, the least interesting of the three, covers the period October 25, 1966, to August 9, 1967. The book also includes some fascinating photographs of Che himself, and the guerrilla camp, a useful chronology of the eleven-month campaign, and a complete list of the guerrillas, all of whom have been identified. (As is now well known from sensational newspaper stories, Tania [Laura], the only girl among the guerrillas, killed in August, 1967, was Haydee Tamara Bunke Bider, an East German double-agent keeping an eye on Che for the Soviet K.G.B.)

There is, moreover, a valuable, if poorly organized and at times inconsistent, introduction by the American editor of the diaries, Mr. Daniel James, a journalist and historian, who has had access to all the captured documents and who has for some time taken a close interest in the career of Che Guevara (a biography is expected to appear soon). In his introduction, Mr. James recounts Che's movements from the time of his 'disappearance' in March, 1965, to his arrival at Nancahuazú eighteen months later; he traces the idea of a Bolivian campaign back to the meeting between Dr. Castro and Sr. Mario Monje Molina, the First Secretary of the Bolivian Communist Party, during the Tricontinental Conference held in Havana in January, 1966; and he explains the purpose of the campaign which was to make Bolivia the catalyst for revolution against 'Yankee imperialism' throughout Latin America. Che is on record as saying: 'Bolivia will sacrifice itself so that conditions [for revolution] can be created in neighbouring countries. We have to make [Latin] America another Vietnam, with its centre in Bolivia.'

* * *

The *Diaries* themselves consist of daily jottings and monthly analyses relating to the guerrillas themselves—Che never had a fighting force of more than forty or so (almost half of whom were Cuban)—and guerrilla operations along a corridor approximately 200 miles long and seventy miles wide, within the triangle formed by the towns of Santa Cruz in the north, Sucre in the west, and Camiri in the south. No doubt they were very like the 'hasty notes' from which Che eventually compiled his *Reminiscences of the Cuban Revolutionary War*, which was also recently published in English (reviewed in the *TLS* on June 20, 1968). Without literary pretensions, the *Diaries* make compelling reading. Like the *Reminiscences* they include a great deal of information about the everyday problems of food supply, sickness, discipline and morale, as well as comments on Bolivian and Voice of America news broadcasts relating to the guerrilla war, and descriptions of patrols and skirmishes with Bolivian government troops. Again, as in the *Reminiscences*, Che writes with considerable self-awareness, frankness, modesty and not a little coarse humour (May 13: 'Day of belching, farting, vomiting and diarrhoea; a real organ concert'). As late as June-July Che was still optimistic (on July 7 the guerrillas had one of their greatest successes when they took Samaipata on the main Cochabamba-Santa Cruz highway), but it was from that time that things began to go wrong: the guerrilla force was gradually reduced in number and Che himself suffered a serious physical deterioration. The end came at Quebrada del Yuro early in October.

The most important question to be asked about Che Guevara's Bolivian campaign is why did it fail? The diaries themselves provide a number of clues. In the first place, and perhaps the most important, the peasants of south-east Bolivia failed to support the guerrillas. On the contrary, they seemed more disposed to assist the Bolivian army in tracking them down. Secondly, the guerrillas maintained little contact with the Bolivian miners, students and other urban revolutionary groups. One important reason for this was the deep rift which opened up between Che and the leaders of the Bolivian Communist Party. *Pombo's* diary reveals Che's bitterness over what became in effect communist sabotage of the guerrilla campaign, and in his introduction to the Guevara diaries Fidel Castro goes out of his way to denounce the Bolivian Communists for 'narrow and vulgar chauvinism'. And thirdly, the Bolivian army, hopelessly ineffective at first, improved its counter-insurgency methods as a result of intensive United States training and, in the end, had little difficulty in mopping up what remained of the guerrilla force.

*   *   *

Is it possible therefore to argue that the kind of guerrilla struggle and 'war of national liberation' which Guevara described in his handbook *Guerrilla Warfare* (based on his experiences in the Sierra Maestra) and upon which he himself embarked in Bolivia (the theoretical basis of which was discussed so brilliantly by the young French student of revolutionary theory and practice, Régis Debray, in his book *Revolution in the Revolution?*) has finally been discredited by the failure of the Bolivian campaign? This would certainly be the view of most of the contributors to an interesting collection of essays on Debray's ideas edited by Mr. Leo Huberman and Mr. Paul M. Sweezy (nine of which first appeared in the July-August issue of the *Monthly Review*).

While sympathetic to the Latin-American revolution and hostile to the Moscow line (they agree with Debray that there is 'no metaphysical equation in which vanguard = Marxist-Leninist party') they are for the most part highly critical of *focismo*. Many of them deny that 'the revolution is formed in the struggle itself' and argue that guerrillas alone cannot create the 'objective conditions' for successful revolution. They reject as 'psychogeographical mystification' the idea that the pivotal focus of the revolutionary struggle is the country-side and the *sierra*. They distrust the romantic elitism and persona-lism of the guerrillas. They argue that the military aspects of the struggle cannot be divorced from, nor elevated above, the political. And on the military issue they are doubtful whether guerrillas alone can defeat professional armies trained to combat them. As Mr. Eqbal Ahmad of Cornell University writes, the *foco* is a 'tailor's fit for the American counter-insurgency program'. Thus, 'by reducing armed struggle to guerrilla struggle, by equating guerrillas with an uprooted and isolated elite, by focusing almost exclusively on the military rather than the political aspects', writes Professor James Petras of Pennsylvania State University, 'Debray predetermines the outcome: defeat'. (Debray himself, of course, visited Guevara in Bolivia in March-April, 1967, as a journalist accredited to the Mexican weekly *Sucesos* and the Paris publishing house of Maspero. According to Che's diary he was soon in a state of 'near desperation to leave'. He was arrested on April 20, his political and military importance was grossly exaggerated by the Bolivian authorities and in November, at Camiri, amidst a blaze of international publicity, he was sentenced to thirty years' imprisonment.)

Above all, the contributors to this volume on Debray and his ideas are critical of the way in which Cuba has been held up as a model for Latin America and the rules and principles of the Latin-American revolution deduced from Cuban experience. 'Wherein does the magic of the Cuban Revolution reside', asks Cléa Silva, a Brazilian sociologist writing under a pseudonym, 'that it should be conceded the power of contradicting the others?' (like, for example, that of China).

For support of the view that Cuba was indeed highly *untypical* of Latin America, students of the Latin-American revolution could profitably turn to a little book by Professor Ramón Eduardo Ruíz, a Mexican-American professor of history at Smith College, which, while virtually ignoring the making of the Cuban Revolution (in spite of its title), offers an unusually searching analysis of Cuban history in the twentieth century and of the genesis of the Revolution.

Professor Ruíz draws attention, for example, to the country's long and almost continuous struggle for social and economic change combined with intense nationalism (first anti-Spanish, then anti-American), to its tradition of violence and guerrilla warfare, to the strong, militant and communist-influenced working class, to the bitter and alienated Marxist-inclined intelligentsia, to the 'fragmented' nature of society and the absence of either a homogeneous landed ruling class or a self-conscious middle class, to the unstable 'colonial' sugar economy, to the feeble state of the Church, to the predominantly lower-class military structure, to the traditional power structure, and, finally, to the widespread distaste felt for the Batista dictatorship during the late 1950s. This combination of political, economic and social factors favourable to revolution, together with the personal factor, the presence of an outstanding revolutionary leader, made Cuba unique among Latin-American countries. Elsewhere the revolutionary struggle will necessarily be longer and harder, not least because both the United States and the conservative forces in Latin America have now been alerted. In Debray's phrase, the revolution has revolutionized the counter-revolution.

3

THE DOUBLE LIFE
OF DR. WATSON CRICK

JAMES D. WATSON'S account of how he and Francis Crick came to suggest the correct structure for DNA is already a best-seller. So what is there about the book that induces both scientists and non-scientists to buy it? Among scientists, *The Double Helix* is enjoying a completely predictable *succès de scandale*; for it is always fascinating to discover the personal weaknesses of eminent colleagues. The book is vividly written; it has flashes of wit and of insight; and it succeeds remarkably well in creating the suspense that a good detective story requires. Sherlock Crick and Dr. Watson, by dint of superior intelligence solve the mystery and leave their competitors flatfooted and tongue-tied. (There is a Professor Moriarty in the piece too; and, for a moment, it looked as if there might be a Mata Hari.) In a curiously sympathetic way, the heroes also have a good deal in common with the heroes in *Grimm's Fairy Tales*: it is the slightly ludicrous Crick (still struggling to get his Ph.D. at the age of thirty-six) and the wide-eyed Watson (with no serious knowledge of chemistry at all) who succeed in winning the hand of the Beautiful Princess DNA (no bigamy here, as you shall see) against the competition of more learned, more distinguished and more plausible suitors. The book is certainly worth a couple of hours in the train; and there is no doubt that, for a few weeks, it will be talked about by scientist and non-scientist alike.

But there are other questions. Is it an accurate account of the discovery of the structure of DNA? Does it give credit where credit is due? Does it give the non-scientist a true impression of how scientific investigation is carried out? Are scientists as a whole as ambitious and as ruthless as Watson appears to have been? Is the motivation which drove Watson in 1951 an essential part of scientific

---

JAMES D. WATSON: *The Double Helix*. A Personal Account of the Discovery of the Structure of DNA. 226 pp. Weidenfeld and Nicolson. 35s.

discovery? Does the book illuminate the workings of an interesting and a creative mind?

Scientists who, like Watson, use the word 'breakthrough' (to say nothing of the word 'scoop') to describe their own discoveries, forget how much they owe their predecessors; and to understand the precise significance of the work of Watson and Crick it is more than ever necessary to appreciate just how much was known about the structure of DNA before these workers made their contributions. DNA consists of two long chains twisting around each other to form a double helix. Each link in these chains is a compound called a nucleotide, which is made up of a base attached to a phosphate group. DNA contains only four kinds of bases, which are called adenine, thymine, guanine and cytosine. It was Oswald Avery, Colin McLeod and Maclyn McCarty who, in 1944, established beyond reasonable doubt that genetic material was DNA; and were it not for their work chemists and crystallographers might well not have turned their attention to the structure of this substance. Alexander Todd and his collaborators had already shown, before 1951, that the nucleotides in the DNA chains were all joined together by the same kind of bond, and they had determined the nature of this bond. Rosalind Franklin had shown that the position of the nucleotides in the DNA complex was such that the phosphate groups and not the bases were on the outside. Erwin Chargaff had shown that in a wide variety of different kinds of DNA the amount of adenine present was always equal to the amount of thymine, and the amount of guanine equal to the amount of cytosine. It was Maurice Wilkins who produced the crucial evidence that DNA was a helix. The two essential decisions which permitted Watson and Crick to construct the correct model for DNA in the light of the data already available to them were first that the helical structure was composed of two chains, not three; and second that the bases in the interior of the structure were arranged in such a way that adenine was joined to thymine and guanine to cytosine. The construction of a molecular model embodying these two features at once permitted the conclusion that the two chains ran in opposite directions. With the acuity of hindsight one might say that two chains might well have been presupposed on biological grounds; and Chargaff's observations strongly suggested a link between adenine and thymine on the one hand and guanine and cytosine on the other. Yet the fact remains that other workers in the field failed to put two and two together, whereas Watson and Crick did. But let there be no mistake about the nature of their achievement. They solved a puzzle in which all the crucial clues had been provided by other people; and there is little doubt that the puzzle would, in any case, have shortly been solved, even if Watson and Crick had not turned their attention to it. The solution of the structure of DNA was a biological discovery of the greatest possible importance; but the intellectual achievement involved in making that discovery was in no way comparable to the intellectual achievements of a Darwin or a Mendel or a Rutherford or an Einstein, as Watson, modestly, and others, foolishly, suggest. It was a case, as Chargaff puts it, not only of the scientist making the discovery, but also of the discovery making the scientists.

How accurate is Watson's account? Well, it is called a personal account, so one must not expect the balanced analysis of a good historian. There is little doubt that each of the other characters in the tale would tell parts of it in a very different way; and perhaps, if a good scholar with a long view of history ever does sift the evidence, an account will emerge in which the whole emphasis may be altogether different. But Watson's version does make one claim of historical importance. The crucial idea underlying the success of the Watson-Crick model for DNA is that the two chains of the double helix are held together by pairing of adenine with thymine and guanine with cytosine in the interior of the helix. Watson claims that this idea was essentially his and that the first attempt to build a model embodying this principle was made by him alone. We may never know whether Crick would agree with this claim, but it is an important one, for, in other respects, Watson's contribution appears to have been concerned largely with generating excitement about DNA in Crick's mind and with gathering information, both published and unpublished, from other people's laboratories. Whatever the ultimate truth may be, Watson and Crick provide a striking example of what geneticists call 'complementation'. This is a phenomenon in which two sets of genes, each deficient in a different way, none the less permit normal function when they are present together in a single cell: each set of genes makes up for the deficiency in the other set. In the case of Watson and Crick it is quite clear that the great discovery would never have been made by either alone. Watson, on his own admission, did not have the intellectual equipment; and Crick would not have been working on DNA at all, and would not have continued to work on it once he had started, without the stimulus of Watson's unremitting ambition. Watson and Crick together, in one brief moment, made history; but Watson or Crick alone would certainly not have been enough. In this respect, if in no other, Watson and Crick are a very different proposition from Darwin or Mendel or Rutherford or Einstein. Watson contends that 'important biological objects come in pairs'. Perhaps some day someone will write an essay on why so many prominent molecular biologists come in pairs.

Writers of memoirs may throw more light on themselves than on the events which they describe; and the picture of James D. Watson which emerges from this book is none too attractive. He appears from an early age to have been consumed with the desire to win a Nobel Prize, and he pursued this goal with single-minded devotion. Most young scientists no doubt dream from time to time of winning a Nobel Prize; but it must very rarely happen that a scientific investigation is carried out in quite the manner described by Watson, and with such purity of motive. Peter Medawar, in a recent review of this book, makes the point that the desire to be the first to make a particular discovery is an integral part of scientific motivation. Of course it is, but the point is trivial. For ambition is an integral part of the motivation of young men in all walks of life, and the same ambition which spurs one scientist to greater effort in the investigation of an important scientific problem may induce another to produce a rash of premature and spurious papers. And the increased competitiveness of the modern scientific life also generates a large class of scientists who have little talent in advancing knowledge in their subject, but a great deal of talent in drawing attention to themselves. In Watson's case, the juvenile ambition is still there. For whereas Crick is now the co-director of one laboratory, Watson is the director of two laboratories in two different places; and he seeks fame in literature as well as in science.

There is one unpleasant feature of the book which indicates that Watson, although he poses as a rebel, is in fact swayed by conventional attitudes. His treatment of Rosalind Franklin in the body of the book is little short of vilification; but now that Rosalind Franklin is dead he finds it essential to write an epilogue about her which can only be described as fulsome. A greater display of moral courage wouldn't have come amiss here. *The Double Helix* does indeed show us, if it really needs showing, that scientists are human; but it also shows us that James D. Watson is more human than most.

Two people come out of the story very well: Wilkins and Lawrence Bragg. Wilkins, who shared the Nobel Prize with Watson and Crick, provided the essential crystallographic data on which the Watson-Crick model was based. Without Wilkins's work we might well never have heard of either Watson or Crick; and Wilkins made his unpublished data available generously and without demur. His behaviour alone demonstrates that there are scientists whose motivation is not as simple as Watson's own. Bragg was the head of the department in which Watson and Crick worked. He appears to have tolerated their idiosyncrasies to a degree which went well beyond the line of duty; and although he is not sympathetically treated in the book, he has nonetheless written the foreword. This, apparently, because he believes that a personal account of a great discovery should not be tampered with, or suppressed. He is surely right. And there is a third, unsung, hero: the English academic scene, benign and tolerant of eccentricity, without which this improbable story would never have been written.

4
ORWELL IN EXTENSO

LIKE THACKERAY, one of his boyhood idols, George Orwell requested in his will that there should be no biography of him; like Kipling, another early favourite, he wanted to be judged solely by his books, and he might well have echoed, in less brusque tones, the older man's warning to literary trespassers:

> Seek not to question other than
> The works I leave behind.

But in practice such admonitions usually only serve to whet the curiosity they are meant to stifle and sooner or later there is bound to be a full-scale scholarly life of Orwell. Meanwhile a number of his friends—notably Mr. Cyril Connolly, Mr. Rayner Heppenstall, Mr. Christopher Hollis and Sir Richard Rees—have already published their reminiscences of him, while we are now offered a four-volume edition of his *Collected Essays, Journalism and Letters* which is explicitly designed, according to the editors, Mrs. Sonia Orwell and Mr. Ian Angus, 'to give a continuous picture of Orwell's life as well as his work'. Even without such encouragement, however, this is what many readers will inevitably be looking for in the new collected edition—a substitute autobiography, a kind of extended 'Orwell par lui-même'.

*   *   *

In some respects they are going to be disappointed. Whole stretches of his career are very imperfectly documented; comparatively few of his letters have survived, for instance, and most of those which have date from the last two or three years of his life, when he had neither the time nor the strength to do much more than write about the

---

GEORGE ORWELL: *The Collected Essays, Journalism and Letters*. Volume 1: An Age Like This, 1920–1940. 574 pp. Volume 2: My Country Right or Left, 1940–1943. 477 pp. Volume 3: As I Please, 1943–1945. 435 pp. Volume 4: In Front of Your Nose, 1945–1950. 555 pp. Edited by Sonia Orwell and Ian Angus. Secker and Warburg. £2 10s. each volume.

immediate business of the day. Nor, apart from the classic account of his prep school, 'Such, Such Were the Joys'—now made readily obtainable in this country for the first time—are there more than a few crumbs of new information about his childhood, although these are interesting enough as far as they go. (How odd a juxtaposition it seems in retrospect, for example, that he should have been confirmed by Bishop Gore, the venerable editor of *Lux Mundi* giving his blessing to the future author of *Down and Out in Paris and London*.) An even more conspicuous gap is the Burmese period, about which very little has ever been made known except, indirectly, through *Burmese Days*. Yet there must still be a fair number of people alive who were acquainted with Orwell in Burma, although this is obviously much less likely to be true in a few years' time. Here, if anywhere, is a good case for a potential biographer getting to work quickly with notebook and tape recorder.

Despite the unavoidable lacunae, however, the new edition does succeed in providing the fullest and clearest picture of Orwell's development that has so far been made available, at least from around 1930. The Orwell who first comes clearly into focus in its pages is a young man in his late twenties trying to write novels, contributing occasional reviews to the *Adelphi*, earning a fitful living as a schoolmaster. In many ways he is still tentative and unsure of himself; the letters in which he gives his friend Brenda Salkeld lectures on modern literature, for instance, often sound as though they were written by a clever adolescent (one might single out the imitation-Shavian harangue against Shaw), while when they touch on larger issues the early reviews tend to read like dutiful undergraduate essays. At the same time, along with the naivety there goes a natural-ness which at its best can already be distinctly impressive, as in the review of *Angel Pavement* which puts that non-masterpiece (then being likened by other reviewers to Dickens) firmly in its place, without begrudging it its deckchair entertainment-value or falling into Q. D. Leavisite shrillness.

And while Orwell was still groping his way towards an independent critical position, he was maturing much more rapidly as a social observer, a first-hand reporter of the lower or lowish depths. His situation in the years 1930–1932 was a rather curious one—when he wasn't exploring doss-houses and tenements, he was mostly living at home with his parents—but there is no taint of slumming or looking for cheap thrills about such austere narratives as his hop-picking diary and his account of tramps in 'the spike'. Both pieces were later worked by Orwell into books (*A Clergyman's Daughter* and *Down and Out in Paris and London* respectively), although in altered and reduced form; while the editors have also unearthed a hitherto completely unknown companion-piece, 'Clink', a description of Orwell's successful attempt to get arrested and unsuccessful attempt to get gaoled on a drunk and disorderly charge which is informed by a certain sardonic humour through its very dourness. Another discovery is the lengthy journal which Orwell kept while collecting material for *The Road to Wigan Pier*. This is interesting both for what it includes—numerous details and incidents which didn't find a place in the finished product—and for what it omits: there is scarcely a trace in it of the nagging caricatures of besandalled, fruit-juice-drinking Socialist intellectuals which gave so much offence when the book was originally published.

* * *

From the period of the *Wigan Pier* rumpus onwards Orwell was to spend much of his life embroiled in political controversy, and in no respect are the new collected papers more useful than for the light which they throw on his shifting political outlook, a light which should effectively dispel a number of widely-held misconceptions and widely-circulated distortions.

Perhaps the first point which ought to be made is a purely negative one: it is very striking how few references there are in these 2,000 pages to political theory or traditional political philosophy. The occasional exception, such as the comments on Franz Borkenau, a writer who seems to have had a genuine if limited influence on Orwell, stands out all the more clearly by way of contrast. Orwell's reactions to public events were blunt, impressionistic, ethical, visceral; he worked with a limited stock of general ideas, and only in the most popular sense could he be called a political thinker. Nor are there any signs that he was ever enamoured of Marxism as an intellectual system, even at his most radical—which no doubt saved him from a good deal of heart-searching once he had definitely broken with the Communists. Never having immersed himself in theology, he refused to be unduly haunted by the God that Failed.

On the other hand, he was haunted by the possibility of some kind of root-and-branch social revolution for much longer than has commonly been realized. If one hesitates to call him a romantic revolutionary, it is largely because he was the last man to dwell on shining utopian prospects; he tended to invoke the Revolution as though it were a salutary cold bath for the bourgeoisie, and there were times when he was in this mood, as at the end of *The Road to Wigan Pier*, when he came close to glum self-parody. It could be plausibly argued, in fact, that he was driven less by a constructive vision of the future than by class-guilt and self-dissatisfaction. Yet whatever the psychological sources of his attitude, he did undoubtedly hate the inequalities of the *status quo* and long to see them redressed. Coupled with this he had a conviction—dating, he says, from around 1931—that the future was bound to be catastrophic: 'I could not say exactly what wars and revolutions would happen, but they never surprised me when they came.'

* * *

His experiences in the Spanish Civil War, as every reader of *Homage to Catalonia* knows, completed his disillusionment with the Communist Party; but they did not initially shake his faith in either the inevitability or (given that it remained democratic) the desirability of revolution. As a result, the period between his return from Spain in June, 1937, and the outbreak of the Second World War found him more than usually out of step with the rest of the world, even by his own nonconformist standards. His determination to denounce Stalinism whatever the cost, and to expose the dishonest reporting he had become aware of in Spain, brought him into collision with what might be termed the orthodox left-wing intelligentsia: Victor Gollancz declined to publish *Homage to Catalonia* before so much as a single word of it had been written, and he had a notable clash with Mr. Kingsley Martin over his rejected *New Statesman* review of Borkenau's *Spanish Cockpit* (an incident now publicly documented from Orwell's point of view by the inclusion here of an important letter explaining his position to the then literary editor of the *New Statesman*, Mr. Raymond Mortimer, who was not directly involved).

At the same time he not only felt enthusiastic as never before, after his contacts with working men in Spain, about Socialism as an ideal; he also continued to cling to the original Communist interpretation of Fascism as simply a variant form of capitalism. At bottom the two systems were the same, and it would be worse than pointless to support a capitalist war against the Axis: there are a succession of remarks to this effect in the letters and articles which he wrote at this period, while he was pessimistic enough about the probable effects of a war on civil liberties to suggest to Herbert Read early in 1939 that 'the dissident left' ought to start making plans for setting up an underground press.

As for countless others, the news of the Nazi-Soviet pact (preceded in his case by a strange premonitory dream) marked a decisive turning-point in his opinions. He now accepted that the war was indeed well worth fighting, and it was with considerable relief, as he makes clear in 'My Country Right or Left', that at last he no longer felt obliged to suppress his natural patriotic instincts. In the years which followed he was also to show something of a convert's scorn for those who still believed that there was nothing to choose between capitalism and Fascism, and to spend what was arguably a dispro-portionate amount of time criticizing pacifists of the Middleton Murry stripe—not that he did not do it very effectively. His literary essays, too, began to show more tenderness than before towards the Englishness of everyday English life.

However, it would be quite mistaken to think of him as a single-minded wartime patriot who put his radicalism in cold storage for the duration. On the contrary, his diaries for the years 1940–42 reveal a split personality: while he was vigorously supporting the war, and faithfully recording the general day-to-day public mood, he was also preoccupied with the idea that the wished-for revolution was immi-nent. Within a year or two, if we had not been conquered, we would be 'a Socialist republic fighting for its life'; within a few months the red militia would be quartered in the Ritz. Nor were such fantasies confined to his diary; they also crop up regularly in his 'London Letters' for the *Partisan Review*, where he spoke, for example, of the 'revolutionary situation' which had unfortunately not been taken advantage of after Dunkirk, without appearing to consider what a revolution would have done to Britain's military position at the time, even assuming that such a situation had really existed. Later, the obsession faded, and with characteristic candour he went out of his way to reopen the subject and remind readers of the *Partisan Review* that he had been quite wrong about the impending revolution, as he had about the suppression of civil liberties—disarmingly, though without altogether satisfactorily analysing the false reasoning which had led him astray.

By the later stages of the war, the period when he was writing *Animal Farm*, one increasingly encounters in the journalism reprinted

here a more familiar Orwell, the scourge of fellow-travellers and the
relentless critic of doublethink. His main polemical writings on this
front are too well known to call for comment, but the editors also
include numerous minor examples of him in action, and very invigorating they are: swashing asides, head-on attacks, jibes at the
'mouthing' quality of totalitarian language. One hardly knows which
to admire more, his courage or the speed with which he goes straight
to the point. A good instance of his ability to ask the simple, devasta-
ting question is his intervention in a *Tribune* correspondence over the
abortive 1944 Warsaw uprising, at a time when many left-wing
commentators were automatically siding with the Moscow-based
Polish Liberation Committee against what they referred to as the
'émigré' Polish Government in London: 'Why does one become
an *émigré* by emigrating to London and not by emigrating to
Moscow?'

*   *   *

Those who have cause to resent the deadliness of Orwell's aim have
sometimes tried to retaliate by firing back the accusation that in his
later years he was a crypto-reactionary, a man of the right. They will
find no additional ammunition in these pages. His position was
unequivocal: declining an invitation to address the Duchess of
Atholl's 'essentially Conservative' League for European Freedom, he
insisted that 'I belong to the Left and must work inside it'. Of
course, critics are still at liberty to assert, as Professor Conor
Cruise O'Brien has done in a somewhat sly essay (reprinted in
Writers and Politics), that Orwell was 'very far indeed from being a
"progressive" ', that taken together his most distinctive qualities form
'a Tory pattern', but at least they now have a good deal more
evidence to explain away. This is particularly true of what, on the
face of it, is Professor O'Brien's most damaging contention—that
Orwell was a Little Englander, and even to a considerable degree a
xenophobe. 'He turned towards foreigners', writes Professor O'Brien,
'especially Asians, that part of his mind which brooded darkly about
sandals, beards and vegetarians.' The only specific illustration cited
is 'Shooting an Elephant', which records 'fantasies about sticking a
bayonet into the belly of a sniggering Buddhist priest'.

Professor O'Brien might have mentioned that these 'fantasies' take
up precisely half a sentence, that in the other half Orwell condemns
the British Raj as a tyranny, and that he immediately goes on to

comment that such feelings are the inevitable byproduct of imperialism. Still, he was a complex man; it seems fair to say that he had at
any rate a Toryish element in his make-up, and no doubt even the
passing fantasies which he himself condemned are not without
significance. Whether they have anything like the significance which
Professor O'Brien attributes to them, however, readers will now have
a chance to judge for themselves, by assessing them in the context of
those other 'parts of his mind' which Orwell turned towards foreigners, especially Asians. A good start might be to consider the regard
which he showed for Indian susceptibilities while working in the
Eastern Service of the B.B.C., or the fierce attack in his essay 'Not
Counting Niggers' on those advocates of Western political union
who left colonialism out of account. It was specifically because it
didn't criticize British imperialism, incidentally, that he refused to
have anything to do with the League for European Freedom.

Orwell's strictly literary development was much more straightforward. It is mildly interesting to find the future champion of plain
words writing in 1936, apropos of Conrad, 'I like a florid style'; it is
mildly interesting to see him describe reading a long-forgotten sentimental novel, not very aptly, as being like taking 'a dive into the
sewers', and then treasuring up the image for more appropriate use,
years afterwards, in his essay on *Miss Blandish*; enthusiastic students
of literary genetics may perhaps wonder why he should have singled
out Flaubert, of all people, as one of his favourite novelists, or
whether his admiration for Lawrence's story 'Daughters of the
Vicar' may not indicate a possible minor 'source' for *A Clergyman's
Daughter*. He himself would have laughed at such speculations, and in
general he is not a writer who repays either close textual analysis or
hunt-the-symbol ingenuity. As a critic, certainly, his virtues were all
on the surface, and by the end of the 1930s, when he wrote 'Charles
Dickens' and 'Boys' Weeklies'; he had perfected his semi-sociological
method. (It was an inspired editorial stroke, by the way, to reprint
the Bunter essay here along with Frank Richards's entertaining
rejoinder.)

Two points come across particularly strongly from the minor
literary journalism. One is the extent to which Orwell plainly felt that
the most useful job of work a critic could do was draw attention to
books which the reader might otherwise have overlooked or brushed
aside; he himself had the knack of making almost anything he
recommended, from an underrated Thackeray short story to a

forgotten novel by Leonard Merrick, sound immediately attractive. The other is the way in which he managed to combine lightness of touch with fundamental seriousness when he wrote about popular classics, 'good-bad' books, the borderline cases of literature. How he would have ridiculed attempts to train the heavy guns of *Kulturgeschichte* on music-hall songs and detective stories! And how he would have loathed camp and all its ways: there wasn't an ounce of whimsy in him.

*　　*　　*

The general standard of the writing throughout these four volumes is remarkably high. Inevitably there are occasional descents into platitude, and places where Orwell starts repeating himself: he was, after all, a fully paid-up member of the N.U.J., and he must often have written against the clock. There are also, from time to time, outbursts of bloody-mindedness or plain silliness; but by comparison with the overall achievement, they count for very little. One comes away, finally, with renewed respect for Orwell's courage and sanity. 'Genius' may seem too big a word for him but he did at any rate have something like a genius for hitting nails on the head.

With the present edition the publishers have handsomely atoned for the catchpenny *Collected Essays* of 1961, which were in fact no such thing. Even now, they include only a representative selection of the minor journalism: every so often there is a reference to a piece which has been omitted—Orwell's review of *The Wound and the Bow*, for instance, or his earliest articles, 'La Censure en Angleterre' and 'John Galsworthy', both published in Henri Barbusse's *Monde*—which one would very much like to see, however slight its intrinsic value. Doubtless fifty years from now some American university press will bring out a really comprehensive collected Orwell, by which time the ephemeral writings will have lost their interest. A pity; but it is hard to see how an edition for the general reader could reasonably have been expected to run to greater length than the present one.

Mrs. Orwell and Mr. Angus have made an admirable job of the editing, arranging the material skilfully and supplying explanatory notes and bibliographical information with the minimum of fuss. Each volume has a useful biographical résumé outlining Orwell's life during the period which it covers, and an exemplary index, compiled by Mr. Oliver Stallybrass.

5

THE LITTLE MAGAZINE

(a) THE NEW AGE

ALFRED ORAGE was a man who, as Shaw observed, 'did not belong to the successful world'. He was an editor who never ran a profitable paper, a socialist who backed Guild Socialism against the Fabians, an economist who preached Social Credit against the Keynesians, a literary critic who found *Ulysses* repellent and disliked the poems of Yeats, a mystic who expected the Second Coming. In thirty years of public life he never supported a winning cause, or profited from a losing one; the movements that consumed his energies are dead, and so are the journals that he edited, and the books that he wrote.

Yet when Orage died in 1934 he was remembered, and mourned, by many men more celebrated than he. The memorial number of the *New English Weekly* (of which he was the founder and first editor) included elegiac notes from Eliot, Chesterton, Shaw, A.E., Pound, Wells, Augustus John, Richard Aldington, Herbert Read, Middleton Murry, G. D. H. Cole, Frank Swinnerton, Edwin Muir, and St. John Irvine, all expressing a sense of loss, and all for different reasons. Eliot praised the literary critic, A.E. the *guru*, Pound the economist; others admired Orage's brilliance as an editor, his flair for discovering talent, his prose style, his disinterestedness, his obstinacy. There is no doubt that to his contemporaries Orage was important; the question is, what importance, if any, remains?

One might say, first of all, that Orage is important as a representative of a type—the lower-middle-class provincial intellectual who turned up in considerable numbers around the beginning of this

---

(a) PHILIP MAIRET: *A. R. Orage*. A Memoir. 140 pp. New York: University Books. $6. WALLACE MARTIN: *'The New Age' under Orage*. Chapters in English Cultural History. 303 pp. Manchester University Press. 35s.

(b) *The Criterion*. 1922–1939. Reprint in eighteen volumes, with index. Faber and Faber. 60 guineas.

(c) *The Little Review*. 12 Volumes. 1914–1929. New York: Kraus Reprint Corporation. $283.50 (Paperback, $256.50).

century and gave a new thrust and tone to English literary life. He belongs, that is, with Wells and Bennett and Lawrence. And he had all the characteristics of the type: he was learned but half-educated, arrogant and quick to take offence, charming but humourless, grimly serious about art and ideas ('a judge of literature cannot afford to indulge in witticisms', he said, and he never did). He was extremely susceptible to conversion, and it could be said of him, as Wells remarked of Nietzsche, that he was so constituted that to get an idea was to receive a revelation. He had many revelations, and like Wells and Lawrence he had a messianic itch to turn his revelations into dogmas. Part radical reformer and part heterodox evangelist, he helped to give Edwardian intellectual life its characteristic tone of strenuous but sombre zeal.

*   *   *

Orage is most representative of his type in the variety of his enthusiasms. Like many another man of his time he had gone to the two sources of Victorian values—science and liberalism—and had found them bankrupt.

Spencer and Darwin had mechanized the world [he wrote] and carried the industrial revolution into thought. Tennyson on his lawn had prettified it and hung it with paper garlands. But nothing could conceal the fact that the new world was repellent and that *nothing* was better than the only certainty promised by it.

For a born believer like Orage, such nihilism was not in fact possible, and he turned instead to newer, less orthodox systems in search of values. In his earlier years he was a Theosophist, a Nietzschean, and a Fabian Socialist; later he tried psychoanalysis, Social Credit, and Gurdjieff's 'institute' at Fontainebleau. Some of his spiritual restlessness one must attribute to the temper of the time, but the eccentric forms in which it was expressed is a function of the type; a man like Orage, rooted neither in a traditional education nor in a fixed social role, will regard society and its ideas as infinitely revisable because he has no stake in either. And he will set few limits on the intellectual instruments that he employs to re-build society and its ideas so that they will include him.

Orage's own roots were in Yorkshire, and in poverty. His father was an improvident schoolmaster who died when his son was a year old, and his mother supported her family by taking in washing. Alfred, the clever child of the family, was encouraged by the local squire, who sent him to a teachers' training college. He became, like Lawrence, a schoolmaster, and settled in Leeds. There he joined the Theosophical Society, the Fabian Society, and a 'Plato Group', and helped to found the Leeds branch of the Independent Labour Party and the Leeds Arts Club. This is a remarkable range of intellectual activities for a provincial city in the 1890s, but for Orage it was insufficient. In 1906 he left Leeds, his teaching career, and his wife, and went up to London to become a full-time intellectual.

In London Orage entered first into political activities, and became at once two kinds of socialist: he joined the Guilds Restoration League, a William-Morrisy movement 'to make aesthetic poverty impossible', and he re-joined the Fabian Society. This mixing of romantic medievalism and statistical rationalism may strike one as improbable, but socialism in 1906 was a slumgullion of fads and dissensions that could accommodate any view, so long as it was unconventional. It was, Orage later recalled:

a cult, with affiliations in directions now quite disowned—with theosophy, art and crafts, vegetarianism, the "simple life", and almost, one might say, with the musical glasses. Morris had shed a medieval glamour over it with his stained-glass *News from Nowhere*, Edward Carpenter had put it into sandals, Cunninghame Graham had mounted it upon an Arab steed to which he was always saying a romantic farewell. Keir Hardie had clothed it in a cloth cap and a red tie. And Bernard Shaw, on behalf of the Fabian Society, had hung it with innumerable jingling epigrammatic bells—and cap. My brand of socialism was, therefore, a blend or, let us say, an anthology of all these, to which from my personal predilections and experience I added a good practical knowledge of working classes, a professional interest in economics which led me to master Marx's *Das Kapital* and an idealism fed at the source—namely Plato.

If this socialist anthology seems an odd account of a Fabian, one need only remind oneself that the society began as The Fellowship of the New Life, a front-parlour discussion group that included communists, spiritualists, psychic researchers and single taxers, and that for a long time it remained receptive to members from the queer fringes of radicalism.

*　　　*　　　*

Orage's conception of his role in the Fabian Society became clear very quickly; he was to be a leader of the philosophical and aesthetic wing. With his friend Holbrook Jackson he created the Fabian Arts Group, with the ostensible aim of making an appeal to 'minds that

remained unmoved by the ordinary Fabian attitude', and of providing 'a platform for the discussion of the more subtle relationships
of man to society which had been brought to the front in the works
of such modern philosopher-artists as Nietzsche, Ibsen, Tolstoy, and
Bernard Shaw'. One might think that the Fabian leaders, faced with
this frank contempt for their methods and opinions, would have
discouraged Orage, but instead they encouraged him to buy a paper.
In the spring of 1907 Orage and Jackson raised enough money to
buy *The New Age*, a failing weekly of uncertain convictions and no
circulation, and the *Fabian News* announced the birth of a new
socialist journal, to be run strictly 'on Fabian Lines'. If the Fabians
had paused to consider the sources of Orage's funds, they might have
viewed the birth of his paper with less confidence; he had got £500
from Shaw, but the other £500 had come from a theosophical banker
in the City. This curiously mixed parentage one may take as symbolical; for from birth *The New Age* was at best a bastard socialist.

The New Age gives Orage another kind of importance. He edited
it, almost without help, for fifteen years. During those years he published a more impressive list of contributors than any other British
journal: among more than 700 were Belloc, Bennett, Bierce, Brooke,
Burns, Carpenter, Chesterton, Cunninghame Graham, Havelock
Ellis, Ervine, Galsworthy, Gogarty, Harris, Hulme, John, Mansfield,
Murry, Pound, Herbert Read, Sassoon, Shaw, Sickert, Swinnerton,
Webb, Wells, West, and Zangwill; art work reproduced included
drawings by Epstein, Gaudier-Brzeska, Wyndham Lewis, Sickert,
and Picasso. 'Great editorship', Orage said, 'is a form of creation,
and the great editor is measured by the number and quality of the
writers he brings to birth—or to ripeness.' By this standard, Orage
was the greatest English editor of this century; nowadays, when that
title is often awarded to Ford Madox Ford for his *English Review*,
it is worth noting that Ford ran his review for little more than a year,
lost £5,000, and was fired, while Orage kept *The New Age* going for
fifteen years with an initial investment one-fifth the size of Ford's,
and resigned. Ford was brilliant, but Orage lasted.

*   *   *

Orage's notion of a great editor says nothing about ideas, principles, or editorial policy, and the paper that he edited had little
intellectual coherence; it was, like its editor's socialism, an anthology
of views. It first appeared as 'an Independent Socialist Weekly' with

D

impeccable socialist credentials—the first issue carried letters of congratulation from Sidney Webb, Edward Pease (the Secretary of the Fabian Society), and Prince Kropotkin. But it also contained an editorial that those congratulators must have read with sinking hearts. 'Socialism as a progressive will', the editors observed,

is neither exclusively democratic nor aristocratic, neither anarchist nor individualist. Each of the great permanent moods of human nature, as imperfectly reflected in the hierarchy of society, has its inalienable right to a place in the social pyramid.

Believing that the darling object and purpose of the universal will of life is the creation of a race of supremely and progressively intelligent beings, *The New Age* will devote itself to the serious endeavour to cooperate with the purposes of life, and to enlist in that noble service the help of serious students of the new contemplative and imaginative order.

This untidy mixture of socialism, Nietzscheanism, and mysticism is a fair expression of Orage's untidy thought, and the journal that he edited was similarly eclectic. It published, for example, the reactionary philosophical essays of T. E. Hulme as well as the heretical socialism of Wells, and found space both for Ford's support of women's suffrage and Orage's fierce opposition to it. If it had an editorial policy at all, it was simply an open-door policy. 'One used to write to *The New Age*', Belloc later recalled, 'simply because one knew it to be the only paper in which the truth with regard to our corrupt policies, or indeed with regard to any powerful evil, could be told.' And when Hulme was asked why he wrote for such a radical journal, he replied simply, 'Because they'll print me'. *The New Age* may have set out to be an 'independent socialist weekly', but the emphasis was on 'independent', and one can see why the Webbs soon gave up hope of seeing it run on Fabian lines, and founded the *New Statesman* to serve that purpose.

The greatest appeal of such a farraginous chronicle was to people like Orage, provincial intellectuals in search of a faith, and it is not surprising that such people made up a substantial number of both its contributors and its readers. The regular writers—the now forgotten journalists who attended Orage's salon in the basement of the Chancery Lane ABC—were mostly, like Orage, poor intellectual outsiders. And the subscribers included people like young D. H. Lawrence, who shared the paper with the Eastwood intelligentsia and liked it more for its literature than for its politics. One may guess that it was far better read in Eastwood than in Westminster, because it meant more there; it was the voice of rebellion and liberation, not clear, perhaps, but loud.

This point of authorship and audience may in part account for the fact that *The New Age*, for all its vigour and occasional distinction, seems to have had little impact on the direction of English thought in its time. But a more important factor is that it had little direction itself. Eclecticism may stimulate, but it does not move, and *The New Age* left behind vivid impressions of its editor's personality, but no impressions of its policies.

When Orage left the journal in 1922, he left a remarkable record of achievements. He had run a weekly journal for fifteen years virtually without capital. He had persuaded most of the important writers of the time to write for him, and to write for nothing (Arnold Bennett, that most cash-conscious of writers, wrote a weekly piece in *The New Age* for eighteen months without payment). He had not only published Ezra Pound, but had made him into a music critic. He had encouraged many young writers, and had published the first works of a number who later made names for themselves, including Katherine Mansfield, Richard Aldington, and Middleton Murry. He had taught and demonstrated the importance of good writing, the style, as he called it, of 'brilliant common sense'. But most important, he had brought new ideas to a new audience, and had helped to redefine the English intellectual class.

Having said so much, one should note also *The New Age's* limitations. It never published an excellent poem, rarely a good story. It opened its pages to a good deal of rubbish, simply because it was *new* rubbish. In the post-war years Orage indulged his strong mystical streak, and published the incomprehensible writings of a Serbian prophet called Mitrinović; at the same time he was giving space to Major Douglas and Social Credit, and the result was a concentrated unreadability that nearly destroyed the paper. Orage's own contributions were sometimes the brilliant common sense that he preached, but he was capable of crude brutality in his criticism, and of windy vagueness in his philosophizing, and as his causes failed he became more and more negative and abusive in their defence.

*   *   *

Orage's last years, after his resignation from *The New Age*, are puzzling and sad. He became a disciple of Gurdjieff and laboured for him for a year at Fontainebleau. Then he went to New York as

Gurdjieff's representative and stayed six years, teaching and raising funds for the 'institute'. In 1931 he returned to England to found a new paper, the *New English Weekly*, which he edited until his death. Looking back over Orage's life, one can see that his need to follow was as great as his need to lead, and that his submission to Gurdjieff's beliefs and discipline was inevitable. But to the unconverted the spectacle of a strong mind capitulating is depressing, and Orage's later life seems a waste of a lively intelligence. In his memoir of Orage, Eliot remarked his 'restless desire for the absolute'; the desire one may call a strength in Orage's character, but the restlessness dissipated that strength, drove him aimlessly from faith to faith, and made his life, in the end, incoherent. 'Gurdjieff once told me', Orage said, 'that he knew my ambition. He said I wanted to be one of the "elder brothers" of the human race, but that I had not the ability it required.' That observation will do for Orage's epitaph.

Mr. Philip Mairet, whose biography of Orage has been reissued, worked on the *New English Weekly* and shared Orage's esoteric philosophical interests. His book, which first appeared in 1936, is informed and sympathetic; it provides all the facts about Orage that anyone is likely to want. Its limitations are implicit in the author's relation to his subject; the book is not detached enough to be critical and it is focused on Orage's spiritual history rather than on his place in the history of his times.

*   *   *

One might expect to find Orage-in-history in Professor Martin's book, which is subtitled 'Chapters in English Cultural History'. Such an expectation would only partly be satisfied. Professor Martin confesses in his preface that he has emphasized literary matters, and on these—the 'New Drama', Realism, Imagism—he is instructive and interesting. But *The New Age* was not primarily a literary paper and the centre of its interest and importance cannot properly be reached through the conventional categories of modern literary history. Professor Martin has contrived an approach that is simply too orthodox for so queer a journal as *The New Age*, and one must conclude that he has captured more of English cultural history than he has of his particular subject. His book will be valuable to the historian, but the true biography of Orage's odd offspring remains to be written—its stumbling childhood, its vigorous maturity, and its soft-headed old age. That biography, if it ever is written, will also be a biography of the Orage-type, the English provincial intellectual in the twentieth century.

(b) THE CRITERION

EXPOUNDING (in 1926) his 'Idea of a Literary Review', T. S. Eliot warned against the dangers of both the 'narrow' and the 'comprehensive' kinds of periodical. Magazines ought not to devote themselves to promoting the views of a small group; nor should they be miscellanies, sprawlingly inclusive. The proper aim of a literary review should be to 'represent the development of the keenest sensibility and the clearest thought' of its age. It should have an identity of its own but ought not to be sealed off in it. It should range undogmatically but not at the expense of 'critical value'. A cautious, compromising recipe. It is characteristic that, in spite of it, Eliot's own magazine (available now in a well-produced reprint, with a prefatory note by Eliot, and an excellent index) should be now almost solely valuable because of what it tells us about Eliot.

Defining his role as editor of *The Criterion*, Eliot was careful to point out that objectives are not programmes. *The Criterion* had no programme; it could merely be said to represent a 'tendency'. He was content to sound fairly vague about how this tendency might be described. The most he would allow was that it was 'toward something which, for want of a better name, we may call classicism', 'toward a higher and clearer conception of Reason and a more severe and serene control of the emotions by Reason'. One gets the sense from this, as from many other of Eliot's more abstract pronouncements, that the tentativeness has more to do with phrasing than with feeling. In a letter, written earlier to Herbert Read, he had been somewhat more distinct and fervent:

If I say generally that I wish to form a 'phalanx', a hundred voices will forthwith declare that I wish to be a leader, and that my vanity will not allow me to serve, or even to exist on terms of equality with others. If one maintains a cause, one is either a fanatic or a hypocrite, and if one has any definite dogmas, then one is imposing the dogmas upon those who cooperate with one . . . . I wish, certainly, to get as homogeneous a group as possible; but I find that homogeneity is in the end undefinable. For the purposes of *The Criterion*, it cannot be reduced to a creed of numbered articles. I do *not* expect everyone to subscribe to all the articles of my own faith, or to read Arnold, Newman, Bradley or Maurras with my eyes. It seems to me that at the present time we need more dogma, and that one ought to have as precise and clear a creed as possible, when one thinks at all.

Although nervous of seeming to impose his own views too autocratically, Eliot all the same envisaged the ideal contributor to his pages as one who held an 'impersonal loyalty' to 'some faith not antagonistic to my own'. There is barely a single issue of *The Criterion* that could have left anyone in much doubt as to what 'my own' faith consisted of, and few of the magazine's critical contributions could not in one way or another be regarded as acceptably supportive of that faith.

*   *   *

Eliot's defence against accusations of programmatic narrowness would presumably have been that his was not a narrow faith. It was a faith which sought nothing less than to maintain the continuity of culture in an age inhospitable to culture, to keep alive those traditional values which, in past ages, had guaranteed the highest cultural possibilities. It was thus profoundly anti-democratic, profoundly hostile to any liberal-progressive efforts to unseat traditional authority. 'The aristocracy of culture' must be protected against 'the demagogy of science', 'the governors of the people' must be encouraged to sustain 'the conviction of their right to govern'. And, since the artist's role was in jeopardy, it was no longer enough for him to be an artist; he must define and protect the conditions in which art might continue to work as an effective civilizing agent. These, very roughly, were the main articles of Eliot's creed. They are familiar enough from his poetry, but *The Criterion* gave him the opportunity to test them out with more discursive and polemical explicitness.

But before going into how this worked out in detail some facts and dates are necessary. *The Criterion* had a relatively long and secure life; rarely needing to worry much about mere survival, about advertisements and new subscribers. The circulation is said to have been unusually small, even by little-magazine standards—somewhere around 400. It was launched as a quarterly in October, 1922, with financial assistance from Viscountess Rothermere, while Eliot was still working in a City bank and therefore 'not in a position to accept a salary'. This happy arrangement lasted for three years, and then Lady Rothermere withdrew her subsidy. Eliot allowed himself some mild resentment on this score: 'The idea which was present to the mind of Lady Rothermere was that of a more chic and brilliant *Art and Letters* which might have a fashionable vogue among a wealthy few'. Then followed the magazine's only major financial crisis. This was resolved, according to the publisher Frank Morley—who acted as go-between—in the offices of the *TLS*, then edited by Bruce Richmond:

'All right' said Tom. 'I'm tough. Who pays the bills?' I don't believe I answered. I was already on the way to find Bruce Richmond. Richmond was the Secret Agent of the whole thing ... [he] permitted himself one chortle of amusement, then took about ten minutes to list a dozen names which were to be ever anonymous, and another twenty minutes to give me notes to some of them, making a memo that he would attack others. There was nothing for me to do but bank the fund in a separate account at the bank.

The magazine was kept going for a time with the help of these mysterious benefactors (Eliot later named two of them: Charles Whibley and Frederick Scott Oliver), and then in 1926 it was taken over by the firm of Faber and Gwyer, where Eliot had meanwhile started his new career as a publisher. Eliot had felt nervous of involving his employer earlier, and it was at Faber's suggestion that the deal was arranged. (It is curious that Eliot was later to single out 1926 as the year when 'one began slowly to realize that the intellectual and artistic output of the previous seven years had been rather the last efforts of an old world, than the first struggles of a new'.) From that year—although there was to be another whip-round some time after—*The Criterion* was firmly on its feet. It became *The New Criterion* and ran for a further five issues as a quarterly before changing to a monthly. *The Monthly Criterion* appeared for just over a year, but by June, 1928, Eliot had come to the conclusion that 'whatever editorial talent I possessed did not extend to the preparation of a review oftener than four times a year', and reverted to quarterly publication, and to the magazine's original title. *The Criterion* continued as a quarterly until its death in 1939. Seventy-one issues had been published, each of about a hundred pages, and the price had crept up from 3s. 6d. to 7s. 6d.

There were few changes in the planning and scope of the magazine during its seventeen-year life. Essays, short stories and poems usually formed the bulk of it. There was a book review section, small and very selective at first but expanded in later issues. There were regular columns on music, art and broadcasting, and there were valuable round-ups of foreign periodicals. Most important of all the regular features, though, was the editor's own 'Commentary'. This elegant, often witty, often hopelessly wrong-headed column first appeared in 1924 and from then on it provided Eliot with the platform, or pulpit, from which he could apply his beliefs to the practical issues of the day. Reading these 'commentaries' straight through, the obsessive strain is very marked. Whatever the topic, however immense or trivial, it tends to get treated in much the same way, and with much the same weight, as grist for Eliot's dark, dogmatic mill.

Browsing, for instance, through a scientific periodical, Eliot finds nothing more deserving of comment than one scientist's passing notion that 'we may look to the isolated as the source of fresh individuality and power, to be paid for in time, however, with the inevitable price of diminished progress'. There is a certain pathos in the editor's lusty cheer: 'We do not know what other zoologists say to this, but it looks as if one distinguished authority thought that a uniform civilization . . . was hardly a prospect to be desired.' On another occasion, Eliot announces that he has been reading a magazine called *Youth* (which, even from his respectful description of it, manages to sound somewhat crankily boy-scoutish) and has been cheered to learn 'of the amazing spread of folk dancing throughout Britain'. Predictably enough, Eliot detects the influence of Sir James Frazer and finds in the phenomenon a 'note of breakers on the reef'. 'This note', he concludes bizarrely, 'is not "the great middle-class liberalism" or the great lower middle-class socialism; it is of authority not democracy, of dogmatism not tolerance, of the extremity and never of the mean.'

Not all Eliot's 'commentaries' were as amusingly eccentric as these. A brief anthology of his reactions to, say, the Spanish war, Fascism, slum clearance, censorship, &c., would make sinister reading these days. In 1928, he was writing in fulsome admiration of the British Fascists, and only regretted that 'a nationalist organization should have had to go abroad for its name and symbol'. In the same year, he was claiming for Britain the leadership of the cultural Common Market: Britain not only provided a bridge between Latin culture and Germanic culture but 'she is the only member of the European community that has established a genuine empire—that is to say, a world-wide empire as was the Roman empire—not only European but the connection between Europe and the rest of the world'.

*   *   *

There was indeed a strong element of what John Gould Fletcher called 'Hellenic paranoia' in Eliot's careful nurturing of the European idea. The views of his hero, Charles Maurras, no doubt sound uglier now than they did then, but even in the middle 1920s one would have thought that Henri Massis's article 'Defence of the West' (published, with some reverence, by *The Criterion* in two instalments) might have been found slightly disconcerting: 'In order to overcome the dangers that threaten us, we must be able to name them. To put it briefly, they are Bolshevism and Asiaticism. The whole of civilization is reduced to defending itself against this dark barbarism which is so powerfully organized.' But there is much of this kind of thing throughout *The Criterion*, and we can see now that some kind of Fascist ideology was the inevitable upshot of the magazine's central 'tendency'. It is distasteful to read an analysis of Marxism that employs as its chief premise the view that since Marx was a Jew and since Jews had become 'more and more openly the exploiters of the Western World today', Marx's world revolution merely represented 'the desire of the inferior to revenge himself on the superior (as Nietzsche points out, characteristic of the Judaic psychology)', but we have to acknowledge that such an analysis might have seemed to fit, humanely, with the magazine's main, anti-materialist doctrines. Knowing the consequences of such doctrines, it is almost impossible not to represent Eliot's championing of them as not merely short-sighted but in some way evilly shortsighted. And that, of course, would be unfair. Reconciling the 'aristocracy of culture' with the 'demagogy of science' is as complex a difficulty now as it was in 1920—our advantage over Eliot is that, knowing what we do, we are unlikely to come up with any easy answers—or perhaps, indeed, with any answers.

Rather more damaging to *The Criterion* than the Fascist views it promoted during the twenties is the complete silence it maintained throughout the thirties about Hitler and developments in Nazi Germany. With the magazine's theological bias becoming more acknowledged and pervasive, it was fairly obvious that Eliot would take the clerics' side during the Spanish war—this was, for him, barely a matter of politics at all. But during the last few years of the magazine's life, discussion of Nazi Germany was persistently avoided in favour of cagily sympathetic dissertations against Communism. (At one point, in fact, Eliot does suggest that Communism would be a less acceptable political system for Britain than the system operating

in Germany and Italy because these were systems devised for predominantly middle-class societies; Communism was all right for
predominantly proletarian societies.)

Sympathetic references to Nazism can be found here and there
throughout the final issues of the magazine: the Broadcasting
Correspondent, writing about a radio discussion of 'Freedom',
remarks that 'nearly everybody took the opportunity to have a bang
at the Nazi ideal of the State and [Wyndham] Lewis alone had a
good word for the German "solution" ' (Lewis is therefore praised
as the 'most penetrating' contributor to the discussion) and Hugh
Gordon Porteus can be heard complaining that 'To give a sympathetic appraisal of Fascism today [October, 1937] would be to put
The Criterion on the black list, to be blackballed by "all decent
thinking people". That is surely a disquieting feature of our intellectual life.' On another occasion Mr. Porteus advised a disgruntled
refugee from Nazi Germany to 'pause sometimes to ask himself how
much better his lot might have been if the Nazi had *not* come to
power . . . the Communist has a more thorough method of disposing
of intellectuals than the Fascist generally feels obliged to employ.'

Eliot himself was content to leave comment on these matters to
his contributors, and we can only assume that he was beginning to
recognize that the magazine's whole programme was being over-
taken by events—events which had not been envisaged and which
The Criterion could take no useful part in. By 1939 the game was
evidently up. *The Criterion* could not continue to pretend that
Nazism did not exist, but neither—apparently—could it bring itself
to oppose it. There was no point in continuing publication: 'In the
present state of public affairs—which has induced in myself a depression of spirits so different from any other experience as to be a
new emotion—I no longer feel the enthusiasm necessary to make a
literary review what it should be.'

The Criterion's missionary self-consciousness was such that one
tends to be rather more aware of what it 'stood for', in terms of
ideology, than of what it actually achieved, in terms of publishing
imaginative literature. There was no talented group of writers contributing to it regularly, no sense of its encouraging any particular
literary movements. It is noteworthy, for example, that *The Criterion*
took no part in encouraging the resurgence of interest in Imagism
around 1930. The 'neo-Imagists' tended, of course, to be those
Americans like William Carlos Williams whom Eliot had 'betrayed'

nearly twenty years before. When the *Imagist Anthology* appeared Eliot sent it to Harold Monro, a critic whose eye for the experimental he had special reason to remember (Monro once turned down the chance to publish *Prufrock*). Monro responded with fine Squirearchical contempt: 'for the rubbish of William Carlos Williams what excuse can be made by anybody? This kind of nonsense is enough to damn any book. The Twentieth Century has grown too old to include it any more in its magazines and anthologies. The joke has been made and the laughter has died away.'

One would be hard put to name any valuable *Criterion* discoveries. Good things appeared, of course—poems by William Empson and Hart Crane; Auden's *Paid on Both Sides*; Eliot's own *Waste Land*—and Eliot was particularly proud of having been the first English editor to publish Proust, Valéry, Cocteau and other Continental (mainly French) writers. During the 1930s he took up most of the good new poets and had many of them writing regular reviews. Geoffrey Grigson, George Barker, Charles Madge and Kenneth Allott were welcomed to the fold, along with Auden and Spender. They injected some needed rigour into literary-critical pages which had been dominated for too long by such figures as Humbert Wolfe and John Gould Fletcher. But none of these young writers could be described as Eliot's discovery. They graduated to *The Criterion* by way of smaller and more adventurous periodicals. Most of what seem to have been Eliot's own protégés have since completely disappeared from view. T. O. Beachcroft, for example, who wrote:

> Here no spring breaks,
> No warmth the barren stone unlocks;
> No herbs, grasses nor such green things breaks
> Through the iron rocks.
> Here no roots hold
> No fruits to bear
> But year by year
> No season of living or dying can be told
> Here.

This is not an uncharacteristic contribution. One likely way of getting poems published in *The Criterion* was to lift lines out of *The Waste Land*; Eliot had a deep weakness for pastiche of his own work.

*   *   *

In spite of its essential and, retrospectively, its debilitating faults, *The Criterion* enjoyed immense prestige, particularly during its early years, and mostly in literary quarters. The important thing about it, of course, was that it was edited by T. S. Eliot. Hart Crane wrote, on hearing that his 'Tunnel' section of *The Bridge* had been accepted: 'I have been especially gratified by the reception accorded me by *The Criterion*, whose director, T. S. Eliot, is representative of the most exacting literary standards of our times.' This must have been a fairly general view. Eliot was the leading poet and critic of his generation; his approval had to be some kind of guarantee of excellence. The magazine's dubious ideology, the frequent turgidity of its set literary essays, the gradual drift away from literature into politics and finally into the dense labyrinths of theology—none of this was likely to deter the admirer of Eliot's poetry from placing a high valuation on his practice as an editor. In 1930 Ezra Pound— who appeared in *The Criterion* surprisingly infrequently—was instructing the editor of the *Hound and Horn* (a magazine which had set out to model itself on *The Criterion*):

Don't sink into Criterionism. Criterion has printed in seven years about enough live stuff for one; if that . . . One cannot indulge continually in a diet of dead crow without its tainting the breath . . . You cannot spend so much of your time analysing the imperfections of dead and moribund writing without some odour of the undertaker's establishment penetrating the pages of the review.

Pound had an excellent nose for such odours, but it was to be a few years before his view was unignorably justified by the actual contents of the magazine. In 1938 Julian Symons was probably speaking more than his own mind when he complained that the 'moral scale of values by which [*The Criterion*] judges literature and life is one that no longer has much meaning'.

It is ironical and appropriate that as *The Criterion's* 'tendency' petered out into ludicrous irrelevance, the magazine began to show more vigour and purpose on the 'creative' side—the irony being, of course, that the writers who introduced this new vitality could hardly have been more hostile to the *Criterion* ideology. It is some kind of tribute to Eliot's open-mindedness in matters of purely literary criticism that he should have allowed this to happen in the dramatic way it did. But the last thing *The Criterion* will be remembered for is open-mindedness.

(*c*) THE LITTLE REVIEW

THE *Little Review* ran from March, 1914, to May, 1929. In its first numbers it was probably the worst and the most pretentious literary magazine in America. Its editor, Margaret Anderson, began by filling her pages with nonsense; a letter from Galsworthy, coy prose for Alice Meynell and Rupert Brooke, twenty-five fan-letters in the second number. In the issue for September, 1914, as a fair example, there was not a single item worth a second reading; while in the same month *Poetry* printed Ford Madox Ford, Sandburg, Robinson's great poem, 'Eros Turannos', Frost, Fenollosa, Yeats and Tagore. But Margaret Anderson had the sense to post a copy of the issue for January-February, 1916, to Ezra Pound, who replied with polite encouragement and a hint that *The Egoist* was worth watching. In November, 1916, Margaret Anderson was joined by Jane Heap, who soldiered on to the end; Margaret Anderson gave up in 1923.

The immediate result of Pound's letter was that both editors read Joyce's *Portrait of the Artist as a Young Man* and became new women. There was no more talk of Galsworthy or Mrs. Meynell. Pound moved in, directing attention to the merits of Joyce, Eliot, Henry James, de Gourmont, Wyndham Lewis, Yeats and Ford. The *Little Review* was converted to the new literature: it became Pound's voice, in effect, competing with *The Egoist* and *The Dial* for news that was likely to stay news. As long as Pound persisted, his mark was indisputable: in May, 1917, he became foreign editor, and the magazine printed Eliot's 'Eeldrop and Appleplex'. Readers accustomed to the prose of Arthur Davidson Ficke now found themselves coping with Lewis's *Imaginary Conversations* and Pound's *Jodindranath Mawhwor's Occupation*. A reader from Cambridge, Mass., wrote to the editors:

It seems to me that the last few numbers of the *Little Review* have been below your earlier standard—almost below zero. What sympathy can the majority of readers feel for the foreign editor, Ezra Pound, with his contemptuous invective against the 'vulgus'?

M.C.A. answered, with the fervour of recent conversion:

A contempt for the 'vulgus' is the inevitable reaction of any man or woman who observes the antics of the 'flies in the marketplace'.

So the magazine went Pound's way; printing Eliot's French poems, a batch of Yeats from *The Wild Swans at Coole*, Pound's review of

Joyce's *Portrait*. The October, 1917, issue was held up in the post because of the alleged obscenity of Lewis's *Cantleman's Spring Mate*. Then in March, 1918, on Pound's suggestion, the editors published the first chapter of *Ulysses*, other chapters to follow. Joyce was Pound's private jewel, lent to the *L.R.* for the good of its soul.

In Volume V the *Little Review* had its great year (1918–19), printing Joyce, Lewis, Pound, Ford, Stevens, Williams, an entire issue on James, more Eliot, more Yeats, a de Gourmont issue, stories by Sherwood Anderson. After the fourth instalment of *Ulysses*, a subscriber, S.S.B., wrote from Chicago:

Really now: Joyce! What does he think he's doing? What do you think he is doing? I swear I've read his *Ulysses* and haven't found out yet what it's about, who is who or where. Each month he's worse than the last. I consider myself fairly intelligent. I have read more than most. There are some few things I expect of a writer. One of them is coherence. Joyce will have to change his style if he wants to get on.

But by the middle of 1919 Pound had left; Jules Romains became French editor, at least in theory, and John Rodker sent pieces from London. The magazine was on the way down. As long as Pound remained, it was propelled by an idea, the search for good work; if most of that work came from Europe, that was not Pound's fault. With Pound gone, the magazine had no governing idea. For the moment, the lack was concealed by spectacular events: *Ulysses* was still running, and after the thirteenth instalment (Leopold Bloom watching Gerty on Sandymount Strand: 'For this relief much thanks') the editors were arrested, the preliminary trial set for October 13, 1920. (In the event, the gesture led not to gaol but merely to a fine, $50 each on the editorial ladies.)

Volume VIII was virtually a different magazine. One issue was given to Brancusi, the *Little Review* was now a quarterly, there was still a certain amount of good stuff; but the new tone was all Narcissus. The current names were on show, Stein, Cocteau, Apollinaire, possibly as a result of Francis Picabia's influence, but the editors were obviously lost. They could be forgiven readily because they knew not what they did. One of the immediate signs of distress was the fuss over Baroness Else von Freytag-Loringhoven, the frenetic attempt to present her as a major writer. The only explanation for this madness was that the Baroness was the most complete imitation of a Dada that the *Little Review* had ever met. John Rodker wrote in July-August, 1920:

Paris has had *Dada* for five years, and we have had Else von Freytag-Loringhoven for quite two years. But great minds think alike and great natural truths force themselves into cognition at vastly separated spots. In Else von Freytag-Loringhoven Paris is mystically united to New York.

There is no evidence that the editors had the faintest clue to the Baroness's procedures, but in a country which had one of everything, a feminine Tristan Tzara was essential. In the next issue L. Lozowick announced that the Russians had one, a male, Alexander Krutchenich. Back in Manhattan, the *L.R.* printed a long piece by the Baroness, 'Thee I Call Hamlet of Wedding-Ring', ostensibly a critique of William Carlos Williams's *Kora in Hell*. The editors, let it be said, were doubtful about this piece, perhaps because it appeared to be prose, and in printing it Margaret Anderson made one of her classic observations:

The policy of the *Little Review* has always been: a free stage for the artists. There are moments when I believe this to be an uninteresting policy.

So the thing was printed; at this distance it hardly calls for comment, it is not amenable to description. At one point the word 'meticulous' is used, with a footnote: 'this word dedicated solely to Marcel Duchamp. Gave it to me with tongue lilt emanation of spirit—*it is he*'. Replying to Harriet Monroe, who suggested in *Poetry* that the *Little Review* might consider dropping the Baroness, Jane Heap retorted:

. . . we do intend to drop the baroness—right into the middle of the history of American poetry. . . . When she is dada she is the only one living anywhere who dresses dada, loves dada, lives dada.

After this, the magazine never recovered its sanity. It still found good work, but rarely; pieces of Hemingway, Cummings, Hart Crane. The last years were squandered, bad money thrown after bad, novelties hoarded as if they would always be new, bright ideas for the Machine Age; anything, glass, theatre-design. 'The Aesthetic of the Machine and Mechanical Introspection in Art', Futurism, Open Volume; until the whole enterprise, dying of its own too much, expired in 1929.

The last issue was entirely commemorative and lugubrious, offering 'Confessions and Letters: More than Fifty of the Foremost Men in the Arts Tell the Truth about Themselves in this Number'. In fact, few truths were told; most of the items were diplomatic, unless the participant thought that this might be the Last Chance.

Margaret Anderson explained that she had lost faith in art: the artist no longer knew what he was doing:

And I can no longer go on publishing a magazine in which no one really knows what he is talking about.

Jane Heap's version was even more direct; there were no longer any 'good writers and the manufacture of silk purses was impossible':

For years we offered the *Little Review* as a trial-track for racers. We hoped to find artists who could run with the great artists of the past or men who could make new records. But you can't get race horses from mules.

The next sentence says everything:

We have given space in the *Little Review* to 23 new systems of art (all now dead), representing 19 countries. In all of this we have not brought forward anything approaching a masterpiece except the *Ulysses* of Mr. Joyce. *Ulysses* will have to be the masterpiece of this time.

Ben Hecht shed tears, Gertrude Stein wrote a flurry of gratitude, Gide sent two letters. Djuna Barnes declined. The Baroness was already dead, but they printed a piece of suicidal prose. Pound wrote to accuse the editors of suppressing one of his manuscripts; J.H. answered that she threw it away for the good of his reputation. Wyndham Lewis sent a photograph. Joyce could think of nothing he chose to say. Marianne Moore, asked why she went on living, answered that the surrender of life did not seem to be demanded of her.

The whole episode is bizarre. Pound was the only participant in the *Little Review* who knew what he was doing and had the executive force to do it. The editorial women were heroines, but at the same time children. Pound was replaced by Rodker; that is, no replacement could be found. The demise of the magazine did not leave America entirely bereft; several of the more serious writers were already welcome in *Hound and Horn, Poetry, The Symposium*, and other magazines. Besides, in its later years the *Little Review* was so crazy that it was useless to American writers for any important purposes. By the time it stopped, it was time for it to stop; perhaps the editors realized this, through their tears. So there is a certain propriety in its going down with the more resounding and more notorious Crash: it was always too happy making a noise. In the great days it was, indeed, great. Even in its bad days it had good moments, as if by mistake: in Volume X Gertrude Stein wrote of

Juan Gris: 'he has black thoughts but he is not sad'. Eliot said in his obituary letter that it was the only periodical, during those years, in which he cared to appear; a touching avowal, rendered possible by his choosing to forget *Poetry*, *Others*, and *The Egoist*. Still, the *Little Review* was special, while its critical power lasted. It offered an affront to New York and Chicago, not merely to *Vanity Fair* and *The Smart Set*. It could not topple the skyscrapers in Manhattan, but it helped to keep the lines of intelligence open in a bad time. Eliot's idiom seems appropriate.

6

FICTION OF 1968

(a) IRIS MURDOCH

The Nice and the Good

THE ONLY SURPRISES in Iris Murdoch's eleventh novel are those which her previous ten would lead you to expect, and the appearance of *The Nice and the Good* will not do much to resolve the current disagreement over the quality and importance of her work. Despite the increasingly mixed reception of her more recent novels, it seems clear that Miss Murdoch is set on her ways and is not going to be deterred by critical hostility; in fact she appears quite oblivious of it. *The Nice and the Good* is entirely characteristic of the kind of novel Miss Murdoch has been writing since *A Severed Head*, and its presentation is neither defensive nor apologetic. On the contrary, it is the work of a writer thoroughly confident of her intentions and energetically engrossed in realizing them. Iris Murdoch continues to write on her own terms.

Even by Murdochian standards, however, *The Nice and the Good* is a relatively relaxed affair. Its action is not obscure, although it is occasionally bizarre. The relationships between the characters are quite elaborately patterned but they are also reasonably straightforward (no incest, for example), and they terminate happily for the most part. Although it is not witty—Miss Murdoch seems nowadays to distrust the sparkle of *Under the Net* and *A Severed Head*—it is fundamentally benevolent; it is a comedy.

The most nearly central character is John Ducane, a civil servant in his forties who wants to end what has become a morally untidy

---

(a) *The Nice and the Good.* 350 pp. Chatto and Windus. 30s.
(b) *The Undiscovered Country.* 307 pp. Constable. 30s.
(c) *Tunc.* 316 pp. Faber and Faber. 25s.
(d) *The Junkers.* 314 pp. Secker and Warburg: Alison Press. 35s.
(e) *The Public Image.* 192 pp. Macmillan. 25s.
(f) *The Crying Game.* 286 pp. Eyre and Spottiswoode. 25s.

affair with Jessica, a younger art teacher. He loves rather than is in love with Kate, the wife of Octavian, the head of Ducane's department. She is quite happy to 'love' him back within the ostentatiously successful context of her vigorously rewarding relationship with her husband. Kate is the queen of a large household by the coast in Dorset which includes her child and two other women—a widow and a divorcée—and their children. Then there is Theo, who left India under some sort of unspecified cloud, and Willy, who was once in Dachau and now lives a hermit-like existence editing Propertius. The narrative structure of the book is based on the repercussions on these people of a sensational event in London: the suicide of a man in Octavian's department. Ducane is given the job of finding out, informally, what was behind this desperate action; he uncovers some strange goings-on, and precipitates further catastrophes.

The plot, although moderately intriguing, is not very tightly developed. Its chief function, as one might expect, is to provide narrative justification or at least narrative occasion for a series of amorous encounters and confrontations. *The Nice and the Good*, like all Miss Murdoch's novels, is a love-story, that is, a story designed to discover more about the character of love by analysing, mobilizing and juxtaposing characters in love. Ducane, for instance, is appalled by the power over Jessica that her love for him permits, and part of Kate's attraction for him is that the solidity of her marriage gives him no power over her.

These manoeuvrings are not continuously gripping to follow in the text itself. Miss Murdoch's sometimes remarkable narrative momentum—evident for instance in the first half or so of *The Unicorn*—has either deserted her here or been voluntarily laid aside. The action is dispersed and often desultory; there is a prevailing impression of thinness; the novel's considerable length seems inadequately underpinned. There are, certainly, one or two exciting sequences—notably the trapping by the tide of two characters in a coastal cave—and there are odd twists and striking developments. Nevertheless there is a basic dislocation between Ducane's investigation in London and the life of the Dorset household; the two main cogs of the action do not satisfyingly mesh. With so many personal dilemmas to resolve, an episodic structure may have been to some extent inevitable, but a deeper perfunctoriness is betrayed by the author's tendency to analyse—often with real if fitful authority—the salient features of one person's situation, only to abandon him while some other necessary case is gone into.

This narrative lassitude is associated with a lack of imaginative intensity. Ducane is an interesting character, but he is only *theoretically* interesting. In many ways he resembles Michael Meade in *The Bell*: he wants to act justly; he tries honourably to maintain an idea of himself as a good man; he wants a life that is morally coherent and decently self-contained. But he is put in positions where he cannot avoid judging and exerting power over others—positions which he feels as false but which are all the same obligatory and with which he must come to terms. His situation perhaps bears some relation to Camus's judge-penitent. His dilemmas are interestingly discussed by the author, but—unlike Michael Meade—Ducane never becomes independent of the terms of Miss Murdoch's discussion.

Although *The Nice and the Good* is not as rigorously organized as some of her recent novels—one does not quite have the sense of characters being positively chivvied into choreographic chases—the pairings are still rather remorselessly enforced. Miss Murdoch has not here justified her assumption that a sense of the mysterious possibilities latent in the personality can be plausibly demonstrated by working characters through an implausible series of sexual permutations. Her often liberating apprehension of the miraculous impenetrability of other people has so often been conveyed by making them do wildly unexpected things that the authenticity of her persons has become compromised by the ostentatious formality of the patterns in which she has involved them. In *The Nice and the Good* this technique is not pushed to extremes but it is evident enough to prevent the characters from seeming free from authorial manipulation, although there are passages of finely dispassionate sympathy.

This novel also relies too much on familiar items from its resourceful author's battery of effects. A picture (Borzino's 'Venus, Cupid, Folly and Time') plays a central part in one relationship (compare the Gainsborough in *The Bell* or the Tintoretto in *An Unofficial Rose*); binoculars are used (as in *The Unicorn*); there are patches of philosophical chat (though not as sustained or interesting as in *Under the Net*); there are twins again—children, admittedly, and unburdened this time with androgynous significance. The use of these and other previously deployed motifs is more casual than before, and takes less weight. Then there are episodes which seem seductively mythical and look as if they are clues to some quasi-allegorical level of significance which would, of course, constitute the book's *real* meaning. Ducane descends to an underground region below Whitehall where Black Masses have been celebrated, and then might be said to be 'cleansed' by immersion in the sea-cave. Someone else mentions Book VI of the *Aeneid*. Kate and Octavian have a generally Olympian style of hedonism, and Kate and the other two Dorset women are explicitly referred to as the Three Graces. Another temptress is nicknamed Helen of Troy. These allusions are, however, more likely to be mere episodic intensifications or simple playfulness than coded hints for explicators.

Despite the dispassionate relaxation of manner which Miss Murdoch now clearly prefers to the much more self-conscious obscurities and intensities of her earlier work, and despite a conclusion which is not far from being soppy, *The Nice and the Good* remains oddly undismissable. It does not do justice to Miss Murdoch's talent but, when all reservations have been made, it still sufficiently exhibits those rare enough qualities which sustain all her novels: an unusual if often recklessly trusted power of imaginative invention, and a serious, generous, and indefatigable attention to the problems of the moral life.

(*b*) JULIAN MITCHELL

The Undiscovered Country

MR. MITCHELL's sixth novel comes in two parts: a 'memoir' of a best friend, written in a relaxedly non-fictional style, introducing several palpably non-fictional persons and places; and a surrealist novella, called *The New Satyricon*, allegedly the friend's literary testament discovered after his suicide. Either we have two pieces of fiction, both Mr. Mitchell's own work; or one which is his but not fiction and another which is fiction but not his. Critics have been known to panic over such challenges.

This reviewer would settle for the diagnosis of pure fiction—taking a hint from the cover, which welds two profiles of Mr. Mitchell, one with glasses and one without, into a half-tone Janus. 'Charles Humphries', on this reading, really is the *alter ego* which Mr. Mitchell's 'memoir' calls him. The whole thing is less Nabokovian charade than Isherwoodian mirror-writing. Indeed, the first half would blend easily with *Down There on a Visit*. Both writers excel in deadpan comic observation of their own class in exotic surroundings; both cast themselves as torn between hedonism and a secular-Puritan conscience. Both have wrought a flat conversational style to a high pitch of technical subtlety; both can fall down heavily on the further sentimental side of simplicity. As here:

He was six feet tall and his hair was black and his eyes were brown and his eyebrows met over the bridge of his nose. His name was Charles. He made me laugh and cry. He is dead. He used to astound me. He said I looked like a magistrate in a Turkish bath. I failed him, and he is dead.

There is rather too much of this in *The Undiscovered Country*. Playing games with factuality suggests a certain nervousness. One might even maliciously wonder whether Mr. Mitchell wrote the memoir first and then adorned it with pastiche, or wrote an experimental novel first and then bolstered it with a narrative in his more accustomed manner. Certainly the first half does not stand up on its own. Charles's succeeding existential crises are too thinly recorded, his obstinate passion for authenticity too tidily counterpointed with the narrator's success and rationality; even the scenes of their meetings, from Los Angeles to Aldermaston, are something of *Zeitgeist* on the cheap. Mr. Mitchell can do schools, or minor changes of mood, very fluently. We know this, and he knows that we know. *The New Satyricon* is presumably a self-criticism of just these minor virtues; a flight from 'compulsive readability'—and much the more interesting half of the book.

Its style is like Cleland, or Defoe, or any master of classical picaresque; its arrangement and content is more like William Burroughs—not actual cut-ups, but a string of episodes which tend to begin and end in the middle of sentences. They take a narrator-hero through a series of fantastic adventures in a vast hotel, where the management and the restaurant are in open civil war, but which is still doing enough business to accommodate a society devoted to sexual pleasure, a pop-concert, a dress-rehearsal of anti-theatre, an Ideal Mother competition, a Lucullan banquet, the narrator's father, and the most beautiful creature in the world. Henry—the narrator—has fallen in love with him/her (since Henry himself later changes sex, the pronouns do not matter) after one glimpse on arrival in the unnamed, undiscovered and presumably eponymous country in which these horrors and delights take place. His progress, in fact, is also a quest.

As a gallop through modern absurdities, it is at least a welcome change from the stranglehold of contemporary realism, and sometimes a little more. As an allegory, even a string of allegorettes, it is not so happy. Henry, for all his elegant simplicity and wide-eyed innocence, is finally less than *Candide*. Mr. Mitchell as narrator flits in and out of *The New Satyricon*, jogging our elbows with hints of the author's—or 'author's'—intentions: Henry is an epitome of self-consciousness, the style sets traps for the over-inquiring reader, the final tableau is a mixture of Freud and the story of Abraham and Isaac. But the fantastic form leaves us dry-eyed and indifferent to interpretations; Henry may swoon, but we shall not be moved. The desire to move is not always the best creative impulse. If Mr. Mitchell had followed it less, he might have produced a less uneven and no less interesting book.

(c) LAWRENCE DURRELL

Tunc

A READER coming across this sentence in Lawrence Durrell's new novel might well think that he was still in the steamy, decadent world of *The Alexandria Quartet*:

Gradually leads up from Salamis the smell of baked bread, melons, tar, borne on the breath of the evening freshets which will soothe wet armpits and breasts.

But although *Tunc* has many points of connexion in both method and material with its author's earlier fiction, its intentions are sufficiently different to make some revision of expectation and attitude necessary.

Durrell's sharp, sensual evocation of place has always been a strength and a stand-by, but the description of Athens just given is not altogether typical of the texture of his new book. None of the localities of *Tunc*—and they include Athens, Istanbul, London, Paris, and Salisbury Plain—benefits from the caressing touches formerly given to the highly erogenous zone of Alexandria. Such atmospheric sequences as rowing through the watery vaults of a palace on the edge of the Bosphorus or driving through early morning Wiltshire mist are vivid enough but a little perfunctory in execution, as if the writer's attention were partly engaged elsewhere.

The principal characters, too, have a diminished vitality. Benedicta, the woman whom the narrator Felix Charlock marries, is as
enigmatic as Justine was, but her enigmas are more left to look
after themselves. There is no repetition of the earlier attempt at
'prism-sightedness', so that one person is seen from various points
of view. The oracular writer Pursewarden has a successor in Koepgen
who has a similar style of cloudy knowing—in fact, he is said to have
been influenced by Pursewarden—but his aphorisms are less frequent
and less germane. A comic deviant named Sipple is a poor relation
of the old Scobie; his patter is feeble when compared with Scobie's
rich and idiosyncratic vocabulary.

Other familiar Durrellian ingredients can be found: comedy at the
expense of the English governmental establishment, bawdy farce at
the Blue Danube brothel in Athens, and some genial jeering at
literary fashion—a publisher instantaneously transforms the French
novel by bringing out a translation of *Bradshaw*. But since these
aspects of *Tunc* also betray a certain loss of energy it would be easy
to conclude that, as a writer, Durrell is simply not quite the man he
was; and this may partly be so.

However, it is also clear that the author is more preoccupied with
abstract matters than he used to be. Of course, the *Quartet's* structure was justified by an appeal to the relativity proposition—an
aspect of the work taken with particular seriousness by Continental
critics—but the resulting 'soup-mix' of the Alexandrian word-
continuum was always more convincing as a practical stock-pot into
which left-overs could conveniently be thrown than as a rigorously
applied theory of perception.

Lawrence Durrell himself has referred to *Tunc* as a 'shadow-play'
containing much more 'hidden theology' than his previous work—
deodorized theology, as he hastened to add. The novel is intended as
an inquiry into the nature of a culture and into the possibilities of
individual freedom within or without the culture. Durrell attempts
to convey such ideas through the history and situation of Charlock,
his inventor-hero, and his relationship with Merlin's, usually referred
to simply as 'the firm'.

We first meet Charlock in Athens, waiting for Koepgen, an errant
theologian-monk. With the help of a computer he has invented,
called Abel, Charlock recalls the stages which led to his present plan
to disappear. Abel seems partly to be a sort of memory-bank (the
Quartet too was an exercise in memory). Charlock's invention of a

deaf-aid for the Greek politician Graphos has brought him to the attention of Merlin's, a vast international organization apparently run by the Pehlevi brothers. He goes to meet Jocas Pehlevi at Istanbul (referred to, for some reason, as 'Polis'), and signs a staggeringly generous contract with 'the firm'. He should be happy; his name is not Felix for nothing. He is also enthralled by Benedicta Merlin, the founder's daughter, and they decide to marry. Her conquest of him largely takes place during a hawking expedition; when he first meets her she has a falcon on her wrist, and it is clear that she herself is a lure. (At the end of the book, after separation from Charlock, she is seen setting out again for Turkey to ensnare another promising scientist.)

'Merlin' signifies both bird of prey and magician. At first Charlock is principally conscious of the firm's beneficent aspect. He is given every conceivable facility for his research, and overwhelmed in luxury. He and Benedicta—whose wealth is so great that to her the word 'cost' is meaningless—go on a honeymoon cruise round the world. But, increasingly, Charlock feels frustrated by the firm, and in particular by Julian, the other, London-based Pehlevi brother, whom he can only talk to by telephone. He makes several rather absurd attempts to see Julian, but the most he ever glimpses is a cigar-holding hand in a retreating railway-compartment. The uses to which Charlock's discoveries are put, without his consent, include a new gunsighting system; his desire simply to give away one of his inventions to mankind is blocked by Julian.

Felix's relationship with his wife deteriorates as she is withdrawn by bouts of neurasthenia; she retires to the Paulhaus clinic at Zurich. After the birth of their son, reconciliation seems hopeless. Charlock's relationship with the firm being now also intolerable, he thinks of escape. He also wants to perfect his computer Abel which will serve as his instrument of revenge against Julian.

Other characters are seen partly and often mostly in the omnipresent context of the firm. The celebrated architect Caradoc, who gives a drunken lecture on the relation of buildings to bodies to a select but baffled audience on the Acropolis, is sent by the firm to build a new university in the south seas; he is reported killed in an air crash, but it later seems more likely that he has made a getaway and gone native. Charlock's Athenian former mistress, Iolanthe, becomes an internationally famous film star, and immediately uses her riches to buy creative independence from the firm. Koepgen is finally (but mistakenly) convinced that the firm has relinquished its hold on him.

'The firm' clearly stands for the culture to which we are all subject and by which we are all modified. According to Julian the firm 'has always existed in one form or another . . . it's a fact of nature, man's nature . . . It's not in itself malefic, just neutral . . .'. The narrative development of the novel—as this bald synopsis may help to indicate—backs this up well enough. The firm is visibly seen to provide opportunities for great advances in human knowledge; it receives many testimonials, even from Caradoc, who is trying to escape from it but who owes to it the opportunities he has had to make fine buildings. It is therefore ungrateful not to acknowledge the firm.

Besides, the firm is very extensive. It embraces the whole of Europe: the stationing of the two Pehlevi brothers (if they *are* brothers) at its extremities is not accidental—indeed their respective spheres of operation are likened to the division of the church between east and west. And wherever Charlock and Benedicta go on their round-the-world trip, the firm's representatives are unobtrusively on hand. Caradoc's flight to a Pacific island no doubt represents a deliberate abandonment of civilization in favour of the primitive, but the firm tries to seek him out even there.

Is it in fact possible to escape from it? At the end of the book Koepgen conveys to Charlock a message given him by an old man dying in a leper colony on an island off Crete who may be the founder of the firm, Merlin, himself. Charlock is told that 'The firm only exists to be escaped from' and that 'There are two kinds of death open to the living'. *Tunc* is announced as the first deck of a two-decker novel and presumably its sequel will show what, in effect, such propositions mean and how they are to be reconciled. Charlock, by the end of this book, has laid misleading clues indicating his death: his clothes have been found on a Mediterranean beach. Felix is once jokingly referred to as 'Charlock Holmes', and his apparent demise as a result of his struggle with Julian may be meant to recall Holmes's apparent end while wrestling with Moriarty. We are likely to see a revivified Charlock in the next book, and it is also probable that we have not seen the last of Caradoc.

Such further adventures will presumably demonstrate whether freedom outside the firm is possible. 'Free' is at one point said to be the only four-letter word that matters, and many of the characters either seek it or knowingly abandon the quest for it. Even Benedicta

Merlin herself, the firm's lure, seems to have fleetingly hoped that Felix would free her from its golden chains. Some indication of what freedom outside the firm means can be gained by considering the fate and death of Iolanthe. Her career as a film star is said, by an admittedly biased witness, to be a travesty of civilization; she coarsens the culture because she makes it available to the modern mob who cannot understand it in its true form. Originally a true Greek, unselfconsciously at home in both brothel and Parthenon, Iolanthe buys her freedom at a ruinous price.

For Charlock, the question of freedom is bound up with his computer, Abel—his reply to the firm. He claims 'Give Abel a sigh or the birthcry of a baby and he can tell you everything', and even though he is drunk at the time, his ambitions for his machine are as ambitious as his remark implies. If Abel is fed with every possible scrap of sound-data it will then process the material so as to recall the past and predict the future of individual lives. The aspiration is towards a total vision of experience, and Abel has obvious affinities with the multiple-mirror devices of the *Quartet*. Charlock himself is not unlike Darley, the narrator of *Justine*, and he thinks of his inventive powers as analogous to those of the artist.

The clear presence of an over-riding thesis behind the novel makes it difficult to know where to call an interpretative halt. What parts of the book are parts of its argument, and what parts are there simply for kicks? The making of this distinction is hampered by the fact that in *Tunc* as elsewhere in Durrell the thought itself is often a function of physical experience. Benedicta, says Charlock, 'ached in my mind like an abstraction'; 'Caradoc ached on like a bad tooth'. Durrell is a sensational writer, and the expression of his thought through the experience of his senses means that it can be fitful, undisciplined and inconsistent.

The notions of culture and freedom implied by *Tunc*, when detached, seem rather thin and shaky, though it is easy to see what attracted Durrell about them. As the *Quartet* showed, he needs some conceptual hold-all to contain the variousness of his gear. But although in the *Quartet* we might be content to regard the relativity business as a fair admission price for the vitality displayed at the different booths within, in *Tunc* the performance is deliberately subdued in the interests of the theory of the novel. When the theory itself is not made convincing, we are bound to be left with a relatively pallid effect.

It would be wrong, however, to imply that *Tunc* is made hard to read by such concerns: if it has not quite the narrative drive of *Mountolive*, it is more coherently organized than *Clea*. What gives the story much of its considerable force is the mythic simplicity of its elements. Felix experiences two women, one dark, the other fair; he passes from the power of one benign brother to the thraldom of another malignant one. He is initiated into a magical world, marries and is discarded by its queen after begetting a son. He appears to die by water, but seems certain to be washed up on some strange coast. *Tunc* is a romance.

(d) PIERS PAUL READ

The Junkers

CYRIL JOAD wrote a story, *The Highbrows*, in 1922, explaining that it was not really a novel. He offered 'rhetorical exercises and didactic discussions . . . the characters are mere puppets for the writer to hang his polemical hat on'. Continuing his apology, he suggested that it was possible for a man interested, like himself, in the form of the modern novel, 'to develop that form to its logical conclusion by writing a novel which is far more like a modern novel than any novel ought to be, and in so doing, to pass a commentary upon it more significant than the most searching of reviews'. Although Piers Paul Read is a far more accomplished story-teller than Joad was, his detachment from his material, his refusal to suspend the reader's disbelief, his straightforward insistence that he is merely making up a neat tale, containing ideas, all recall that cool mood of the 1920s— made still cooler by his rejection of explicit moral judgments. Ethical standards are taken for granted: there is no rage expressed, a valuable and difficult self-denial when dealing with the cruelties of Nazism.

He concentrates on aristocrats. No one has done more to rescue the image of the German officer class (for the poetic imagination, which is predisposed to admire knightly and patrician qualities) than Claus von Stauffenberg: he is one of several conspirators against Hitler who appear, mingling with fictional characters, in these glimpses of Germany from the 1920s to the 1960s. It is typical of the author's straightforwardness that he should insert short bio-graphies of the real-life characters (in italics, between square brackets) into the body of the text. The chapters are made up of brief sections, with headings like 'Edward von Rummelsberg: 1942' or 'Klaus von Rummelsberg/Günter Strepper: 1943–1944'. The author is at his most unconventional when he ignores the convention of feeding necessary information to the reader in a supposedly 'natural' way—that is, by pretending to be doing something else, recording conversation or describing a landscape. Deliberately or not, he alienates as Brecht's slogans do: he is, also, at once terse and comprehensive.

The von Rummelsbergs mentioned above are two of three aristocratic brothers from Pomerania, Edward being a brave and religious soldier who is drawn into the anti-Nazi circle of Stauffenberg and his friends, while Klaus becomes adjutant to an exceptionally loathsome war criminal, Günter Strepper, the local dentist's son. After the war, Edward, who had deliberately surrendered to the Russians, becomes a respected member of the east German establishment, while Klaus works in west Germany as political leader of the right-wing refugees from the Communist sector. Klaus is subjected to investigation by the Occupation forces, in 1963, trying to guard against neo-Nazism. An unusual aspect of this investigation is the attitude of the young Englishman in charge, the narrator of the novel's story. Talking to Klaus, he is reminded of admirable Edward: 'I liked Klaus von Rummelsberg as instinctively as I liked his brother, and I saw no reason to give up either of them as friends'. Klaus talks of British errors in conquered Germany, and the young Englishman remarks: 'I expected to feel irritated that this ex-Nazi should talk about our mistakes, but I did not. What did I care? . . .' These are statements of fact about his feelings: he tells us no lies, expresses no 'righteous anger' that he does not truly feel.

Yet political considerations and moral judgments affect his sexual life—which he describes in a manner both clinical and poetic. Before Klaus and Edward, he had met the third brother—Helmuth von Rummelsberg who spent the war as a diplomat in Japan and, in 1963, is running cabarets: with Helmuth is a young girl, Suzi, and the narrator loves her. She turns out to be the daughter of Katerina Strepper, a Pomeranian aristocrat who married the infamous war criminal, but the young girl might conceivably have one of the von Rummelsbergs as a father; and this possibility offers no physical obstacle to love-making. But when the narrator first realizes that she must be the daughter of Strepper, he is unable to make love to her.

The same thing happens, later, when she becomes a Communist. Earlier in the book, we have seen Klaus as a young man, unable to make love to a Jewess. The narrator records these phenomena with an air of mild surprise. He is cool and aloof even when describing Strepper's atrocities, or the sado-masochistic tendencies apparent in his own and Suzi's sex life. (Constantly he offers links between minor failings and terrible crimes.)

At the book's end he finds himself shaking hands with Strepper, secretly returned from Argentina, and is wincingly prepared to accept the notion of this dreadful person as his father-in-law. He does not find Klaus von Rummelsberg dreadful at all. Having discovered that Klaus is quietly collaborating with Edward and the Communists, in the interests of a united Germany, the investigator decides to conceal this information from his British superiors and from the Americans, to keep it as a secret between himself and his French colleague. This narrator is extraordinary, taking responsibilities himself, ignoring obedience, contemplating with the same air of quiet wonderment events which most people would think unbearable, situations which most people would take for granted. Sometimes he is like Klaus, observing with a pained stare the obscene Nazi-sponsored experiments on guinea-pig women: sometimes he is like Helmuth listening to a Japanese friend, 'I know, if we lose this war, we shall be blamed for savagery and cruelty: our adversaries, I think, will blame their cruelty on machines'.

The oddity of the viewpoint relates to a refusal to consider motive, a refusal to blame. Results are what count. The results of Hiroshima cannot be preferred to the results of Auschwitz. Death on the road is no different, for the victim, from death by murder: moral horror can only be judged by the results—if, for instance, it is more difficult to make love to a murderer than to a careless motorist. Erotic feelings are so complex, however, that a murderer may be especially stimulating. The style of writing is appropriate to the author's determination to face facts unexcitedly: it is pure, unaffected, pre-Victorian. Other writers who have taken a similar tone when constructing moral fables include David Garnett, Edward Hyams, William Plomer—and, most of all, the author's father, Herbert Read, in his novel, *The Green Child*. It is a youthful tone, likely to be thought heartless by older readers. Some will hope, after this second *tour-de-force*, that Piers Paul Read can keep it up.

(e) MURIEL SPARK

The Public Image

The Public Image is a novella, and, like many another novella, it is set in Rome. But not, as might have been the case in earlier times, a Rome that is half consumed by its history, a Rome that is still ancient. This is a Rome whose only Colosseum is a 'communications' circus consisting of film people and of the press that is parasitic on them. Images are projected, reputations promoted. Only once does the past intervene.

Mrs. Spark's leading character is an actress by the name of Annabel Christopher, a mousy girl whose eyes photograph well: her *beaux yeux* take her into films, where her image is blown up into that of 'the English Lady-Tiger'. She is married to Frederick, who thinks himself of finer grain and is offended by her success, seeking shelter in an image of his own: that of the serious writer, among thieves. They settle in Italy, where the publicity notion of an intriguing couple smouldering behind their national reserve finds great favour. This is not, perhaps, an image that your average actor's agent would expect to work wonders with, but there it is. The marriage suffers, in the conventional way: he has a mistress and she has a baby; a hanger-on called O'Brien keeps visiting them.

One evening Frederick saddles her with some sordid guests, an expatriate rout of the sort that figures in Fellini's *La Dolce Vita*, then casts himself from the Church of St. John and St. Paul into the caves beneath, where workmen are digging and where the martyrdom of the latter saint is traditionally located. Afterwards there is the hysteria of image-protection, the hushing up of the various incriminating letters deposited around Rome by the suicide, and the problem of what to do about O'Brien's perfidious photostats of the letters. The inquest is being directed 'like a movie' by Annabel's aides and mentors, but she loses faith in the scenario, forgets her image and flees to Greece with her baby.

The circumstances of Frederick's suicide may seem symbolic, and so may Annabel's surname; they may appear to resemble the crosses and martyrdoms symbolized in Muriel Spark's earlier works. But it is unclear what is symbolized here, and the resemblance is more likely to be a matter of the survival of certain habits of expression than of any persistence of underlying aims. In important respects

The Public Image is unlike her other novels. It is a plain story
straightforwardly told. A spade is a spade; a catacomb is a catacomb—or at any rate cannot lightly be taken as a metaphor for
some spiritual state. Her previous novels are fantasies, in which much
hangs on the preservation of a manner and on the freshness and
individuality of the verbal wit. *The Mandelbaum Gate* is, of course,
an exception. It is more of a true story, and tends less towards
poetry; it is personal and even confessional in tone; wit becomes
artifice or is supplanted by a kind of piety. In the present book that
personal note is absent, and so, too, is the fantasy of her first book.
But she has not given up making jokes.

In those early days when she was working in small parts her stupidity
started to melt; she had not in the least attempted to overcome her stupidity, but she now saw, with the confidence of practice in her film roles, that
she had somehow circumvented it. She did not need to be clever, she only
had to exist; she did not need to perform, she only had to be there in front
of the cameras. She said so to Frederick, as if amazed that she had not
thought of it before. He was exasperated, seeing shallowness everywhere. . . .

The word 'shallowness' is a triumph, and it recalls the flair, and
economy, with which the bachelors of her earlier novels were
presented. Frederick has something of the odour of these bachelors.

  In one respect, however, the new novel *could* perhaps be called
confessional. Much is owed to the circumstances of Muriel Spark's
new life as an international star novelist, with a public image of her
own to bear. There have always been novelists who became stars,
and recent decades have brought closer relations between authorship
and show business. Novels are made into films, and novels are
written about films. Kingsley Amis's next novel is reported to be
about a television personality; and when Edna O'Brien left Ireland,
became a star—though not exactly an Irish Lady-Tiger—and shed
her Irish locations, these were replaced, at times, by scenes in such
places as film colonies. Muriel Spark has been exposed to similar
environments, and in the same way these environments have now
entered her fiction.

  The newness of her themes has left its mark: it is as if the novel
were still warm, or reeking, from the experiences it records. It has a
way of seeming improvised, blocked-out, rather than composed. A
short book by a concise writer, it manages, surprisingly, to ramble;
it makes no mysteries, yet it manages to appear rather cryptic. The
portrait of Annabel herself is its best feature: she is a convincing

waif, with nothing of the cinematic orphan about her. An endearing humility is established chiefly through her relationship with Frederick, in the course of which it becomes apparent that there are worse things than shallowness, though shallowness is, indeed, everywhere. It is a pity that Muriel Spark passes from this relationship as soon as she does, spending more than half the novel on the tumultuous outcome of Frederick's suicide.

At the end of the book she might almost appear to have succumbed to doubts about the value of this artless account of disorderly conduct. Annabel is at the airport:

She was pale as a shell. She did not wear her dark glasses. Nobody recognized her as she stood, having moved the baby to rest on her hip, conscious also of the baby in a sense weightlessly and perpetually within her, as an empty shell contains, by its very structure, the echo and harking image of former and former seas.

The use of grandiose language is sudden and incongruous, though that phrase about 'former and former seas' could only come from a remarkable writer. The shell represents a private image, after the public image by which Annabel's life has been ruled. But the story cannot be said to support its conclusion, which reads a little desperately, like a flight into the poetic. The book does not end. Like Annabel, it takes off.

(f) JOHN BRAINE

The Crying Game

THIS VERY READABLE NOVEL deals with the misadventures of a young journalist from the north who gets mixed up with a rather fast set in London. Though tall, handsome and soldierly in appearance, Frank Batcombe is a little shy: he frequents King's Road pubs, longing to be invited to join some circle, convinced that grand private parties are available somewhere in the neighbourhood. He returns to his dismal flat at World's End and counts his suits—which, from their description, would appear to have been selected by Jeeves. His habit of pricing everything he sees, of consciously noting the names of smart shops and restaurants, is enough to explain to the reader why Batcombe is not universally welcome. He gives the impression of a humourless man glumly, boringly, on the

F

make—a sad fact which does not seem apparent to Batcombe, as narrator.

All this changes when he meets dashing Adam Keelby, a public relations officer whom Batcombe comes to hero-worship. He gives Batcombe pertinent advice: 'We've got to be doubly clean because we went to a grammar school. . . . Either don't use cologne and all the rest of it or use stuff that you can only get at Floris or Trumpers or Harrods.' A.K. introduces the country mouse to a company of tall, lean bachelors in the £5,000 a year bracket, all holding the same political opinions—'extreme right or, to be more accurate, derisively anti-left'. They have invented the Society for the Propagation of Reaction, Arrogance and Stubborn Prejudice, to be known by the initials R.A.S.P. They have chosen Franco, Salazar, Vorster and Ian Smith as their executive. Their slogan is 'Down with Oxfam'. Somehow, when reported with stolid admiration by Batcombe, these jokes do not seem so funny as they do in the Peter Simple column. Their favourite game is 'Prog-baiting'—'prog' being short for 'progressive'. (No doubt this usage relates to 'trog', a word used by national service officers to describe rankers.) The framework of thinking here recalls Amis's novel, *Take a Girl Like You*, where the failings of left-wingers and other low types are enumerated: they are labelled as 'the stooges' and punishment-fantasies are devised by their enemies.

Other new friends include a fiercely independent journalist, A.K.'s conscience, who says things like: 'All my beliefs are working-class beliefs. Hang the murderer, flog the thug, jail the thief, distrust all foreigners and keep Britain white.' Another new friend, a leader-writer of 'meticulous cleanliness' who lunches at Rules, is described as 'a James Cameron with a head or a Peregrine Worsthorne with a heart'. Batcombe admires him for being 'all that I could never be. . . . He was of an old English Catholic family, and I was of Irish extraction on my mother's side'. But, if we are to sum up people and label them on the basis of accumulated details, Adam Keelby remains the most resistible of all. He has a tray containing the visiting cards of dukes, a collection of children's books and handcuffs.

Batcombe is an odd sort of journalist. He conducts long interviews without taking notes: no need for research or reporting. (How did he get this good job?) His principal task in this novel is to sneak into the press rumours about an affair between a Labour M.P. and a 'prog' novelist. This attempt is foiled by the treacherous

Keelby, who has been engaged to improve the image of a homosexual photographer. He puts it about that the prog lady is having
an affair with this client. It is almost the last straw for Batcombe:
he can't abide all this disloyalty, nor all the sexual perversity going
on in Keelby's vicinity. He wasn't too comfortable, either, when
Keelby brutally assaulted his client's delicate boy-friend. Now, tears
start in Batcombe's eyes; he slaps Keelby on the face and goes off
to make a good Catholic marriage, with a girl from one of the good
old English Catholic families.

Earlier there were signs of some kind of debased puritanism in
Batcombe. He went back to his solid family's home and drank with
his respected father ('next in line for a manager and earning over
£2,000 a year') in the homely Conservative Club, under a portrait
of the Queen. Father heard a 'suitably edited account' of Batcombe's
attempt to expose the M.P.'s love-life and commented: 'A dirty lot,
these bloody socialists, and cunning with it, not like poor old
Profumo.' This passage is clearly intended to represent Batcombe's
idea of a simple, high-principled environment, the basic decencies of
life. Yet more repulsive is Batcombe's trip to a council house in
South London. ('I felt sick. . . . The most frequently used term of
disapproval at our home was *Council House.*') But this is an important job. His paper is anxious to attack leniency towards murderers
and other criminals, and Batcombe must enter the noisome home
and interview the parents of a murdered child. The house is smelly,
the mother a slattern, the father a layabout; to look at the surviving
children 'was almost physically painful. Pity hurts'. Batcombe
handed out a Mannikin 'and the prosperous clubroom smell helped
to fumigate the atmosphere a little'. His tears flowing, Batcombe
writes a passionate anti-murder article, quoting: 'All I know is, my
Miriam's dead, and the man who did it is still alive. It won't seem
right to me if he doesn't die.' His article is 'a real cracker'. Batcombe
feels quite noble. Solid provincial virtue has triumphed over the
corrupt metropolis. . . .

Surely this crude novel is the melancholy climax of the Angry
Young Man phenomenon, all that mindless moaning against the
upper classes now directed against the so-called 'liberal establishment'.

7

THREE CONFESSIONS

(a) NORMAN MAILER

A FEW YEARS AGO Norman Mailer gave a lecture to an audience of
Cambridge undergraduates. It was perhaps the best attended talk
of the year—*An American Dream* had already received the kind of
attention that placed it immediately in that special area between
notoriety and critical recognition that turns out to be the top of the
best-seller list, and Mailer himself, with his flair for turning adventure into misadventure, had recently run for mayor of New York
and knifed his third wife on the street after a party. He had also, it
was rumoured, become a prophet of the new message, the key
symbols of which were cancer, pot, the orgasm, bull fighting and
boxing, so if there were some pre-lecture jokes about the oldest
hippie and the whitest Negro, there was nevertheless a genuine air
of anticipation in the austere and over-crowded room in which he
was awaited. That very few of the undergraduates present had read
any of his novels—or even much of his journalism—only became
evident halfway through a harrowing evening. What had really
brought them to hear him was their own version (secretly conceived
in the cinemas of their childhood) of the American dream. They
wanted neither the critical pieties of a highly gifted writer, nor the
moral analyses of a highly intelligent American citizen. They wanted,
above all, to be liberated for a short time from their education and
their English decency. They wanted glamour.

What they got was dressed for the occasion in a baggy blue suit,
a white shirt, a strangely institutional tie fatly knotted, and a waistcoat behind which a shirt and some other loose garments had

---

(a) NORMAN MAILER: *The Armies of the Night*. History as a Novel. The Novel
as History. 288 pp. Weidenfeld and Nicolson. £2 5s.

(b) WILLIAM STYRON: *The Confessions of Nat Turner*. 429 pp. Cape. 30s.

(c) NORMAN PODHORETZ: *Making It*. 384 pp. Cape. 36s. *The Commentary
Reader*. Edited by Norman Podhoretz. 763 pp. Rupert Hart-Davis. £5 5s.

apparently been stuffed—as if, in fact, two or three vests and the shirt had somehow been put on after the waistcoat. With his short, powerful body, his muscular paunch, this muddled respectability of clothing, and a flushed and shrewdly beaming face, he closely resembled one of those honest cops—Dennis O'Keefe's superior perhaps—from American films of the mid-1950s; which made him of the right period but from the wrong film. His very entry thus dispelled the glamour of his reputation. If this man was hip or of a negroid psyche, then there was still much to be said for the burping sourness of a Kingsley Amis, the camp asceticism of an Angus Wilson. Within the time it took Mailer to walk from the door to the centre of the hall he had lost his hold on the audience. Worse, its mood had turned against him. The embarrassing but potent dream had been hurriedly disowned, and Cambridge was fastidiously ironical once again. He was accompanied, it should be added—for the entourage helped define the impression of the man—not by any racy equivalent to James Baldwin's mysterious travelling companions but by a very pretty blonde lady with a cute smile (his fourth wife and a television actress) and a sleek fellow, himself fastidiously ironical, presumably a publisher's representative.

The lecture was, inevitably, it seemed, although in a smaller way, as complete a disaster as the novel it was intended to advertise. If Mailer had possessed the rhetorical gifts of a Baldwin (the master cat who seemed simultaneously to be purring in the audience's lap and smiling down at it from a high leafy branch) or if he had been deeply and truly and contemptuously drunk, in the manner made famous by Brendan Behan, then he might still have turned the newly regained aloofness of the audience to his advantage. But he was mainly inarticulate, and when he was articulate he was mainly strange (especially on cancer and the orgasm) and sometimes he was both inarticulate and strange, as for instance when he delivered a flurry of punches in the direction of the audience, checked himself with a chuckle, and then with a wink to his wife, ducked imaginary retaliations. At other times he simply stood, his arms hanging down and his face thrust out, in what seemed a positive stupor of stupidity. And all the while the audience, deceptively fresh of face and calm of voice, were polishing up their own positions, and were baiting him from behind them. It took the merest concentration on the memory of a Goya etching to give the implied metaphor a full and hideous life. The bear, sadistically got up in a suit designed to caricature its physique; cuffing the air harmlessly or falling into dazed incomprehension. The spectators, egging each other into bold bad manners from behind their joined defences, inflicted their mean wounds almost at will, though tirelessly. For anyone who had come to find out how the author of *The Deer Park* could have written *An American Dream*, the agonies of the evening lasted long after Mailer, once again crudely shadow-boxing, had been led out of the ring by his two companions who had themselves begun to take on—infected perhaps by the metaphor—the aspect of keepers. Anyway it seemed clear that *An American Dream* had been produced by a writer at the end of his tether. Its willed, self-obsessed rhetoric portended the fall of a major talent as a sudden and vulgar shopping spree might portend the bankruptcy of a stylish millionaire. The lecture itself had merely been the last desperate shaking of an empty cup. The sensation of loss—at least to the admirers of *The Deer Park* and the journalism—was far sadder even than that reminder of how much complacent spite lies, like a sac of poison, at the roots of the English urge to score moral points. At least Mailer, stumbling and ultimately forlorn, had been as much without malice as he had seemed to be without genius.

That evening is worth recording now, when Mailer has just produced so fine a book that only the author of *The Deer Park* and of the best of the journalism could have written it. For among the many incidental successes of *The Armies of the Night* is the way in which Mailer places the inept and insensitive side of himself in a perspective that is at once comic and convincing. In fact, the evocation of that Mailer among many Mailers is part of his complex intention, and if *The Armies of the Night* is a deeply serious account of the effect on the American artist of the war in Vietnam, it is also a deeply serious comedy about the distance between what we are and what we long to be.

It is written in two sections, the first of which deals with the Washington Peace March of October, 1967, in which Mailer, against much of his will, so spectacularly figured, and goes on to a description of his arrest (deliberately provoked), his subsequent imprisonment, and the negotiations in the court-room that culminated in his release. The second and much shorter section is an account of the political manœuvres and counter-manœuvres that led to the staging of the march, along with a documentation of police action against the marchers. The first section is written as if by a novelist, with the incomparably human Mailer—Mailer *louche*, Mailer nervous, Mailer bold and Mailer cerebral—as the third person protagonist, while the second section is written as if by a journalist whose immediate concern—to give a concise history of the preliminary negotiations and the subsequent horrors—in no way betrays the ultimate and complex judgment to which he is working. The two sections, so seemingly different in tone, nevertheless complement each other and make for an astonishingly effective unity. For example, the moral comedy of a meditation on thirst (after only a short time in prison) moves from an awareness of physical discomfort to a confident celebration of the spiritual possibilities of thirst—'How good to know that a little hunger and a little thirst were tonic for a day of battle, and discipline for dull hours in jail'—and concludes with:

Yet on these thoughts, he took a drink of water. It was characteristic of him to make such a move, and he hardly knew if he did it for the best or worst of reasons, did it because in recognizing the value of thirst he had a small panic to destroy the temptation to search such a moral adventure further, or did he do it precisely because he was now aware of the value of thirst, and so thirst by such consciousness had lost its value. Or did he take a drink because he wished to study his new state after satisfying thirst? He noticed only that he was a trifle sad on the first sip, and couldn't stop going to the sink for more and more water afterwards. . . .

But our embarrassed and yet delighted recognition of this kind of self-betrayal is recalled with an intensification of embarrassment, and with no delight at all, when in the closing pages we read of a group of Quakers who had reached 'the last rite of passage' in a jail in Washington, where having refused to wear prison clothing and refusing to eat or drink, they were stripped naked and forced into cells so small that 'not all could lie down at once to sleep. . . . Dehydration brought them near to madness'. The frequently genial comedy of the first section through which Mailer invites us to share his knowledge of his own weaknesses, and thus smile fondly on our own, proves to be a trap in which Mailer, catching himself, also catches us. We, too, yearn—

> O to break loose, like the chinook
> salmon jumping and falling back,
> nosing up to the impossible
> stone and bone-crushing waterfall—
> raw-jawed, weak-fleshed there, stopped by ten
> steps of the roaring ladder, and then

to clear the top on the last try,
alive enough to spawn and die.

The quotation is used superbly, in the early pages, in bland juxta-position to a brilliant bitchy description of its author's participation in the pre-march meeting at Washington's Ambassador Theatre:

And Lowell, with a look of the greatest sorrow, as if all this *mess* were finally too shapeless for the hard Protestant smith of his own brain . . . now threw his eyes up like an epileptic . . . and fell backward, his head striking the floor with no last instant hesitation to cushion the blow, but like a baby, downright sudden, savagely to himself, as if from the height of a foot he had taken a pumpkin and dropped it splat on the floor. 'There, much-regarded, much-protected brain, you have finally taken a blow', Lowell might have said to himself, for he proceeded to lie there, resting quietly, while [Dwight] Macdonald went on reading from 'The White Man's Burden'. . .

then wonderingly, as 'Mailer' and Robert Lowell stand before the Pentagon, and wait, to the beat of the Fugs' exorcizing music—a music that Lowell finds 'so damned repetitious'—for their separate moments of choice before the marshals and the police; and finally, as part of a lament for that group of Quakers brought near to mad-ness by their noble intransigence. And the lines sound backward, through the whole journey from New York to a Washington gaol, commenting sadly on the short distance Mailer knows himself to have come, and the great distance, 'to the last rite of passage', that a handful of others had travelled. For Mailer teaches us what we would prefer not to know—that for most of us the conscience is not a pure and separate instrument, but captive to our egos, even to the silliest of our vanities, and that only on rare occasions and as if by chance does it break free, possibly 'to clear the top on the last try', but more likely, after expressing itself in a gesture that might be heroic but might also be rendered ludicrous by the inextricable rest of our natures, falls back inert into its old prison.

Mailer knows, too, that the war in Vietnam is a barbarous war, a war in which American atrocities abroad are defended by American atrocities at home, and he condemns it as best he can with all 'the cutting edge of his style'. But most of us are like him in that we could not go to 'the last rite of passage' either; and less than him in that we could not admit to what it is that would prevent us—nor therefore make out of the admission a work that, for all its darkly pessimistic notes, is nevertheless liberating.

Finally to return to that helpless, shadow-boxing figure of the Cambridge disaster. It is impossible to understand now what the real Mailer—the author of *The Deer Park* or of *The Armies of the Night*—made of the audience, but it was likely to have been more generous than what the audience made of him. Perhaps *An American Dream* was really the result of a desperate groping for the data that history was shortly and horribly to provide, and the real prophet— the novelist—was brought to a temporary paralysis somewhere between what he felt and what he knew. But what is certain is that trapped within that apparent ineptness was a voice more genuinely representative of civilization than all the voices that sounded confidently out at him then and that in a more sophisticated form have begun to sound out at him once more.

(*b*) WILLIAM STYRON

SOME WRITERS REGARD a first-person narrative the way a film director would consider making a movie with only one camera. Yet the technical restrictions of the narrative 'I' vary a good deal, depending on whether the confining ego is the author's autobiographical self or an imaginary character created by him. When he is writing as himself, he is presumably limited to the facts and fictions of his own experience; when he is writing as an imaginary character, he is limited only by what he can persuade the reader to accept. Even the autobiographical ego, however, seems wonderfully free when compared to a first person which belongs to someone who actually lived and whom the author is attempting to revive with his imagination: his sense of confinement as a writer must then be almost unbearably intense. We cannot check the detail of the author's own life nor that of an imaginary character, but we *can* track down his lies and evasions in the case of a literary Lazarus, and we can also be more sure about his achievement in drawing character. We knew of the real Lazarus; has he been brought back to life? Or is he perhaps another person using the same name, the same ego?

Although it is justifiable to base a novel on a real character, it is not as easy to justify writing such a novel in the first person. At one extreme in this biographical kind of novel is *The Moon and Sixpence*, in which Somerset Maugham built so much on his Gauguin base

that he even used another name for the character and thus didn't
have to worry about respecting the facts of Gauguin's life—or
respecting Gauguin. Then, more in the middle of this group, come
the floods of novels about artists with romantic, dramatic lives so
popular in the last generation. Typical of these was *Lust for Life*
about Van Gogh, which was written in the third person and usually
had good documentary evidence for ascribing certain 'thoughts' to
its hero, 'Vincent'. We were in fact let in for a minimum of that
kind of embarrassment we feel on reading trashy, patronizing
interior monologues ostensibly put in the head of some hero we
admire by a scribe lacking the hero's genius and eloquence. We can
most easily understand the whole problem when we remember how
little we know about even the way our own parents think and
behave. Would the reader like Irving Stone or a contemporary
Somerset Maugham to write a novel about his father or mother
describing their allegedly intimate thoughts and actions?

It is reasonable to pose this question in considering William
Styron's new novel, *The Confessions of Nat Turner*, for which he has
just been awarded the 1968 Pulitzer prize for fiction, because Mr.
Styron has not only chosen as his chief character a man who actually
lived but he has written in the first person as if from Nat Turner's
viewpoint. Most American critics when the novel first appeared
applauded this as an extraordinary feat of the imagination, but
unfortunately it appeared that they were greatly influenced by the
fact that Nat Turner was a Southern Negro and Mr. Styron is a
Southern White; and the twain never usually meet; they were really
seeing it not in literary or even in human terms, but in a purely
racial context. Nobody seemed to care what Nat Turner the man
would have thought about having another man's thoughts—particularly some repressed puritanical ones—ascribed to him. Trying to
repeat Mr. Styron's feat of imagining Mr. Turner's reactions, one
suspects that he would not have liked it at all.

The essential drama of Nat Turner—the slave revolt he led in
Virginia in 1831—is a great story, even in the bits and pieces left us
after most of the evidence was suppressed. It naturally would attract
an American novelist of our time because he might find in it so many
reflections of today's racial tragedy. For those who read only newspaper headlines, Stokely Carmichael will seem to follow in the foot-
steps of Nat Turner: ten years ago Malcolm X might have seemed
a successor. It would be impossible to convince such a reader that

the real Nat Turner, in fact, would have had more in common with the late Dr. Martin Luther King, because they shared a great religious sense, although in action Nat Turner was more an Old Testament man and Dr. King was strictly a son of the New Testament. It is a story, in short, that has the raw material of all the great historical novels; it is a marvellous tale and also is very relevant to our own time.

But why tell it from Nat Turner's viewpoint in the first person? Firstly, it shows scant respect for Nat Turner, who was obviously an extraordinary man; secondly, hardly any documents remain, except his own brief confession, to justify guessing his thoughts or feelings; thirdly, he lived over 100 years ago as a slave, and we know very little about the day-to-day domestic lives of slaves, so that the author not only had to throw his imagination back over a century but also into an almost unknown society; also he is a white Southerner and therefore had all kinds of personal, social blocks to overcome in tackling this particular subject from the inside. Technically, too, there seem to be enormous advantages in giving us a third-person narrative without any of the restrictions of the first person, for surely there are restrictions enough without any purely technical ones: in this case, one would have thought the novelist needed all the help he could give himself.

Having raised the question of why this form was chosen—the first novel, in fact, Mr. Styron has written in the first person—we need now to consider how it works out in practice over 429 pages. Well, let us say this at once. Lazarus (that is, Nat Turner) hasn't been raised from the dead. This combination of Old Testament prophet and Southern white puritan isn't the Nat Turner who has so sturdily resisted the White South's attempts to erase him from history. And one wonders in the end, as he clearly isn't Nat Turner, whether he is anyone, or whether perhaps the author hasn't rolled back the gravestone and found the body arising in his novel to be no more or less than William Styron himself. Almost at times one can imagine the book as *The Confessions of William Styron* by Nat Turner, for the style is biblical (in a contemporary translation), though more rhetorical than Nat Turner's own confession (which anyway was taken down by a lawyer and may have been only a curt summary by an amateur stenographer); the style *could* be Nat Turner's on a garrulous day, but the person reflected there seems so often to be an outsider posing as an insider, i.e., Styron himself. The details of slave life, what a Negro slave thought (or thinks) of a white person, the racial smells, and so on down through the documentary details, are often expressed too badly in the way a white outsider often tells one some things about Negro life which he imagines are some great original discovery. Mr. Styron, who has come late to an appreciation of Negro life, might well write that way, but Nat Turner, who was born knowing all of it, would have written or talked much more naturally about it all and so fitted it more closely into the body of his narrative. It is the difference between knowing something at first hand and merely learning it at second hand. One might add, of course, that Mr. Styron presumably had to bear in mind that he was writing essentially for a white book-buying public even more ignorant of Negro life in America, then or now, than Mr. Styron, and therefore these bald explanations were necessary in his mind, however much they strike the wrong notes in a narrative pretending to be Nat Turner's.

Mr. Styron perhaps sought to defend himself from such a charge in his prefatory note, in which he calls his book 'less an "historical novel" in conventional terms than a meditation on history'. Call it a novel, and perhaps Mr. Styron will reply: 'Now, now, didn't I tell you it was a "meditation on history"?' But unfortunately *The Confessions of Nat Turner* is a novel or it is nothing, although one leading American weekly did choose to have it reviewed by an historian. Its history, however, is at a freshman level and its meditating is no more profound than that of most talented novelists, even great ones. And this is no criticism of it as a novel, for history and literature serve different gods. History must at its most basic level be accurate as regards facts even if it is incapable of recapturing atmosphere. But a novel at the same basic level has to involve us in its atmosphere; it can dispense with facts altogether. If Mr. Styron's Nat Turner were a giant who involved us in his tragedy as if it were our own, we might have reservations about writing of someone who has lived in the first person (surely it is always condescending), but we would excuse it as the price for the writer's art. But Mr. Styron's Nat Turner does not so involve us. There are long stretches of fine descriptive writing—and when 'Nat Turner' is involved simply in action, it is often moving—but the sum total is not a man, not a slave in nineteenth-century Virginia, but, as Mr. Styron suggests himself, the author meditating on slavery in his own home state, and perhaps his sense of the white Southerner's guilt in himself, though surely *The Confessions of William Styron* would have been more to the point there (how seldom white Southerners are willing to give us the kind of soul-stirring personal confessions we have come to expect from American Negro writers).

Some American Negro critics have questioned its historical accuracy (some think, for example, that rather than being the repressed puritan of Mr. Styron, Nat Turner was, in fact, married and deep in family life) but we must insist on considering it as a novel and therefore much more relevant to us is the liveliness of the chief character—call him 'Nat Turner' or 'Charles Strickland', it doesn't really matter, so long as you reject Mr. Styron's description of it as a 'meditation'. We know enough about contemporary slum life, ghetto life, Southern rural and plantation life, to guess what some aspects of slave life must have been like. Certainly in that kind of environment you must graduate sexually much earlier and take most sexual forms of expression much more for granted. Mr. Styron has his 'Nat' and one of the other slaves trying to communicate with each other through a feeble little touch of homosexuality. The scene, though prettily written, was more like certain scenes that used to appear in novels about English public schools—or perhaps white Southern private schools. Nor is 'Nat's' hungering for white womanhood and apparent rejection of Negro girls very convincing even in contemporary terms. Slave life by its very nature could not support such artificial, genteel, puritanical repressions. It is an essentially dry, reserved attitude and what one senses above all in the very little we know about slave life is the flood of soul feeling waiting to find an outlet, almost any outlet. Mr. Styron's 'Nat', in the matter of sex, is more like a suburban white boy.

A big point of his characterization is that 'Nat' could not bring himself to kill. Fifty-five white men, women and children were killed by 'Nat's' army of slaves, but 'Nat' himself kept finding his weapons too inefficient and succeeded at last in killing only one person—a young white girl he had yearned after. And after that one killing, the fanaticism that had kept him going seeped out of him. As Mr. Styron has him say: 'My mouth was sour with the yellow recollection of death and blood-smeared fields and walls.' He watches a white girl escape without trying to stop her. 'Did I really wish to vouchsafe a life for the one that I had taken?'

It is a convenient way of looking at all the bloodshed. The ill-treated slaves, led by a biblical fanatic, rebelled and murdered, but their leader, finding action harder than words, is revolted by the bloodshed and gives up. It is the same hope of those white Americans today who fear some great violent act of Negro revenge: a hope that guilt will stop the Negroes. That is why the late Dr. King was admired by so many white people—he condemned the violence even before it began. His religious message, however, was lost. So, too, this way of looking at Nat Turner's revolt is much too convenient. Why accept it any more than the opposite interpretation—that Nat Turner was not a fanatic of the Old Testament who turned into a lover of the New Testament when he tried to carry out his revenge, but that he was really as much of an avenger as Abraham or David and that the slave-owners by their very way of life were human devils good only for fire and sword? Just as Mr. Styron does not delve deeply enough into the slaves' way of life but often seems to be transplanting the way of life he has known in *his* Virginia, so, too, he seems to be taking too easy, too convenient, too complacent a view of Nat Turner's outbreak and those fifty-five deaths, not to mention the execution of Nat Turner and his army and the destruction of most of the signs that they had ever existed. It is a view that obviously will appeal to most established readers—that is, most established whites—but that perhaps, too, is an illustration of how far short Mr. Styron has stopped before the full anguish he contemplated in the tragic life of Nat Turner.

(c) NORMAN PODHORETZ

EMILY DICKINSON was apparently wrong: success is counted sweetest by those who *do* succeed. Counted, and re-counted, and recounted, like a king's money rather than a miser's; and most ostentatiously in dollars. Norman Mailer has already offered a glittering prospectus for himself; now, in *Making It*, Norman Podhoretz, the thirty-eight-year-old editor of *Commentary* magazine, has written an autobiography that sounds like the official history of a profit-swollen company. The similarity between Norman I and Norman II is quite explicit.

For several years I toyed with the idea of doing a book about Mailer that would focus on the problem of success, but in the end I decided that if I ever did work up the nerve to write about this problem, I would have to do it without hiding behind him or anyone else. Such a book, I thought,

ought properly to be written in the first person, and it ought to constitute a frank, Mailer-like bid for literary distinction, fame, and money all in one package; otherwise it would be unable to extricate itself from the toils of the dirty little secret. Writing a book like that would be a very dangerous thing to do, but some day, I told myself, I would like to try doing it. I just have.

The stylistic debt is the last of many. Mr. Podhoretz is something of a ventriloquist, as any good editor or critic should be. His own literary personality bends to influences and performs imitations. Now Mailer, at Cambridge Leavis, at Columbia Trilling: at the beginning of this book his high-school English teacher tries to 'develop' her brightest pupil by weaning him from his Brooklyn background, and he finds himself unwillingly responding, becoming 'a facsimile WASP', beginning the long treacherous American climb. Now, identity buttressed with prosperity, he tells himself and the audience that it was all worth while, a world well won; that ambition is our 'dirty little secret', as sexuality was the Victorians', and an equally disastrous repression; that making it, like making out, is a glory rather than a shame.

*   *   *

As a life story—or even as a confession—it is less than full. It is inexhaustibly intelligent, in the muscular manner of the American serious journalist whose stock-in-trade is an argument developed over four or five thousand words. (His English counterpart has to convey a sense of effortless superiority in eleven hundred.) But Mr. Podhoretz is not by instinct either a narrator or an observer. Only when events fit a thesis, or when telling them is itself a moral posture ('ruthless honesty'), does his prose catch fire; and when the thesis is clear or the posture established, he moves on to the next chronological patch. On his home ground—the New York literary scene, the power-and-influence struggles in magazines and publishing houses—he can use this technique illuminatingly. For the description of his non-professional life, it is a handicap. Like many others, he found conscription a depersonalizing, humiliating, infantilizing experience, and muses heavily on it. None of his musings conveys as much as his drill-sergeant's remark:

You see that guy there? He got about ten degrees from all kinds of fancy colleges all over the place, but when I say 'Shit!' he shits.

However, Mr. Podhoretz is not in the anecdote business. 'I am a man who at the precocious age of thirty-five experienced an astonishing revelation: it is better to be a success than a failure.' Even the circumstances of the revelation are themselves revealed, with more detail than St. John ever gave to the island of Patmos. In 1962 an international cultural congress was held on Paradise Island, off the coast of Nassau, and the boy from Brownsville was among the elect.

This was what it meant to be rich: to sleep in a huge bright room with a terrace overlooking an incredibly translucent green sea, to stretch one's arms out idly by the side of a swimming pool and have two white-coated servants vie for the privilege of depositing a Bloody Mary into one's hand, to sign checks (which we had to do, though of course we would never have to pay them) without giving money a second thought.

Paradise indeed; although, as the author admits, it had previously been named Hog Island, which didn't suit the developers. If the sty fits. . . .

One's first reaction to this copywriter's prose might be how very little it took to change Mr. Podhoretz's heart. As More says to Rich in *A Man for All Seasons* (Rich, newly made Attorney General for Wales, perjured himself for More's conviction): 'It profits a man nothing to give his soul for the whole world. . . . But for Wales!' It is not just a question of will—clearly the High Life did not exactly have to rape Mr. Podhoretz—but of scale. Hog Island is not Persepolis, and a luckier man in a less ambitious society might even treat it with a certain disdain, not because it was wicked but simply because it was not that much of a ball.

* * *

Mr. Podhoretz quotes some advice from a friend who had grasped the distinction between the merely successful and the very rich— nine-tenths of whom, even in mobile America, have inherited at least part of their wealth. Since the very rich are *spending* around sixty thousand dollars a year, it is a mistake to think one can keep up with them merely because one is asked to a few of their parties. Even worldly intellectuals should therefore learn to 'think poor', to 'take it a little easier and settle for three-dollar shirts and the cream-cheese sandwiches at Chock Full O'Nuts'. Sound advice, but delivered, as the next paragraph points out, 'over many martinis, applejacks, and the best and most expensive steak which can be had in New York or anywhere else in the world'. Only Europeans, as Mary McCarthy pointed out in a famous essay, are materialistic enough to ration their material self-indulgence in order to make it go farther. Americans will spend beyond the satiety of physical desire—on two-seater marble lavatories, mink fountain-pens, 'his' and 'her' midget submarines—to feed a spiritual hunger accumulated by centuries of being the European poor; particularly the European Jewish poor.

It is, as they say, no coincidence that Mr. Podhoretz came to public notice with a review for *Commentary* of *The Adventures of Augie March*, which is both a story and a proof of Jewish integration into the American dream. After two disciplined, European-Jewish novels commenting on the human condition in a North American setting (*Dangling Man* and *The Victim*), Bellow, like Augie himself, was prepared to take America on its own exuberant terms: a very significant act for a member of the 'literary family' centred on *Partisan Review* and *Commentary*, since the family found the problems of 'being American' difficult even by the standards of that self-conscious continent. Mr. Podhoretz was acute enough a social critic to take up this point; but he also had a fine ear for prose, and rightly maintained that much of the lyrical spontaneity of *Augie March* sounds forced and false, that Augie protests too much and Bellow is pushing it as well as making it. The upshot was a fine specimen of the literary quarrel, lovingly described, matching the later eruptions when James Baldwin accepted *Commentary's* commission for *The Fire Next Time* and then sold it to the *New Yorker*. The family throve on feuds.

But there is also a note of moral restraint in Bellow's version of success which is singularly lacking in Mr. Podhoretz's. When Augie finally repulses the patronage of Mrs. Renling, he reflects:

Listen to her, and I was made for easy conditions, and to rise from a soft bed to the comfort of a plentiful breakfast, to dip my roll in yolk and smoke a cigar with coffee, in sunshine and comfort.

Listen to Mr. Podhoretz, and he tells himself something similar: not that he was made for it, but that he has reached it with an *almost* preordained clarity which defies criticism. Augie left comfort for questing; Mr. Podhoretz has had the quest, and will now take the comfort.

The element of complacency in him is not quite exorcized by his well-aimed thrusts at the gibing orthodoxy of his less successful contemporaries, simon-pure and simon-simple. Anybody who has

G

had even a whiff of success must know how many people protect their envy, their idleness, their cowardice, or their sheer lack of talent behind a *cheveux-de-frise* of righteousness. But their motives do not flatten their case, any more than Mr. Podhoretz's overcoming his youthful puritanism makes cavaliers of us all. There is a certain brutality in his manner. It is perfectly sensible to criticize his own extreme uncertainty in using his editorial power when he was first appointed.

I turned the operation into one of those 'progressive' families in which the father, instead of representing authority, becomes another one of the children himself, vying for their favour and consent.

It is less sensible to follow that up directly with a gruesome anecdote (told, perhaps, with more than a shade of approval) of how Henry Luce crushed a rumoured revolt at *Time* by calling his staff together and announcing: 'In case any of you don't know me, let me introduce myself. I am your boss. I can hire and I can fire. Any questions?' That, according to Mr. Podhoretz, is power exercised not under the aegis of the 'dirty little secret'. It suggests that the two secrets are not quite comparable, that whereas sex can be openly enjoyed, power must be openly exercised—and on somebody. *On ne peut régner innocemment*; which is why liberal shyness of power can be defended more stubbornly than sexual censorship.

But the individual moral issue (will success spoil Norman Podhoretz?) is not the most important one. An individual *arrivé* may or may not become tyrannical and grasping: the wit and brains of this narrative suggest that the worst that can happen to its author is getting fat from those expensive steaks. But in any case, so public an autobiography is not a moral testament of private character. What happened to Mr. Podhoretz happened—in some cases more spectacularly—to a whole stratum of American intellectuals. According to puritans, the perfection of their work, rather than their lives, was thereby endangered. Those steaks are finally no more important than Balzac's oysters or Rembrandt's jewels. What matters is the editorship of *Commentary*; and the editor's representation (rather than the amazing fact of his membership) of a whole successful ambience.

*   *   *

Commentary is, very crudely, a sort of American Jewish *Encounter*: a solid monthly drawing on prestigious talent, partly financed by the

American Jewish Committee to publish articles on 'Jewish and general' topics. The balance was never officially regulated, and the problems of editorial strategy were obviously enormous. Added to some predictable administrative dogfights, they make Mr. Podhoretz's inside story of the *Commentary* office an intellectual horror story. His predecessor, Elliott Cohen, was driven to breakdown and suicide partly by the appalling spiritual burden of creating the magazine's identity. But he settled firmly for two things: literary grace, and an outward looking attitude. At whatever cost, he succeeded so well that when his young successor took over the two horses were virtually harnessed for life. Far from being outsiders, the Jewish intellectual community had become at least a powerful group at the centre of American thinking. Literary discussion could centre on Bellow, Malamud and Roth; criticism by Trilling, political theory by Hannah Arendt, sociology by Nathan Glazer, were both kosher—to be crude again—and the best that America could produce. One can work through the fat *Commentary Reader*, selected from the magazine's first two decades, without any sense of the sectional, the parochial, or the second-rate. A professional eye can also deduce how thoroughly edited *Commentary* has always been. The main evidence is negative: so little writing falling below a certain standard of brightness and cogency, so few really bad patches, all point to a busy blue pencil. Such professionalism is more common in America than in England, but is notably lacking from even such an intelligent magazine as the *New York Review of Books*, whose frequent typographical solecisms infuriate at least one reader.

On the other hand, there are less welcome omissions as well. The cerebral energy referred to above can become wearisome (anti-Semites would probably invoke that notorious 'Jewish' trait, intellect devoid of intuition). Generosity of space is essential for the authority which *Commentary* seeks, but allows some confusion between seriousness and solemnity. There is a certain dominant dryness, exemplified in Mr. Podhoretz's decision to stop publishing poetry altogether 'like Rabbi Plato before me, said Sherry [his editorial assistant] in order to evade the impossibly difficult problem of finding poems that were good in themselves and yet substantively relevant'.

But the real case for corruption would have to prove one of two offences: political cowardice, or intellectual dilution. Certainly *Commentary* in the 1950s, as Mr. Podhoretz admits, displayed more enthusiasm than judgment in its hardline anti-Communism. But his editorship began with some extracts from Paul Goodman's *Growing Up Absurd*; later pieces of self-criticism have included George Lichtheim's onslaught on the *New York Times* and Theodore Draper's patient unravelling of the idiocies of United States policy over the Dominican Republic. The record on Vietnam has been more cautious, but still critical. And the magazine has thriven. But so have others farther left, as Mr. Podhoretz grudgingly admits. Not only the *New York Review of Books* but—to move down a few intellectual notches—*Ramparts* has done well out of middle-class American masochism. A liberal society is notoriously good at engulfing critics: Paul Goodman himself complained of being President Kennedy's court jester. Mr. Podhoretz records a lunch with 'a *very* high member of the Kennedy administration', who asked if he had any ideas on Harlem.

I had, as it happened, a great many of what I would have called 'ideas'— and interesting ones as I thought—on this subject, but I noticed while expounding them over a very good lunch that the great man was growing restless and bored. This puzzled me, for I had thought I was speaking well. Faltering a bit in response to his impatience, I asked him whether he disagreed with what I was saying. 'No, no,' he answered, 'what you're saying is all very well, but what should we *do* about it?'

To be surprised at this is surely as much a mark of naivety as to demand that the editor of *Commentary* should always lunch at Chock Full O'Nuts. The American establishment is one of the most open in the world: indeed, a strident demand that the rules of the club should be changed is almost a precondition of membership. But it is an establishment all the same. What *Commentary* has achieved is the liberalism of the second-generation college graduate. If Elliott Cohen's magazine was the self-made middle-of-the-roader from Iowa State, Mr. Podhoretz's is the Galbraithian radical from Harvard. It is a position which can be defended, but is better not celebrated—at least not from inside. *Commentary's* social criticism is both a genuine, sincere editorial attitude and—objectively considered—a very good recipe for success. Such success no more guarantees integrity than failure would: and boasting of it even less.

The same is true of the magazine's intellectual standards. After his success the editor states:

If anything, *Commentary* was a more difficult magazine to read than it had been when its circulation was ten thousand and it was losing a hundred and fifty thousand dollars annually.

Maybe so, maybe not. But the problem is at least worth a glance. Culturally as well as politically, we are no doubt too resolutely sold on a nineteenth-century model of the lonely rebel, the avant-garde against the bourgeoisie. But what Dwight Macdonald called Midcult is a genuine phenomenon—and a genuine threat—rather than a fantasy of soured drop-outs. Mr. Macdonald himself, incidentally, struck a fine blow against Midcult's own James Gould Cozzens in *Commentary*, and is now, by an entirely typical cycle, accused by some of perpetrating it in the *New Yorker*. The shuffle for leftward position in New York, like the fight for the inside of a race-track, almost persuades one that a little honest vanity is the thing. Hence *Making It*. But American intellectuals are neurotic about success with good reason. Just as Lockean liberalism has become America's conservatism (Hartz's paradox) so the whole American bourgeoisie wishes to join the avant-garde. John F. Kennedy is often accused of raping the country's intellectuals, and leaving them pregnant with confusion. ('Do we belong here or not?') But the problem is far older: as old, in fact, as the generous, earnest, egalitarian society that spawned it, replacing Stendhal's happy few with the Masterpieces of World Literature for You.

Three optimistic propositions—on the surface hard to quarrel with—dominate the Midcult scene. A good writer should have the highest rewards; a good book should be enjoyed by everyone; a good idea should increase the sum of human happiness. Begin there, and you end with the *Reader's Digest*; or with Hemingway, whose writing deteriorated certainly *as* and almost certainly *because* he became The Champ. The line from Hemingway goes through Mailer; Mr. Podhoretz is in danger of extending it, which would be a pity. For all its proclaimed honesty, *Making It* is in some ways an un-self-knowing book, telling as a romantic individual case-history what might also figure in one of *Commentary*'s social essays. What finally happens depends on other factors than one man's vision, or one man's exposure of a dirty little secret. He may not have made it yet.

8

POETS TODAY

(a) MARIANNE MOORE

The Complete Poems

'COMPLETE'? Well, merely in the blurb's sense that these are all the poems Miss Moore is 'willing to preserve'—though the cliché seems inappropriate as applied to the La Fontaine fables, only nine of which appear here. As to the original poems, Miss Moore's epigraph —'omissions are not accidents'—must, of course be, swallowed, though in her eighty-first year what would have been timely as well as most interesting and useful would have been a truly collected edition. For the poetry's bibliographical history is far from satisfactory or straightforward. Miss Moore's first book, published by the Egoist Press in 1921, was brought out by her friends Bryher and H.D. without her knowledge (she said later that 'to issue my slight product—conspicuously tentative—seemed to me premature'). The *Observations* of 1924 was never reissued in its entirety and the English *Collected Poems* of 1951 did not even include all the pieces in the *Selected Poems* of 1935. The English appearance of the translations from La Fontaine was a mere selection from the complete fables published in America by the Viking Press.

In prolonging this fragmentary story no blame can be assigned to hesitancies on the part of the poet's English publishers or public, for the present volume is a photographic reproduction of its American counterpart. Though there are, for instance, two pieces here ('To a Prize Bird' and 'The Student') which were not in the 1951 *Collected*

(a) *The Complete Poems of Marianne Moore.* 306 pp. Faber and Faber. £2 2s.
(b) *The Collected Poems of Theodore Roethke.* 279 pp. Faber and Faber. £2 2s.
(c) *Berryman's Sonnets.* 115 pp. Faber and Faber. 21s.
(d) *Selected Poems.* Translated by Czeslaw Milosz and Peter Dale Scott. Introduction by A. Alvarez. 140 pp. Penguin. 4s. 6d.
(e) *King Log.* 70 pp. André Deutsch. 21s.
(f) *Fidelities.* 103 pp. Faber and Faber. 21s.
(g) *The Night of Stones.* 87 pp. Macmillan. 25s. (Paperback. 8s. 6d.).

Poems, one piece ('Melancthon') is omitted which was. Most of the celebrated 'Poetry' is now relegated to the notes, and the page of 'Errata' at the end by no means exhausts the textual errors—of stanzaic arrangement, initial capitals and the like.

It is not just pedantry or antiquarianism that would wish to see the filling in, the chronological delineation, of Miss Moore's earlier work. There is a mystery here which curiously enough has become of increasing interest and importance since 1938. The question of from where Miss Moore, during the First World War, obtained the authority for using syllabic instead of stress metres seems never to have been satisfactorily answered. She herself has denied that her style has literary antecedents, though retroactively she has found Francis Jammes's titles and treatment a good deal like her own.

Ezra Pound, on seeing her work originally, remarked 'Someone has been reading Laforgue, and French authors'—but apparently it was not Miss Moore. The technical discussion which took place when Miss Moore was interviewed by Donald Hall for the *Paris Review* in 1960 (an excellent document, reprinted in the second series of *Writers at Work*) did not clearly disentangle the syllabic business from other innovations in her verse, such as her use of quotations, so that the last word on its parentage has by no means been said, even by Miss Moore herself. Besides, her very practice of incorporating extracts from prose works into her poetry presupposes, through its extreme extent, a syllabic basis for the poetry's metrics (and one may assume, too, that the device of isolating the first line of a poem, or part of it, as the title, was prompted by a necessity or convenience in the mathematics of syllable counting).

Pound himself never contemplated a metric based on a syllable count. In a note of 1917 (which appeared in the *Pavannes and Divisions* of 1918) he thought that in his own *vers libre* he had gone as far as was profitable towards looseness of stress, and looked towards the authority and discipline of classical quantitative metres for possible further progress (perhaps having in mind the experiments of Robert Bridges which had been appearing during the first two decades of the century). The free verse of Eliot and of Arthur Waley is, each in its different way, based on stress, though in a sense Waley's is the more revolutionary since it was directed against the iambic line (one of his exercises, he has said, was 'translating' the more Miltonic passages of Wordsworth out of blank verse). No doubt the technical freedom of Imagist poetry gave some sanction for the practices of Miss Moore's early verse, but one looks in vain in the work of her friend H.D., say, for anything like the Mooreish syllabics. In the non-syllabic poem of Miss Moore's he quoted in his introduction to the 1935 *Selected Poems* Eliot saw 'a slight influence' of H.D. but really this seems confined to the one word 'splintered'.

The poem itself ('A Talisman') deviates from strict stress metre merely in having a few rhymes on weak syllables (a practice that only becomes significant when regular stress has disappeared from her verse), though it is amusingly prophetic that it shows interest in one of the few aspects of stress metre where the syllable is important—at the start of an iambic line shorter than the pentameter.

In characterizing Miss Moore's mature verse critics usually describe her elaborately arranged stanza, with lines of varying length and of one or two rhymes—the stanza of 'The Steeple-Jack', say:

> Dürer would have seen a reason for living
>   in a town like this, with eight stranded whales
> to look at; with the sweet sea air coming into your house
> on a fine day, from water etched
>   with waves as formal as the scales
> on a fish.

An odd thing is that the stanza's syllabic count (in this case 11, 10, 9, 8, 8, 3) is not always strictly maintained. Though this can be detected not by the ear but only by the fingers, it rather threatens the foundations of what, though primarily a discipline for the poet, is for the reader authorized by ingenuity and symmetry. Again, when, between 1935 and 1951 three and a half lines disappeared from 'The Buffalo', Miss Moore replaced them with a row of dots despite thereby mangling the shape of two stanzas. And in fact a good deal of Miss Moore's verse, particularly the earlier, is not stanzaic at all— or rhymed. Perhaps it is here that her contribution to modernist poetry may be seen at its purest and most remarkable, for what she is writing is not prose or the prose-poem but poetry with prose's rhetoric, complexity and ease, poetry without adventitious musical aid, whose units are arguments and paragraphs:

This animal to which from the earliest times, importance has attached, fine as its worshippers have said—for what was it invented?
To show that when intelligence in its pure form has embarked on a train of thought
  which is unproductive, it will come back?
We do not know; the only positive thing about it is its shape; but why protest?

The passion for setting people right is in itself an afflictive disease.
Distaste which takes no credit to itself is best.
('Snakes, Mongooses, Snake Charmers and the Like.')

When, as we may on disc, we hear Miss Moore reading her poetry it may be found surprising at first that the rapid, rather nasal voice pays no attention to line endings even in stanzaic poems (and even when they rhyme), and that the syllables that have been counted out with (more or less) painstaking accuracy are often slurred over. But soon it becomes apparent that she is reading for sense and, of course, this is how she must be read on the printed page. The baroque cleverness and ornament is to delay and enrich a closely argued journey towards the clinching spire or altar of meaning and emotion.

Miss Moore has said more than once that what she writes can only be called poetry because there is no other category in which to put it. Up to the last war there was a sense in which such a statement might have commanded assent in that she was the sole practitioner of the technique she had invented (or obscurely evolved)—a Schönberg without disciples. But in the Winter 1940 *Kenyon Review* W. H. Auden printed his 'In Memory of Sigmund Freud' whose four-line unrhymed stanzas were in the syllabic pattern 11, 11, 9, 10. This poem (which was reprinted in *Another Time*, first published on February 7, 1940) must obviously have been written soon after Freud's death in the autumn of 1939. John Fuller (in an unpublished paper) has pointed out that another poem in *Another Time*, the rhymed piece later called 'Heavy Date', also sticks rigidly to a syllabic pattern though it is possible to read it as a stressed poem (and that some earlier poems, 'Journey to Iceland', 'Casino', and 'Schoolchildren', are printed in their latest versions without initial capitals to the lines, but, as Mr. Fuller adds, their looseness and odd enjambments are related to the freedom of form of 'Spain' and the 'Epilogue' to *Look, Stranger*, a freedom which goes back to *The Orators*). We know from *The Dyer's Hand* that when in 1935 Mr. Auden first tried to read Miss Moore's poems he 'simply could not make head or tail of them'. Clearly on his going to America closer acquaintance with the poetry or the poet prompted him to adopt the Mooreish technique, and it has since been a most important influence on his manner. Moreover, through Mr. Auden's syllabics have become a freely available procedure, used by many poets indifferently as a change from stress metres or *vers libre* based on stresses.

For most other poets the advantage of syllabic verse to Miss
Moore in accommodating prose quotations does not apply and the
use of the technique, if not dictated by mere fashion, must reside in
its way to a fresh music, to an escape from iambic clichés. It is
curious that Miss Moore (and Mr. Auden following her) does not
avoid writing in lines of an even number of syllables. Even numbers
tend to the iambic—and that, surely, is one thing that the syllabic
is designed to avoid. In the stanza form of 'A Carriage from
Sweden', for example, four of the five lines are eight syllables long,
and the poem starts like this:

> They say there is a sweeter air
> where it was made, than we have here;
> a Hamlet's castle atmosphere.
> At all events there is in Brooklyn
> something that makes me feel at home.

Despite the regular internal rhymes, the impression left here is of
iambic tetrameter gone lame in metre and rhyme-scheme—an impression reinforced by the second stanza and revived later in the
poem—whereas the effect Miss Moore is aiming for is really this:

> Seats, dashboard and sides of smooth gourd-
> rind texture, a flowered step, swan-
> dart brake, and swirling crustacean-
> tailed equine amphibious creatures
> that garnish the axletree! What . . .

The iambics of the former stanza have also led to a flabbiness and
sentimentality which, certainly in the earlier work, is very rare (and
perhaps they have led, too, to the literary lapse in the third line, for
surely the reference should be to Macbeth's castle). Weakness also
occurs when the iambic cuts across the syllabic lines, particularly
when it is emphasized by strong rhymes: 'O / quiet form upon the
dust, I cannot / look and yet I must.' Less frequently some even
more inappropriate metre accidentally intrudes: 'Its leaps should be
set / to the flageolet.' As twelve-tone music must avoid the old con-
cord, so syllabics must in general avoid regular stress, but with more
sense. An exercise like the little poem 'To a Prize Bird' (appearing in
the canon for the first time), where the even numbered syllabic lines
also scan precisely according to stress, seems rather wasted.

What of Miss Moore as a poet 'beyond all this fiddle'? There is
no doubt that in the later work the cosy element in the poet, the
element acceptable to the *New Yorker*, is in greater evidence, and

where a more elaborate effort is made a sense of strain allied to a
certain pedestrianism is sometimes discernible. A near disaster
(which plainly affected Miss Moore severely) attended the La Fontaine translations: the publisher who commissioned them died *in
medias res*; the work in progress was shown to a large American firm
then interested in Miss Moore and they were chillingly discouraging;
the Viking Press stepped in providentially. The completed work is
one of supreme intellectual effort but the impression at the moment
is that it does not warrant the diversion of her talent from the
original verse that might have resulted in its stead. We must also
probably reserve judgment on how far the general corpus of the
poetry comes off having regard to its difficulty and the awkwardness
of reading it with the notes ever in mind. It is still not familiar
enough and requires a deal of exegesis which the American critical
industry might have been expected already to have supplied. What
is now beyond dubiety is a quite substantial number of brilliant and
wholly successful poems—and the truly original technique, fertilized
so timeously by Mr. Auden that Miss Moore has the gratification,
unlike many innovators, of living with an increasingly interesting
and broadly-based progeny.

(b) THEODORE ROETHKE

The Collected Poems

WHEN THEODORE ROETHKE died five years ago his obituaries, very
sympathetically written, tended to reveal by implication that the men
who wrote them had doubts about the purity and weight of his
achievement in poetry. Now that his collected poems have come out,
the reviews, on this side of the water at least, strike the attentive
reader as the same obituaries rewritten. Roethke was one of those
men for whom poetic significance is claimed not only on the level
of creativity but also on the level of being: if it is objected that the
poems do not seem very individual, the objection can be headed off
by saying that the man was a poet apart from his poems, embodying
all the problems of writing poetry 'in our time'. It is a shaky way to
argue, and praise degenerates quickly to a kind of complicity when
what is being praised is really only a man's ability to hold up against
the pressures of his career. Criticism is not about careers.

From the small amount of information which has been let out publicly, and the large amount which circulates privately, it seems probable that Roethke had a difficult life, the difficulties being mainly of a psychic kind that intellectuals find it easy to identify with and perhaps understand too quickly. Roethke earned his bread by teaching in colleges and was rarely without a job in one. It is true that combining the creative and the academic lives sets up pressures, but really these pressures have been exaggerated, to the point where one would think that teaching a course in freshman English is as perilous to the creative faculties as sucking up to titled nobodies, running errands for Roman governors, cutting purses, grinding lenses, or getting shot at. If Roethke was in mental trouble, this should be either brought out into the open and diagnosed as well as it can be or else abandoned as a point: it is impermissible to murmur vaguely about the problems of being a poet in our time. Being a poet has always been a problem. If the point is kept up, the uninformed, unprejudiced reader will begin to wonder if perhaps Roethke lacked steel. The widening scope and increasing hospitality of academic life in this century, particularly in the United States, has lured many people into creativity who really have small business with it, since they need too much recognition and too many meals. Plainly Roethke was several cuts above this, but the words now being written in his praise are doing much to reduce him to it.

This collection is an important document in showing that originality is not a requirement in good poetry—merely a description of it. All the longer poems in the volume and most of the short ones are ruined by Roethke's inability to disguise his influences. In the few short poems where he succeeded in shutting them out, he achieved a firm, though blurred, originality of utterance: the real Roethke collection, when it appears, will be a ruthlessly chosen and quite slim volume some two hundred pages shorter than the one we now have, but it will stand a good chance of lasting, since its voice will be unique. In this respect, history is very kind; the poet may write only a few good poems in a thousand negligible ones, but those few poems, if they are picked out and properly stored, will be remembered as characteristic. The essential scholarly task with Roethke is to make this selection and defend it. It will need to be done by a first-rate man capable of seeing that the real Roethke wrote very seldom.

Of his first book *Open House* (1941) a few poems which are not

too much reminiscent of Frost will perhaps last. Poems like 'Lull'
(marked 'November, 1939') have little chance.

> Intricate phobias grow
> From each malignant wish
> To spoil collective life.

It is not assimilating tradition to so take over the rhythms of poetry
recently written by another man. It is not even constructive plagiar-
ism, just helpless mimicry. To a greater or lesser degree, from one
model to the next, Auden, Dylan Thomas, Yeats and Eliot, Roethke
displayed throughout his creative life a desperate unsureness of his
own gift. In his second book *The Lost Son*, published in 1948, the
influence of Eliot, an influence which dogged him to the end, shows
its first signs with savage clarity.

> Where's the eye?
> The eye's in the sty.
> The ear's not here
> Beneath the hair.

There are no eyes here, in this valley of dying stars. In his five-part
poem 'The Shape of the Fire' he shows that he has been reading *Four
Quartets*, giving the game away by his trick—again characteristic—
of reproducing his subject poet's most marked syntactical effects.

To see cyclamen veins become clearer in early sunlight,
And mist lifting out of the brown cat-tails;
To stare into the after-light, the glitter left on the lake's surface,
When the sun has fallen behind a wooded island;
To follow the drops sliding from a lifted oar,
Held up, while the rower breathes, and the small boat drifts quietly
                                                                shoreward;

The content of this passage shows the pin-point specificity of the
references to nature which are everywhere in Roethke's poetry. But
in nearly all cases it amounts to nature for the sake of nature: the
general context meant to give all this detail spiritual force usually
has an air of being thought up, and is too often just borrowed. In
the volume *Praise to the End!*, which came out in 1951, a certain
curly-haired Welsh voice rings loud and clear. It is easy to smile at
this, but it should be remembered that a poet who can lapse into
such mimicry is in the very worst kind of trouble.

> Once I fished from the banks, leaf-light and happy:
> On the rocks south of quiet, in the close regions of kissing,
> I romped, lithe as a child, down the summery streets of my veins.

In the next volume, *The Waking* (1953), his drive towards introspective significance—and a drive towards is not necessarily the same thing as possessing—tempts him into borrowing those effects of Eliot's which would be close to self-parody if it were not for the solidly intricate structuring of their context.

> I have listened close
> For the thin sound in the windy chimney,
> The fall of the last ash
> From the dying ember.

There it stands, like a stolen car hastily resprayed and dangerously retaining its original numberplates. His fascination with Yeats begins in this volume—

> Though everything's astonishment at last,

—and it, too, continues to the end. But whereas with Yeats his borrowings were mainly confined to syntactical sequences, with Eliot he took the disastrous step of appropriating major symbolism, symbolism which Eliot had himself appropriated from other centuries, other languages and other cultures. The results are distressingly weak, assertively unconvincing, and would serve by themselves to demonstrate that a talent which has not learnt how to forget is bound to fragment.

> I remember a stone breaking the edifying current,
> Neither white nor red, in the dead middle way,
> Where impulse no longer dictates, nor the darkening shadow,
> A vulnerable place,
> Surrounded by sand, broken shells, the wreckage of water.

Roethke's good poems are mostly love poems, and of those, most are to be found in the two volumes of 1958 and 1964, *Words for the Wind* and *The Far Field*. Some of his children's poems from *I Am! Says the Lamb* are also included, and there is a section of previously uncollected poems at the very end of the book including a healthy thunderbolt of loathing aimed at critics. Roethke achieved recognition late but when it came the critics treated him pretty well. Now that his troubled life is over, it is essential that critics who care for what is good in his work should condemn the rest before the whole lot disappears under an avalanche of kindly meant, but effectively cruel, interpretive scholarship.

(c) JOHN BERRYMAN

Berryman's Sonnets

UNDER A CRYPTIC STYLE, this sonnet sequence delivers a familiar story, told as usual in the first person. During the spring of 1946 a thirty-two-year-old lecturer at Princeton University falls in love. His Danish mistress is younger and tougher, bound far more lightly to him than he to her. Both lovers are married; the couples are acquainted; and 'Lise', for all her recklessness and alcoholism, is a mother. So the affair becomes a chain of deceits, separations, furtive meetings, and—for the poet—lacerating guilt. Before autumn Lise decides she can live without him; he is left at the end, therefore, with these poems and his 'helpless and devoted wife'.

If the obvious parallel is *Modern Love*, this is not to say Mr. Berryman had it in mind. But without suggesting that he stands on Meredith's shoulders, we may ask how much farther he sees. In this kind of narrative the direct expression of strenuous emotion rarely succeeds by itself; most readers want freshness of style, dramatic turns of action. Meredith starts with what seem advantages. Adopting an unconventional, sixteen-line form, he shifts his point of view novelistically, speaking either as the husband or as a brooding observer. Meredith's plot is peculiarly dramatic because the husband takes a mistress only after the wife has betrayed him; unlike Berryman's passive sufferer, he dominates the action.

But Berryman's modern attitude of demanding sympathy for a weak, vicious protagonist has more power than Meredith's symmetrical development. Our lingering pity for the wife, our disgust with the poet's submissiveness, give this collection a brilliantly sustained energy. By appealing to self-destructive impulses like masochism and incontinence, Berryman provokes in the reader a fascinated wavering between critical and sentimental responses. In form only a few of Berryman's sonnets are not conventionally Italian. Between the octave and the sestet there is generally the tonal contrast that skilful sonneteers like to create. But over the expected patterns rushes a staccato fury of language and syntax, making a structure beside which Meredith's innovations sound timid.

Admirers of *Homage to Mistress Bradstreet* will know what these exercises led to, because phrases and situations from the sonnet sequence reappear, movingly transformed, in Berryman's

best-known poem. What reappears with them but becomes the ruin
of the earlier work is its verbal extravagance. Puns and imitations
alternate with archaisms and allusions. The texture of sound often
grates on one's ear; the conceits make broken hops from image to
disparate image. Berryman's syntax, para-Miltonic, is so densely
crowded with inversions that one studies many lines like a schoolboy
construing Horace. Such mannerisms reflect the near-hysteria of the
poet and suggest the division in his nature; for even while squirming
deliciously with guilt and anxiety, he cannot help foreseeing the
inevitable moment when those pains will appear properly trivial. In
praise of the style, one may describe it as suitable for chaotic emotions conveyed through an obsession with will and order.

But if Mr. Berryman overworks his words, he badly underpays
them. Neither Lise nor his passion seems deep enough for the care
he devotes to each. Her character receives little analysis; his lust
hardly escapes from the familiar walls of desire, shame, pleasure,
and loneliness. And what should be a virtue increases the damage.
For the subtle particularity that one welcomed in Mr. Berryman's
earliest work pervades the sonnet sequence. Here again time, place,
and public event belong to the design. The Princeton bicentenary
occurs in one poem, a class reunion in another. We even discover the
names of Lise's favourite composers. To a situation so narrowly
defined the application of post-Symbolist devices is unfortunate.
Wallace Stevens treated his Sunday morning as a chance to meditate
on art and religion. Mr. Berryman moves the scene out of doors and
merely lets nature approve of a tryst in New Jersey. At several
points the lover's yearning does become the poet's desire for fame,
and the mistress blends with the muse. But these metamorphoses are
too weak to carry the stylistic effort; and the whole affair remains
a shop window for a display of Mr. Berryman's technique.

(d) ZBIGNIEW HERBERT

Selected Poems

INANIMATE OBJECTS are always correct and cannot, unfortunately, be
reproached with anything. I have never observed a chair shift from one foot
to another, or a bed rear on its hind legs. . . .

Hypocrisy, betrayal, violence: Poles do not need Albert Hall-style poetry readings to remind them of these. A brief allusion calls up quite enough sombre thoughts. What to do in the face of such thoughts, in the face of such facts: that is the insistent question. One of the reasons why Zbigniew Herbert is so highly regarded as a poet in Poland today is because he asks the question so doggedly, so intelligently, and so gently.

Herbert is now in his forties. In his teens he fought in the Polish resistance; he was a student (of law, economics and philosophy) in the worst Stalinist years; he was not able to publish his first book until 1956, though some of the poems in it had been written many years before. But few of his poems simply recount the moral and physical horrors he must have witnessed. They are more directly concerned with virtue than with evil. Many of them are brief mono-logues-in-the-mind of men straining to see and feel with justice and generosity—or simply not to deceive themselves. One may regard these portraits as self-portraits of the poet without loss to him; there is a kind of modesty with which we have grown unfamiliar in presenting oneself as striving for virtue, and being glad to attain it in however small, uncertain a degree, or however belatedly:

> I was talking of battles
> dungeons and ships
> heroes being slain
> and heroes slaying
> and I forgot about that one. . . .
>
> > when he lies down
> > pierced by a javelin
> > and the lips of his wound
> > slowly close
> > he sees
> > neither sea
> > nor city
> > nor friend
> > he sees
> > just before his face
> > the tamarisk

Herbert is frank and rueful enough about the impediments to virtue; and irony—more at his own expense than others'—is a powerful instrument in his hands. But his irony never slips, as it can so easily, into immodest extremes of cynicism and self-disgust. Rather it is a kind of corrective in the name of truth which can round even on itself if necessary (and Poles, it should be further said, have seen it

H

plentifully used at times as—at the other extreme—just a comfort and entertainment):

At the end only superstitious neurotics carried in their pockets little statues of salt, representing the god of irony. There was no greater god at that time.

Then came the barbarians. They too valued highly the little god of irony. They would crush it under their heels and add it to their dishes.

In the inner monologues there is a direct miming of Herbert's efforts to render the complex justice due to different human situations. The strain to realize, the shock of realizing: this is the rhythm that the short lines embody. In other poems the reader's mind is more deliberately and rhetorically forced to consider, and reconsider. A final simile may press a further judgment on all that has preceded, as in the poem on the lovers who 'leapt into each other's eyes' when the forests were on fire:

> To the end they were brave
> To the end they were faithful
> To the end they were similar
> like two drops
> stuck at the edge of a face.

Or, as in one of the prose-poems in this volume, 'The Emperor's Dream', the throw-away line may unsettle a complacent scorn that the whole piece has been drawing one into feeling:

A crevice! shouts the Emperor in his sleep, and the canopy of ostrich plumes trembles. The soldiers who pace the corridors with unsheathed swords believe the Emperor dreams about a siege. . . . In fact the Emperor is now a wood-louse who scurries about the floor, seeking remnants of food. Suddenly he sees overhead an immense foot about to crush him. The Emperor hunts for a crevice in which to squeeze. . . .

Yes. Nothing is more ordinary than the dreams of Emperors.

(We may admire there, incidentally, besides the overt moral drama in which the poet is skilfully engaging with the reader, the beautifully handled, implicit Freudian reduction to common terms of the Emperor's dream and the soldiers' interpretation of it—which is quietly making the same point in a different way.)

But not all Herbert's work consists of examples, in his own words, of 'the moralist's dry poem'. There is also a haunting visionary element in his poetry, offered though it is with caution and often with grief for its fancifulness. 'Arion' is a sketch of the fabulous singer who 'restores world harmony':

The crowns blacken on the tyrants' heads
and the sellers of onion cakes
for the first time err in their figures to their own disadvantage.

More enchantingly:

> in the shadow of one hexameter lie down
> wolves and roedeer goshawks and doves
> and the child goes to sleep on the lion's mane
> as in a cradle
> Look how the animals are smiling
> People are living on white flowers
> and everything is just as good
> as it was in the beginning.

But even here there is a slowly growing hint of clichés being parodied; while some of the phrases describing Arion himself leave the reader free to conclude that the vision associated with him may not lack a moneyed, vulgar character:

> the Grecian Caruso
> concertmaster of the ancient world
> expensive as a necklace
> or rather as a constellation.

(Who is correcting himself in that last line—poet or clever propagandist?) Yet in spite of all his caution the poet grants a legitimate power to the vision, and makes that power come through at us, beautiful and disturbing. We find something similar in the poem of Herbert's that is probably best known in this country, 'Elegy of Fortinbras'. Here Fortinbras takes farewell of the dead Hamlet, to return to his sewer project, his decree on prostitutes and beggars, and his 'eternal watching'; yet even as he does so he has to say

> This night is born
> a star named Hamlet. We shall never meet
> what I shall leave will not be worth a tragedy.

Gravely, and very movingly, Herbert locates the best examples of high human possibilities again and again in the dead and the non-human—fidelity in a wooden stool, dignity in a pebble; while

> The most beautiful is the object
> which does not exist.

This last quotation is in fact the opening of the title-poem in the latest volume of Herbert's poems published in Poland. Yet the corrective to this, too, returns in a still more recent poem:

At first it was to have been different
luminous circles choirs and degrees of abstraction
but they were not able to separate exactly
the soul from the flesh and so it would come here
with a drop of fat a thread of muscle
it was necessary to face the consequences
to mix a grain of the absolute with a grain of clay
one more departure from doctrine the last departure
only John foresaw it: you will be resurrected in the flesh

There are not many love poems in this collection, but in them this tenderness for the unideal clay is as strongly felt as anything in Herbert's poems. 'Silk of a Soul' is about a man who tries to look into his girl's soul while she is sleeping with her mouth open:

I was expecting
branches
I was expecting
a bird
I was expecting
a house
by a lake great and silent
but there
on a glass counter
I caught sight of a pair
of silk stockings.

What is his reaction?

my God
I'll buy her those stockings
I'll buy them.

There is nothing here of the cynicism in the Baudelaire prose-poem where the poet, looking out of the window at the clouds and thinking that his darling's eyes are still more beautiful, gets clumped on the back and sworn at by her because he's letting his soup get cold. The man in Herbert's poem just goes on wondering, yet without much hope and without betrayal of what he has, what will appear on the 'glass counter of the little soul' then:

will it be something
which cannot be touched
even with one finger of a dream.

Herbert's rather dry, guarded diction, with its evocations under tight control, and his use of the line-break for many of his major effects, make him, fortunately, a poet less difficult to translate well than many other poets. These are very good translations, strong in their own right and close in force and feeling to the originals. The volume is introduced by Mr. A. Alvarez, who sums up very precisely and cogently that quality of Herbert's poetry—full of 'fine classical yearning', yet unshakably, practically, politically concerned with the obdurate world—that is representative of the best tradition of Polish literature; representative too, it might be added, of the best art and literature throughout eastern Europe at the present day.

(e) GEOFFREY HILL

King Log

IN HIS FIRST BOOK, *For the Unfallen* (1959), Geoffrey Hill established, with intense care, his credentials: a line packed tight to buckling point, a wide cultural allusiveness, an almost forbidding formality. Soon after publication, when interviewed in a Leeds University magazine, he quoted two statements as 'summing up a good deal' of what he felt. The first was from Yeats:

I took pleasure alone in those verses where it seems to me I found something hard and cold, some articulation of the image which is the opposite of all that I am in my daily life.

The second was Pound's:

The poet's job is to define and yet again define. If the poet doesn't make certain horrors appear horrible who will? All the values come from our judicial sentences.

This belief in literature as begetter and conserver of values, coupled with the desire for a tough, cold excellence of expression, was unfashionable, and there was an embattled feeling, a bristling defensiveness about the book. Certain poems stood inside elaborate scaffoldings of quotes and dedications. Unlike St. Sebastian in one of his poems, Mr. Hill was anything but, 'Naked, as if for swimming'.

The poems were obsessed with heritage, with the European tradition seen as a 'blinded god', a bewildered weakening giant surrounded by auction cries. What he was attempting to register were the shifts, scars ('evidently-veiled griefs: impervious tombs') and cataclysmic landslides of a continent exhausted by history.

If the book was, in its own way, very impressive, it was also disconcerting. Brilliance had a tendency to short-circuit itself and plunge the poem into darkness. The work was at moments so wrought-up that it could hardly speak. One felt the whole enterprise menaced, fore and aft, by ghostly parentheses.

The interest of *King Log* is that while it contains a handful of very fine poems which in some ways complement the first collection, it also reveals probings towards a different kind of achievement. It is a book with marked changes of tone.

The choking, visceral disgust of 'Annunciations' with its 'loathly neckings and fat shook spawn' echoes that fascinated horror about the body's gross appetites which has always permeated Mr. Hill's metaphors. 'Locust Songs' has the indignation, the rhetorical scorn he brings off magnificently. (With, yet again, that intensity close to nausea; 'This must be our reward: / To smell God writhing over the rich scene. / Gluttons for wrath we stomach our reward.') While in 'Funeral Music', a sequence bearing 'belated witness' to an obscure but bloodily savage battle during the Wars of the Roses, he not only finds the occasion round which can cluster his preoccupations (with history's sense, with the brute impingements of world on spirit), but also discovers the method and tone by which the poem can turn on itself, tear itself with implied criticism. The meditation is broken by 'grunts and shrieks'. The 'poetry' is lacerated from within. One is aware of the breathing of obscure protagonists. The effect is of a strong, fiercely arguing rhetoric facing its limits, its ultimate frailty, its possible irrelevance.

One is struck, reading this sequence, by the kinship between Mr. Hill's obsessions and those of that other singular and difficult poet, David Jones. Both sink shafts into what Jones calls 'the complex deposits of these islands'. Both are sensitive to those strata of the language which when touched send up tremors to be recorded at the surface. Both are great turners-up of bones into the light. For each the silence of excavated sites is eloquent.

'Funeral Music' is, then, a culmination which recognizes the limits of its kind. Scattered through the book are stanzas and lines which either recall other voices and look to be blind allies (Wallace Stevens in 'An Order of Service', René Char in the two fastidious prose-poems) or which show a struggle to write more simply and directly of people.

> At nightfall
> My father scuffed clay into the house.
> He set his boots on the bleak iron
> Of the hearth; ate, drank, unbuckled, slept.
>   ('The Stone Man')

And there is the gentle, sad tone of these lines from 'Coplas'

> Oh my dear one I shall grieve for you
> For the rest of my life with slightly
> Varying cadence oh my dear one.

These are new departures. Metaphors no longer crowd the subject. In 'A Song from Armenia' from the Sebastian Arrurruz sequence (Sebastian root-of-arrows, love's martyr—old habits die hard with Mr. Hill), though the poem is about separation, absence, the pain is scaled-down and the conclusion balances between anguish and a tone of relaxed, sensual reverie:

> Why do I have to relive even now
> Your mouth and your hand running over me
> Deft as a lizard, like a sinew of water?

An as yet unsolved problem in the book is how to give a sense of spaciousness to the short poem. Three of the 'Four Poems Regarding the Endurance of Poets' show unsuccessful attempts.

In the first, Tommaso Campanella watches from his cell, 'a slug / Scale the glinting pit-side / Of its own slime'. But the lines are *first* an alliterative and assonantal arrangement, a metaphor, and *secondly* a slug struggling. The feeling of physical space and confinement is not realized.

'A Prayer to the Sun' has three tiny, cruciform stanzas arranged diagonally. There is neither agony nor spaciousness about the poem, only the dry pain of self-regarding composition, a preciousness. 'Tristia' is a better poem but flawed by the same misjudgment as to how to open out. It is instructive to compare the version printed earlier in *Stand* with the revised poem. Beginning with the end of the third line, it ran:

>   There go
> The salutes, dust-clouds and brazen cries.
> Images rear from desolation
> Like ruins across a plain. . .

This became:

>   Too late
> The salutes, dust-clouds and brazen cries.

> Images rear from desolation
> Look . . . ruins upon a plain . . .

The arm flung out to indicate distance in 'There go' is suppressed and resurfaces in the staginess of 'Look. . . .' A diagonal arrangement of stanzas and a line of dots tracking pregnantly, represent space on the page but not necessarily in the poem.

There is achievement of a high order in *King Log*, fruit of a ferociously self-critical talent. There is also promise of a simpler excellence in the future.

(*f*) VERNON WATKINS

Fidelities

TWO EPIGRAMS in this posthumous collection, which Vernon Watkins prepared for publication not long before his sudden death in America, seem to anticipate and invalidate much that a reviewer might say about it. 'Vultures' puts critics in the place which this poet assigned to them:

> Fling bones to vultures, who dissect
> Thoughts of a living man when dead.
> Trust the wide wings to spread his shade
> And win what he hates most, respect.

The fuzzy metaphors here—beginning with the bones flung to vultures, when it is flesh they eat—challenge the vultures to show their talons and do just what Vernon Watkins says they do, dissect the dead man's thoughts. It is hardly possible to conceive of the vultures' wings spreading the dead man's shade and not clear whether they win respect for him or for themselves. The ambiguity is not taut or pungent enough to bear 'dissection'; and the whole epigram is self-defeating, because Watkins's rare resorts to satire and invective exposed the weakest side of this otherwise admirable poet. Wherever he deliberately and obtrusively thought in verse—in order to protest and argue, as in 'Trees in a Town', or to define and assert a religious creed that was also a poetic creed—he laid himself open to those vultures; and not only because what he thought and believed was unacceptable to most of his contemporaries, poets as well as critics and informed readers, but because the very undertaking did not accord with his peculiar gifts.

The second epigram, 'The Stayers', disarms criticism not by challenging or condemning it, but by its patent ingenuousness and sincerity:

> When the trees drop their leaves in frost,
> Old Earth, deep-rooted, knows her own;
> Poets, who loved her, are the last
> To leave her, when the rest have flown.

The epithet in the second line could also be called in question, since it transfers an attribute of the trees to the soil in which they grow, and hence to Old Earth; and a kind of semantic short-circuit between the two halves of this very brief poem makes it more puzzling and tantalizing than epigrammatically cogent. Yet imagination can accept the sense in which Earth, too, is rooted; and it is to imagination, rather than wit, that the poem appeals. Imaginatively, the logical contradiction between the falling of the first half and the staying of the second, the return to earth and the leaving of earth, is arresting. The poem seems to say more, not less, than its argument; and that makes the ambiguity fertile.

Rhythmically, too, 'The Stayers' profits by an irregularly accented first line; and the whole collection could be divided into poems whose cadences were imposed by a ready-made metre, and poems in which Vernon Watkins relied on his extraordinarily fine ear for modulations and improvisations of his own. The ready-made metres, in turn, were apt to impose an excessively formal diction, forced rhymes and awkward syntactic inversions. The same obstinate traditionalism often prevented this poet from drawing on his immediate visual experience, as he did in 'Fisherman', 'Fingernail Sunrise' and 'The Snow Curlew', poems that stand out in this collection because they fuse the real with the imagined. In other poems experience and vision fall apart, either because the immediate occasion remains private, as in 'Poem for Conrad', or because its symbolic extension is elaborated to the point of abstraction or obscurity.

Vernon Watkins's art, like his creed, aspired to timelessness, and this sets him apart from the mainstream of modern poetry in its post-Romantic-Symbolist phase. Many of his most characteristic perceptions were of a kind that defies verbalization, as he recognized once more in 'Means of Protection':

> As plovers trail their wings
> To hide a nest from men's concern,
> Right lovers turn

Talk that nears treasured things.
The best of judgment says
No case is won by what speech proves,
Least of all love's.
We live by silences.

The paradox of language demanded an explanation of the inexplicable, as in the very lines quoted here, an expression of the inexpressible, an articulation and enactment of those silences. No task could be more difficult. Vernon Watkins was equal to it in poems—like 'Cornfields', 'Movement of Autumn' and 'Triad' in this volume—that come closest to Symbolist practice in its liberation of music and vision from the control of prosaic argument. Yet Vernon Watkins's affinities and fidelities were apt to forbid this freedom; they were too generous and too eclectic, and included too much that pulled him in the opposite direction. The tributes in *Fidelities* to Marianne Moore and Heine, poets whom Vernon Watkins admired for being utterly different from himself, show how his various allegiances tempted him into formal exercises close to imitation or parody. The poetic pantheon that meant so much to him in later years, eliciting so many poems of homage and celebration, was at once too isolated and too capacious.

Yet the same isolation is inseparable from the strength and purity of Vernon Watkins's best poems—poems essentially anachronistic in their aspiration to timelessness and their rejection of temporal material which more worldly poets have been able to use. Those best poems are not worldly, but most of them are earthly enough to outlast many changes in the world.

(g) GEORGE MACBETH

The Night of Stones

THE EVENING is probably not far off when Steed will recite verses through the dressing-room door to Tara King as she dons her fighting suit for a new adventure: when he does, *The Night of Stones* could be his text. 'The Avengers' is fancy telly and this stuff is fancy poetry, stylelessly stylish, unoriginally new, each tuneless phrase poised and punctuated so that it *must* mean more than it seems to do. The unwritten guarantee which comes with 'Avengers' drama

assures the viewer that nothing, no event, image or show of character, will force itself upon the memory—only a general air of chic
will remain. With the blood-stone-light-bone poetry here under consideration, the reader is assured that the words will stay safely on
the page. Though the most appalling scenes of carnage and nuclear
holocaust are visited, it is only for the run of the book; usually only
for the length of the page. Atomic bombs go off like crazy, scorching
the *stone* with *light* and playing hell with the *blood*, not to mention
the *bone*. But these atomic bombs are Material for Poetry, and the
killed are Material for Poetry too—their deadness is thematically
handier than their lost aliveness. As in grand guignol, the only
genuine casualties—once breathing, now rigid—are the words
themselves.

> Old, asleep,
> Washing slow hands in water, she was there,
> Grey-haired and guilty, waiting for their thumbs
> To choke her blood and stone. . . .
> Like a dog
> Blood ran between them with its nose to the ground
> Sniffing for a scent. . . .
> Somewhere a faucet dripped
> Water, blood, water on stone. Inside her brain
> The blood beat back.
> Fire was the sign of blood. . . . So he drove on,
> Wading in blood. . . .

(In this last piece one assumes that the car has a very long pedal
travel, thus inducing a wading sensation when changing gears.)

In the longish poem, 'Driving West', which opens the book, the
word *blood* occurs eighteen times, although to some extent monotony
is avoided by supplying it in a variety of colours and textures—red,
black, soupy, oily, watery and with its nose to the ground. In the
book overall the word receives several more mentions than any of
flame, *silk*, *ice* and the ever-popular *groin*, and towards the end
manages to race away even from its stable-mates *bone*, *stone* and
light to amass a total of twenty-five mentions—surely a record for
a single substantive at the distance.

Suspended in this non-evocative vocabulary float inert namings of
gadgets and gimmicks, mostly left-over properties from low-budget
SF serials like *Captain Video*: hypodermics, electric coils and inevitably the dread laser.

> O, my dear one, tempered
> by the beam of the laser, torn
> by the stone body of the gorgon, the man-child
> *lighten my darkness, I*
> *need you now*

None of the *O.E.D.* definitions of *tempered* accords with the actual properties of a *laser*, but no matter: prop gimmicks cost money and must be put to a variety of uses, as when Captain Video employed his personal oscilloscope (the Optic Inscillometer) to detect the political affiliations of the invaders from the Red planet Mongo. The pun count for the book is low, but the instances are revealing. This one is about a German dog.

> his
> jaw swivels, and:
> schnapps!

Schnapps, you see, because the dog is German; and his jaw *snaps*; and *Schnapps* is a German drink. One's response to such felicities sharpens at a second reading, causing, in the fit reader, a tendency to drum the heels on the floor. Nevertheless, this sequence of mini-poems about dogs (called 'At Cruft's') is the best thing in the book: 'characteristic' pix of your favourite pets, taken with one of those cameras which develops the film instantly and gives you a slightly wet but reasonably sharp impression of what the outside of things looks like.

There are a few trick poems included, based on 'vowel analysis' and 'numerical analysis' of other people's work: a dangerous game for this poet since a blood-stone-light-bone analysis of his own poems would uncover the precisely recurring clotted patterns of a radar screen sweeping a herd of tortoise. A poem about Malta which conflates imagery of the two great sieges (1565 and 1940) seems to contain a moment of genuine memory:

> With paired wings, three remain
> Holding the gold walls. . . .

These are Faith, Hope and Charity, the three Gladiators (they were biplanes, hence the 'paired wings') which defended the island at one desperate period. The poet's emotions are at least temporarily involved here, so the verse comes to life for a while: a writer so tough about Death, though, should have avoided giving the planes' pilots

> clean, grey eyes
> Behind the wings, mounting in honour

Biggles, Ginger and Algy fly again, as technical advisers to *Malta Story*.

The combination of recondite information and predictable emotion is characteristic—a narrow intensity of curiosity shared by stereo fiends and those people who wear opera capes and green eyeshadow and who can name you the directors of every Bette Davis movie if you give them half a chance. To draw upon the flat characters, contrived situations and ramshackle properties of B-pictures, Sam Katzman serials and comic strips is the only way to talk about poetry of this type. It is media poetry. It has a great air of living and struggling in the true world of Hitler, Himmler, Stalin and Beria, but a close look reveals that it has been transformed by fright-wigs and plastic incisors into the process-shot world of Bela Lugosi, Boris Karloff and J. Carroll Naish, each lit uncannily among the zapping electric coils. Like horror films, this kind of poetry is the art with which frivolous people fulfil their seriousness quota. 'I was terrified', said the old lady emerging from *Psycho*. 'It was wonderful.' And in all that spookery ('all that' is one of this poet's favourite soggy specificities), not a single haunting phrase.

9

STRANGE CREATURES

(a) SOMERVILLE AND ROSS

BY NO POSSIBLE freak of the imagination could we picture a convergence between the worlds of Bloomsbury and of the Irish writers Somerville and Ross. A party of dons from a plate-glass university would seem to have more in common with the Oxford grind than had—say—Lytton Strachey with Martin Ross (this was the nom de plume of Violet Martin). We cannot see the inmates of Bloomsbury—either 'young' Bloomsbury or 'old' Bloomsbury—at ease in Drishane (Edith Somerville's house) with the rats moving thunderously behind the bedroom walls. 'I caught a flea on my person with amusing brilliance', writes Martin Ross from Ross House. Against this background of rats and fleas, the buns and cocoa of Gordon Square seem to beckon with civilized tranquillity. In one totally unimportant particular (which will be referred to later) there was a junction between Edith Somerville and Virginia Woolf, but in all the recent outpourings about the inmates of Bloomsbury there seems no evidence that they ever turned their cool appraisal on the works of Somerville and Ross. Yet for all the chances of life and habits of mind which sundered Gordon Square from southern Ireland, they were linked by one point which was important and radical. They both played a part in edging forward the fundamental revolution of our day—the overthrow of man's dominance over woman. Perhaps neither was conscious of what they were helping to achieve and their approach was, of course, totally different. Somerville and Ross subtly, but not overtly, treated man to a little gentle ridicule; Bloomsbury helped to elevate woman to the level of man.

In his book, which is convincing because it is easy-tempered and enjoyable, and because it tells the story from the inside, Mr. Quentin

---

(a) MAURICE COLLIS: *Somerville and Ross*. 280 pp. Faber and Faber. £2 2s.
QUENTIN BELL: *Bloomsbury*. 126 pp. Weidenfeld and Nicolson. 21s.
   (b) MICHAEL HOLROYD: *Lytton Strachey*. A Critical Biography. Volume II: *The Years of Achievement 1910–1932*. 754 pp. Heinemann. £4 4s.

Bell notices the point, and tells us that in one sense Bloomsbury was feminist. He means by this that, so far as discussions about sex and morality are concerned, men and women could discuss them in Gordon Square with the openness of a fraternity of undergraduates in Lytton Strachey's rooms at Trinity College. He quotes a letter, written in 1913, from a young member of the Bloomsbury circle; she describes a country weekend and portrays in ample detail the conduct of her host with a choice pair of catamites. Although the Irish partnership may have lacked the argumentative force and 'shock' tactics of Bloomsbury it was, both transparently and latently, feminist. Miss Geraldine Cummins, who some years ago wrote an understanding biography of Edith Somerville, quoted a close friend of the latter who said that she was 'subconsciously jealous of men'. That is almost certainly the case though it has to be deduced rather than proved from the books. For example, is not the severest condemnation of Francie in *The Real Charlotte* intended when her aunt says, 'Any man comes handy to her! Upon my word, she'd dote on a tongs, as they say!'? Rather unexpectedly Edith Somerville was no admirer of Jane Austen; she once remarked that most of the men in those novels are 'male characters dressed up as governesses'. It could well be that this remark sprang from a feeling that Jane Austen was too susceptible to masculine superiority. Did not the weakest of her characters (for instance, Mr. Elton) have the temerity to despise a woman?

Unquestionably Somerville and Ross aimed some unobtrusive blows at man on his pedestal, but are we justified in arguing that these blows sprang from their complete sufficiency to one another based on their androgynous affections? Mr. Collis devotes many pages to this edifying topic and concludes that there was no physical relationship between the two ladies but that when that redoubtable warrior Dr. Ethel Smyth appeared at Drishane after Martin Ross's death she did attempt—although the two doctors were both in their sixties—to place the friendship within a physical setting. How do we know? Mr. Collis goes on to tell us that Ethel Smyth abandoned Dr. Somerville, when she fell 'violently in love with Virginia Woolf'. No doubt these matters appeal to the mid-twentieth-century mind but are they important? There is much speculation in Mr. Collis's book, but no proof. In this connexion there is a tale about a necktie which the enquiring reader will find in *Irish Memories*. In the immediate past (and possibly still) a necktie on a woman was something thought to proclaim a follower of Sappho. We are told that Martin Ross was once given a necktie on which a friend pronounced the following verdict: 'I would not be seen dead in it at a pig-fair'. She goes on to tell us in the charming, inconsequent style of Irish conversation, 'I gradually threw it away'. When we try to give these subtle personal relationships a modern setting, we have to remember the weight of convention in the days that are past, and especially—as Geraldine Cummins reminds us—the very strong inhibitions of Irish people at that period.

If 'that sage blue-stocking Sappho' had clearly influenced the writing of Somerville and Ross, then we might reasonably devote anxious consideration to the effect of such relationships on their work. But there is no evidence whatever of such an influence. Indeed the strength of their greatest novel, *The Real Charlotte*, rests on its complete mastery of natural emotion. About this novel, and indeed all their work, there is the fascinating side-issue, discussed by Mr. Collis, of apportioning the credit among the two authors. There is perhaps evidence that the characterization is Ross's while the background, always beautifully drawn, is Somerville's. Andrew Lang, a great admirer of *The Real Charlotte*, said to Martin Ross at dinner, 'I suppose you are the one who did the writing'. She explained with some care that this was not the case, but Lang was not the only person to wonder how two people could really evolve character. But however the credit for the whole is apportioned the finished book rests on the heights. Orlo Williams, who stood remote from literary fashion but was a most convincing critic, once compared *The Real Charlotte* with Vouvray— 'bright and rather dry, gay and with a little bite in it'. But he thought that the two writers jointly lacked the powers of a great tragic artist—powers which were necessary to give the novel its completely triumphant development. A few of Mr. Collis's readers may well regret that he did not eschew some of his pages about female friendship and substitute for them a closer study of *The Real Charlotte*.

Edith Somerville left seventy-five volumes of diary, and Martin Ross thirty-eight volumes—five million words together. When Edith Somerville wrote *Irish Memories*, after Martin Ross had died, she possibly did not set great store by these diaries because she writes, apropos the material for the book, 'Martin and I were not accustomed to take ourselves seriously. . . . The diaries will not be brought into court'. Mr. Collis has used them to bring out what is most characteristic of the two women, but he tells us that he has concentrated on what is lively, curious, fantastic or tragic. Perhaps one of the chief impressions from his book—and this is no doubt correct and is supplemented from other sources—is that Martin Ross, though the more shadowy biographical figure compared with her collaborator, was the genius within the partnership. Something of gaiety and more of depth seem to have been withdrawn from the partnership when Martin Ross died. *The Big House at Enver*, which was published a decade after Martin Ross's death, was the nearest approximation to the old triumphs, but something is missing. In all her later books Edith Somerville retained Martin Ross's name as joint author and Mr. Collis has some interesting information about her efforts to keep in touch with her friend by spiritualism, and suggests that some of the later books were written under that influence. In one of the seances, Edith Somerville says that she could not write without Martin and the latter significantly adds: 'I can not help thinking that I may be allowed to help.' When Martin Ross died, Edith Somerville sent some lines to *Punch* which seem to sum up her feelings for her friend and the change which her death implied:

> With Flurry Knox and you our guide,
> We learned to laugh until we cried;
> Dear Martin Ross, the coming years
> Find all our laughter lost in tears.

The Irish themselves have always been ungenerous to Somerville and Ross, seeing in their work an example of the Anglo-Irish establishment laughing at the 'natives'. Lady Gregory disliked these books because Edith Somerville was thought to mount her horse and look down. Even so wise a critic as V. S. Pritchett tells us that it was impossible to make a lady of Francie, 'so she had to be killed'.

No doubt Somerville and Ross are dated, and perhaps a weakness of Mr. Collis's biography is that he tries too hard to give Edith Somerville a sixtyish look. His comments on foxhunting illustrate this point. 'I am generally glad when a game-fox gets off', writes Miss Somerville. On this Mr. Collis comments, 'She was humane beyond her period'. Was she? Does not a familiar voice sound in memory? 'It ar'n't that I loves the fox less, but that I loves the 'ound more.' Contemporary and urban prejudices about fox-hunting need not disturb the readers of Somerville one jot or tittle. The point is not what Edith Somerville thought about the fox, but how she describes the hunt. Some have held that, for those unaccustomed to the saddle, her hunting scenes are even more delightful than those of Trollope. Though Mr. Collis's book may not satisfy all tastes—and he certainly leaves room for a wider and more detailed study of the literary achievements of the two friends—he has given us a memorable picture of Dr. Somerville, surrounded by her easy-going family, in the time-honoured country life of County Cork.

Turning to Mr. Bell's book, we can see how his distinguished family and their circle played their part in transforming woman—the sheltered, protected plaything—into the co-equal and co-adjutant of man. Their attacks on established opinion were strengthened by a taste of sex-warfare. Here is Virginia Woolf on Kipling and Galsworthy:

It is not only that they celebrate male virtues, enforce male values and describe the world of men; it is that the emotion with which these books are permeated is to a woman incomprehensible.

She adds that it is 'like being caught eavesdropping at some purely masculine orgy'.

Mr. Bell's book is a serious contribution to our understanding of the intellectual world in the first half of this century. To scandal and gossip it owes nothing for, as he amusingly expresses it, he is disinclined 'to act as Clio's chambermaid'. The author makes two important points. He suggests that Bloomsbury existed primarily for conversation and the exchange of ideas. Though the comparison is inexact, Bloomsbury was something in the style of the Bluestocking Society of the mid-eighteenth century. Both were in a sense flights from upper-class society to a society of the mind. This was once amusingly expressed by the author's mother, Vanessa Bell, when, for the benefit of her fellow-members of the Bloomsbury circle, she described how her family had tried to launch her in society. She described this launching as 'the end of my career in the upper world. I rapidly sank to the lower, and have remained there—if I may say so without disrespect to the present company.'

Mr. Bell's other point is that Bloomsbury had no deep-laid plot to further a particular point of view in either literature or art. It was a conglomeration of individualists rather than a society moving towards a definite objective. He quotes Sir John Rothenstein's attack on Bloomsbury—'I rarely knew hatreds pursued with so much malevolence over so many years' and 'their determination to ruin utterly the "reactionary" figures whom they denounced'. The author deals patiently with this attack, is understanding of Sir John's vehemence and convinces us (and possibly Sir John) that it was based on a mis-understanding because Bloomsbury had in reality no such exciting intention and indeed no explicable intention at all. The most that Mr. Quentin Bell would allow is that its members had a revolutionary purpose but a purpose which was inspired only by a common tend-ency of thought among the circle, and certainly no intention of ramming that thought down the throats of others. This is much what his father said in the *Twentieth Century* in 1954, though Clive Bell was apt to put on the glove of truth and bash his critics till they were wounded rather than convinced. He maintained that Bloomsbury was merely a collection of individuals who liked one another, what-ever 'the riff-raff of Portland Place and Fleet Street' might say to the contrary.

He was especially incensed by a leading article published in this journal on July 17, 1948. This article suggested that Bloomsbury was 'anchored firmly in the faith that nothingness was the destiny of lost mankind'. No doubt it could be argued that this was sometimes the impression which they gave—especially to those who were outside the magic of the society. Though Lord Russell was not strictly speaking a member of Bloomsbury—he was rather an honorary member and a deservedly respected one—there are passages in his autobiography which might justify some such gloomy belief in mankind's future. But the great strength of his views and indeed of the views of the fraternity lies in the fact that they were never rigid. Mr. Bell argues that Bloomsbury was killed by the advent of Fascism. And Lord Russell has also explained how his own views were overset by the spread of those pernicious doctrines. Those who most admire Bloomsbury will recognize that so far as there was a common mind it was never closed within itself, but was always open to the world as it moved and ready to accept correction from events outside itself.

(*b*) LYTTON STRACHEY

THE LIFE OF Lytton Strachey in maturity, which has been patiently pieced together by Mr. Michael Holroyd, reveals in the end a puzz-ling picture and—it must be added—a singularly revolting one. While no one would condemn Strachey for being attracted to his own sex, the indulgence of his fancies at the cost of the happiness of

those he loved (and—what is surely worse—at the cost of the
happiness of those they loved) can only be condemned. As in the
first volume, we are conducted by the author within a very close
circle of Cambridge friends, highly intelligent, highly amusing, highly
irreverent but a little desiccated and somehow leaving the reader
longing for the fresh breezes of worldly fame which these clever men
loathed as the mark—not of the beast—but of Oxford. Spared
nothing by way of revelation of the desires and bodily afflictions of
Strachey and his circle, the reader may be excused for feeling rather
like the judge who, trying a case of unnatural vice, managed to fall
into a light sleep; waking with a start he was heard to exclaim 'Good
God! Am I in Sodom or Gomorrah?' Some of us may feel that there
is much to be said for the biographical reticence of Sir Roy Harrod
in his study of Strachey's associate Maynard Keynes—'that dear nice
Bernard Keynes' as he was called by one of those twaddling hostesses
round whose table these great men somewhat gingerly gathered.

*　　*　　*

Now for the story which has prompted these comments. In 1915
when Strachey was staying with the Clive Bells he met Dora Carrington, an art student of strong feelings and infinite vivacity. About
everything her feelings were passionate, so that a friend once told
her 'Your parents were Huntley and Palmer; you are like a tin of
mixed biscuits.' While not even Mr. Holroyd can unlock the door to
the secret passions of those who fill his pages and there is speculation
in his book whether Carrington (as she was always called) really
loved X or Y or was passingly attracted by Miss X or Mrs. Y, this
much is clear. Carrington devotedly loved Lytton Strachey and was
in turn loved by three men, who were gifted, unusual and important
in the story. They were the artist Mark Gertler, Ralph Partridge
(whom she married) and Gerald Brenan. Some people thought it
incredible that Carrington could have been in love with Strachey and,
when Arthur Waley expressed this incredulity to her, she replied with
the characteristic persiflage of her circle: 'Oh: it's his knees'. But
whether it was his knees, his beard, his splendid hands or some secret
charm, she indubitably loved him. As Mr. Holroyd says, 'When he
was with her, she was alive; when he was away for a week-end, a day,
she ceased to exist.' When Strachey died, Carrington, like some
Chinese potentate preparing to mount the dragon for the next world,
put on Strachey's yellow dressing-gown and shot herself. Do we

catch some glimpse of the human being behind the mask when we read that Strachey, on his death-bed and just conscious, said to her 'I always wanted to marry Carrington and I never did'. In all the tangle of human beings and human emotions involved in the story the individual who may exasperate readers but who will find her way to their hearts is Dora Carrington.

The position was further bedevilled by this fact—Strachey was in love with Carrington's husband, Ralph Partridge. All three lived under the same roof. 'The curious ménage or ménages work, I think, quite well', wrote Strachey complacently. Ralph Partridge was a splendid man; in his tastes and background he was the complete opposite of Strachey, he was a fighting soldier, a rowing man, extremely practical, with a crisp and confident outlook on events which was contagious. His contributions to the *New Statesman* distinguished that journal in its great days. Although his position in the ménage was—to use Strachey's own adjective—'curious', he did not reciprocate Strachey's feelings, and it is some indication of the overwhelming force of Strachey's personality that, although an Oxford man and far removed from everything that Bloomsbury thought and wrought and taught, Partridge put his past behind him and, in that somewhat improbable country between Hungerford and Newbury, long after Strachey was dead, kept bright the traditions of reason and tolerance which he had absorbed from the master. When Partridge's marriage with Carrington showed signs of strain, Strachey kept it from collapse —partly (it must be said) because his domestic comfort depended on their presence. Mark Gertler wrote a letter to Carrington when she proclaimed her love for Strachey. Mr. Holroyd calls it 'half-incoherent', but it makes certain points with almost glaring clarity. 'You have by your love for that man poisoned my belief in love-life . . . the combination of your fresh young self with that half dead creature . . . he will deaden you in time.' No doubt Carrington was infinitely trying to everyone except Strachey—and this biography quite properly does not attempt to conceal the shadows in which she moved—but who can fail to feel compassion for her? History rightly thinks that Effie Gray was a personality deserving all our understanding and sympathy but was her plight in essentials greatly different from Carrington's? Indeed Carrington's tragedy was deepened by her love for the unresponsive partner and by the fact that even if a Millais had arrived he would not have been able to set her free.

By an odd coincidence Strachey, earlier in his life, had been a member of another triangle of love of which Henry Lamb was the base—loved from one side by Lady Ottoline Morell and from the other by Strachey. And what gives this affair its unpleasant tang are Strachey's comments on Lamb—'the most delightful companion in the world and the most unpleasant' ... 'he really looked amazing though of course very, very bad'. Anyone who knew Henry Lamb—the most understanding of friends and companions—would (as Mr. Asquith was fond of saying) rub their eyes with astonishment at these descriptions of him and at Strachey's method of address—'très cher serpent'. Whatever long-buried secrets may be the cause of such strictures the traveller with Strachey for guide must not make the mistake of attempting too closely to follow his foot-prints. Undoubtedly there was a streak of savagery in Strachey and his friends. Here he is on Augustine Birrell—'a certain bookishness gleaned from some rather narrow reading, and then— blank'. On Lady Ottoline, who had nurtured him in his days of adversity, Strachey reports 'her bladder is now gone the way of her wits—a melancholy dribble'. Of Sir Osbert Sitwell, Lady Aberconway and others he writes 'strange creatures—with just a few feathers where brains should be'. And if he wanted to denigrate the excellent Christopher Hollis could he not have thought of something less unoriginal, less Gladstonian than 'but what can one expect from a Roman Catholic?'

*   *   *

As we close this long biography ought we to conclude that Strachey as well as his books is now for the dark? Before attempting to answer that question a word should be said of Mr. Holroyd's distinguished part in the story. He has set Strachey before us as his subject would have wished, with no defect, no unpleasantness concealed. Did not Strachey himself say 'I'm afraid my biography will present a slightly shocking spectacle'? That is correct. But in addition to a portrait of Strachey Mr. Holroyd gives us a far-ranging survey of the most influential minds of the first three decades of this century whose sway is still felt over the background of our lives today. His footnotes are models of accuracy and information. If the reader notices that he confuses the two Walter Runcimans and that Lady Ponsonby (not the obsequious Gosse) was the author of the article in the *Quarterly* on Queen Victoria in 1901 it is only the rarity of such slips that makes them memorable. Just occasionally he may dash off in pursuit of something which seems doubtfully relevant to his story. The roguish review in this journal of Mr. F. A. Simpson's second volume of his biography of Napoleon III is a case in point. (The review was written by Philip Guedalla.) If these dead embers are to be raked over we should also be reminded of the glowing praise with which Mr. Simpson's first volume was received in this journal. But together Mr. Holroyd's two volumes form a portrait of an epoch in literature which will not be superseded. Clear-cut, comprehensive, highly coloured and convincing, it will be recognized by contemporary readers and by those who come after as a splendid piece of work.

*   *   *

The turn of mind of mid-twentieth-century England is greatly exercised by the sexual curiosities of human beings, but we should be quite wrong in thinking that we have exhausted the many-sidedness of Strachey's character which is revealed in this biography, by seeing him too exclusively in relation to those attachments which he noisily trumpeted among his friends. Strachey himself was fond of analysing people whom he did not greatly admire—Asquith is a case in point— and after divesting them of their attainments and accomplishments to proclaim that he finds 'just nothing at all'. Supposing we were to remove from Strachey not only his homosexual friendships but—so far as that is possible—all the mental and personal influences to which they gave rise, should we find 'just nothing at all'? If this were done it is abundantly clear that we could say with the poet 'though much is taken, much abides'. In what abides we may indeed come nearer to the true man. The most attractive thing about Strachey was his perpetual enjoyment of the play of circumstance on human nature. Perhaps it was Mr. Asquith, when he was Prime Minister, bowling up the Haymarket in an open motor-car and looking so happy that 'I immediately became aware of a curious sensation of *bienaise* in the air'. He is amused by the distinguished company he meets at Lady Cunard's and is diverted by contrasting the guests with his hostess's 'frankly lower-class bounce'. We feel also that he would have been the first to enjoy the spectacle of himself and Lady Ottoline playing tennis, with the lobbing strokes of the 1880s, in the gardens of Bedford Square, to the astonishment of the crowd which rapidly collected. He would have been the first to write off to his friends and make fun of the conscientious objector who blew up an air-cushion before facing the discomforts of the seat provided for him at the Tribunal. The fact that he was the man would not have made the slightest difference. We know that this would have been the case from 'the unfortunate occurrence in Ravenscourt Park'.

This was the occasion when he was engaged in a fisticuff brawl with Mark Gertler over Carrington after an evening party. To a friend, describing the scene with infinite gusto, he writes 'anything more cinematographic cannot be imagined'. No doubt it can be argued that in some of his behaviour he was affected and no doubt it is also true that many of his remarks, which sound rather frosty after four decades, were made for effect. But against that it remains true that, although we may be a trifle startled by some of the things he says, we can see that often they spring less from malice than from his never-ending surprise that human beings could really behave in such an astonishing fashion. Lord Annan makes the point when he says emphatically that 'far from despising people Strachey had an irrepressible affection for their foibles'. How exactly this bears out the words of Strachey's own celebrated preface to *Eminent Victorians* about shooting a sudden, revealing searchlight into obscure recesses of human nature and then examining the result 'with careful curiosity'.

If Strachey had been merely an elegant trifler—shall we say (using the words in their kindest sense) a sort of Eddie Marsh?—we could not possibly account for his influence over a varied but powerful circle of friends without hopelessly diminishing their recognized position in the world. 'Lytton Strachey is coming' were the words which often adorned the invitation cards of Virginia Woolf to a frugal little gathering in Bloomsbury. He came and—we may be sure—they came. In reality Strachey was a far more serious and influential figure than his flamboyant private life, his wit and even his books imply. Indeed, in a sense, the parade of these things in Mr. Holroyd's book tilts the balance against the real man. Mr. Raymond Mortimer reminds us that the same individual who could throw off an amusing verse about a cat in the middle of a high-brow paper-game could yet pronounce with effect and authority on matters of literary judgment and on public affairs. People listened to him. He is perhaps the last person to be judged by the external man which he showed to the world at large. He had an unpardoning sense of right and wrong—not of course on morality where he would not have pretended or wished to judge—but on intellectual and political problems. Anyone doubting this should read his letter attacking the *New Statesman* at the end of the first war as 'Northcliffian'; it was powerful and justified.

Lytton Strachey did not like Matthew Arnold who, he said, 'would have been a quite satisfactory collector in an up-country district in India'. But does not Arnold aptly illustrate the fascinating problem which was Strachey's—how far do the externals of a man reveal or hide his innermost feelings.

> Below the surface-stream, shallow and light,
> Of what we *say* we feel—below the stream,
> As light, of what we *think* we feel, there flows
> With noiseless current strong, obscure, and deep,
> The central stream of what we feel indeed.

IO
PAPER TIGERS
THE UNREALITIES OF JORGE LUIS BORGES

IN ONE OF THE EARLIEST and most lastingly provocative of his stories, 'Pierre Menard, autor del Quijote', Jorge Luis Borges conceived a writer of remote and intriguing trifles whose ambition it is to write a book that will coincide in every particular with one already in existence, *Don Quijote*. The coincidence would be a much more glamorous feat than it sounds, because Menard soon realizes that he cannot backdate his memory and start thinking spontaneous seventeenth-century thoughts; instead of a copy of Cervantes's novel he will have to produce a premeditated, twentieth-century re-creation of it. The impediment is not any lack of talent for the task, only the time for its accomplishment; he has chosen, perversely, to fulfil himself on a scale compatible only with eternity, the dimension set aside by Borges for lofty games of escape from chance like fiction or metaphysics. But however ample the facilities for play may be in eternity, time remains a problem somatically, and Menard completes only two chapters and a bit of his novel before his death.

*   *   *

The impulse for his project comes from Borges's proposition that all ideas are compossible for the mind whose modesty is god-like enough to accommodate them, a proposition which, whatever flaws it may have for a neurologist, is particularly bracing for the writer, since it means that there are no limits to his mental freedom, beyond syntactical ones. It is rather less bracing for literary critics, who like to believe that a determinate personality conditions each written word of the work they are studying and renders it expressive. But what contortions such critics would be faced with, says Borges, if

---

JORGE LUIS BORGES: *A Personal Anthology*. Edited and with a foreword by Anthony Kerrigan. 210 pp. Cape. 30s.

they found out that L.-F. Céline had written the *Imitatio Christi*. His own theorem is more liberal: the greater the creator—God, let us say, or Shakespeare—the more smudged the personality. Thus when Borges calls on God he can please himself whether he addresses him as Someone or Nobody.

One of the ideas which the divinely self-effacing Pierre Menard finds himself forced into sharing with Cervantes is that fighting men are superior to writing men, a priority laid down in Don Quijote's famous 'Discourse on Arms and Letters'. But unlike Cervantes, the veteran of the Turkish wars, Menard does not find it easy to sustain a belief so comically out of keeping with a life's practice of literary annotation in provincial France. As an antidote to his reading of Julien Benda and Bertrand Russell, and to acquire the necessary stiffening, he turns to Nietzsche; the point is, in fact, that his *Quijote* is not a rewriting of Cervantes's *Quijote* at all but a reading of it; it is Cervantes read, say, by a contemporary reader who has previously taken in something of *Also sprach Zarathustra*. The function of Menard's story is to make clear that it is the order we read books in that decides their meaning for us, not the order they were written in.

Menard's defence, after Cervantes, of an active and errant principle against a sedentary one is more than just a cunning exploration by Borges into his theory of analogy, because it relates closely to a bifid tradition within his own ancestry. From his father's family he has been stocked with contemplative genes, from his mother's with heroic ones, and Borges has taken the opportunity of presenting himself as the meeting-point of these rival urges, whose reconciliation takes place in his fictions.

He has been free enough, largely and fittingly in his poems, in celebrating the gallantry of certain of his maternal ancestors in the defence of Argentinian causes of the nineteenth century. But he has been freer still in owning up to his extreme bookishness, having been brought up among (largely English) books as a child and having later returned to care for them as a librarian in Buenos Aires. Thus, when he writes, as he has done, 'few things have happened to me and many have I read' or 'life and death have been lacking in my life', he is slanging reality for falling short of some ideal epic, fit for the descendant of a warlike family. Indeed, Borges cannot help identifying himself in his stories as a writing man: in one of the briefest and most sympathetic of his self-portraits he turns up as a Jewish newspaper editor, 'short-sighted, atheist and very shy'—such condensation ought to spur us on to estimating what the exact degree of kinship is between these three attributes.

Having inherited his father's poor sight, Borges is now almost wholly blind, a deterioration which may have offered him a cruel proof of the Schopenhauerian doctrine he has so lovingly under-written, that everything which happens to us is a dark enactment of our own will. For Borges is one of those Romantics who have defined writing as an activity that should take place with the eyes closed. What he has displayed above all is fiction's considerable capacity for transforming the mournful contingencies of direct observation.

*   *   *

One story which he has said is among those he likes best, and which has been placed third in his *Personal Anthology*, is 'El Sur' (The South), where the autobiographical pressures are less diffuse than they are elsewhere and well worth the uncovering. The hero of 'El Sur', Juan Dahlmann, is a third-generation Argentinian and also a point of uneasy confluence between conflicting strains, theological on his father's side, military on his mother's. The story is of his quest to recover the image of his maternal grandfather, who had been killed in battle, the image, in fact of a 'romantic death' (to romanti-cize death is quite certainly the highest of the pen's possibilities for Borges). Dahlmann wants to travel south, the compass-point of colour and vitality, and reoccupy the ruin of a ranch belonging to his mother's family. Instead he falls victim—though his death does not take place on the page—to a destiny rank with the essential themes of Argentinian literature. Having been challenged to a knife fight by a stranger in a bar he is supplied with a weapon in his moment of need by an ancient gaucho.

*   *   *

Yet the whole of the second half of 'El Sur' is blatantly spurious for anyone reading the story with the degree of care needed to keep fully in contact with Borges, because there is a 'hinge' at the moment where an acceptable reality is exchanged for fantasy or nightmare. Tiny symmetries between the two halves of the story betray Borges's literal duplicity, notably a slight head-wound first inflicted on Dahlmann when he walks into a door left carelessly ajar—by an 'accident', in fact, which is also an invitation to penetrate to the other side of the décor. This wound develops, excessively, into septicaemia and an operation in hospital involving an anaesthetic, i.e., a rational moment for reality to be abandoned. The wound is later taken up and used again when the challenge to Dahlmann is issued, bizarrely, in the form of a volley of paper pellets hitting him on the forehead—the paper no doubt being an indication of the purely literary nature of his imminent glorification.

'El Sur' is a privileged guide to Borges's philosophy of fiction because he has said that he turned to writing fictions, having been a poet, essayist and critic, after an attack of septicaemia and as a challenge to a mind he feared might have been sterilized by his illness.

This same elevation of the banal into the mythical often takes a more moralistic form than it does in 'El Sur', since Borges is also fond of showing how a literary transposition of events is enough to make a villain into a hero. In 'Tema del traidor y del héroe' the Irish patriot Fergus Kilpatrick, a traitor to his own cause, becomes the much-mourned talisman of that same cause thanks to the stupendous efforts made in the stage management of his death by the well-read investigator, Nolan; in an adjacent story, 'La Forma de la espada', another Irishman, John Vincent Moon, is a hero in his own narrative but a coward in inescapable fact, and given away by the scar on his face; in 'La Otra muerte' an Argentinian countryman is allowed to make up for his frailty in battle many years before by a delirious projection of valour in the hour of his death.

These stories not only act out the urge to buy back weakness with strength, they also expose this urge for what it is, a fiction. Whatever intimate inadequacy may have set Borges to oscillating between the real world and his own makeweight one, there is also the public fact that, as an Argentinian writer, he started writing fiction against a tradition of another kind, the tradition of *Martín Fierro*, which he himself has faithfully analysed, with its 'religion of courage', its 'generous' knife-fights, and so on. And perhaps because of his seven years in Europe, between 1914 and 1921, Borges has remained highly sensitive towards what he calls the 'ciphers' of Argentinian culture, the gaucho, the *compadrito*, the tango—a dance so debased in its export version that the rest of us are more likely to decipher it as the bent-kneed prowl of Groucho Marx.

Ever since he returned to Argentina, after periods of callow poetastery in Geneva and Madrid, Borges has been a townsman of Buenos Aires, yet the pampas have gone on lapping round his urban consciousness. All idea of local colour as such has become abhorrent to

him, but he has taken over the endless plains, the *llanura*, for his
metaphysical fantasies. Such topography as he has bothered to
preserve in his writing, at any rate since he left behind the gaudier
manner of his early years, has tended morosely towards the barren
and the flat, to the point where even Cornwall, in one story, has been
equipped with some 'sandy hills', preparatory to the erection there of
a labyrinth and the introduction into it of some murderous and
implausible orientals. The relationship of labyrinth to landscape is
the relationship of literature to life: as he creates, Borges is defending
his right to deal with universal themes rather than more recognizably
'Argentinian' ones, as well as bringing imagination into the style of a
country seen as badly in need of *asombro*.

It is because he has restricted himself to supplying imagination to
his country's literature, rather than its political or social institutions,
that Borges has been deplored by a number of his continent's younger
and more committed writers. In the massive compilation put out in
his honour by the Cahiers de l'Herne in 1964 he was paid the guarded
insult at one point of being told that he had taught his successors to
appreciate many forms of writing but not his own. Certainly his
political postures have been indecisive, though he aroused Perón
sufficiently to be sacked from his job as a librarian and put
in charge of chicken sales in Buenos Aires market. (Friends saved
him from this degradation and turned him into a teacher and
lecturer on English and American literature, a fall and resurrec-
tion which Borges himself has yoked ironically together as cause
and effect.)

There has also been an escapologist's wit about his rare statements
of social policy: a rejection of Marxism in its guise of historical
inevitability, on the grounds that a gentleman likes to be associated
only with lost causes; a recent subscription of the conservative, anti-
Castro line, as being the appropriate decision for a political sceptic.
Such ideological levity makes it a nice paradox that Borges should
have become, in Paris, one of the feted predecessors of the critical
guerrillas of *Tel Quel*, who have taken him over as a writer opposed,
like themselves, to the damaging fallacy that writing is expression
and not creation. Some of these young lions have dismantled Borges's
stories with a finesse that has daunted even their author, but they
have had to insist too heavily on suppressing all indication in them
that they were born from the circumstances of Borges's life. However
deafening the cosmic overtones in his fiction, or however persuasively

it can be interpreted as dramatizing the creative process, it does have roots in his biography.

* * *

Appropriately, it was in France, during the series of radio interviews he gave to Georges Charbonnier and of which the texts were later published, that Borges chose to play up the affective element in his stories and so defend them, by implication, against the extremists who believe that an intellectual interpretation of them can be exhaustive. This affective element is one of anxiety and solitude. Solitude is, as Borges makes clear, the condition of creativity: where should his own creature, Ts'ui Pen, be found—English-speaking readers at least can take the hint in his given name and recognize the wily Chinaman as a writer—working away at his labyrinthine novel, if not in a very willow-patterned outhouse called the Pavilion of Limpid Solitude? Others again of Borges's canny self-projections wrestle with the decipherment of the universe in actual captivity, and, their focal length thus shortened, these prisoners degenerate into helpless fantasists. One, a Muslim fakir, sets out to draw himself a map of the world in his prison cell but ends up covering the walls with tigers—the 'dreamtigers' that are a persistent image in Borges and figure the writer's forced suppression of physical reality:

> but still, the act of naming it, of guessing
> what is its nature and its circumstances
> creates a fiction, not a living creature,
> not one of those who wander on the earth

The poem from which these lines come, 'El Otro tigre', starts off in a library, a reminder that the solitary creator, unable to be forever dashing outside to check the promptings of his imagination against the reality, is not deprived of mental stereotypes; he invents against a tradition of such inventions and so puts in his own claim for admission to the literary community. In a book of spoof detective stories, which he wrote together with another Argentinian dabbler in the infinite, Adolfo Bioy Casares, Borges introduced a detective who is actually under sentence of death and copes with a series of mysteries without ever emerging from the death cell. This is certainly out-Poeing Poe, but it is also a grim reminder of the limits of the literary. The name of the detective is Parodi, a pun which proves that true originality lies not with man the unraveller but with Time the mystagogue.

No one has worked more wholesomely than Borges to cut the modern writer down to size, and challenge the orphic labels often pinned to him. (Diligent readers of 'La Lotería en Babilonia' might, for example, find fleeting relief in a 'sacred latrine' called Qaphqa.) He has said that of all his books it is *El Hacedor* that he likes the best, a flimsy collection of 'reflections' and 'interpolations', some of them brief pieces of prose, others poems, defined for the most part by their modest divergence from some existing literary model or philosophical idea. There is something excessive about this self-denial, and the corresponding promotion of traditional tropes above personal ones, as in the essay on the *kenningar* of the northern Sagas; and the fact is that Borges himself, as a young man, was a committed *ultraist* and involved as such in the hunt for wild and telling personal images à la Gomez de la Serna.

Yet the theory he has developed in reaction against this expressionism is not by any means as sterile as it may seem, since to quote an expression from the past does not mean denying or demeaning the present. This theory is best expounded in a story (included in the *Personal Anthology*) called 'La Busca de Averroës''. Here, the Andalusian Arab commentator of Aristotle is in quest of the meaning of two unknown terms he has just come across in the Greek, Comedy and Tragedy; he concludes that the first is a satire or anathema, the second a panegyric. This conclusion is followed by Borges's own, that his story is the narrative of a defeat, the defeat of Averroës's attempt to understand Aristotle and the defeat of his own attempts to understand Averroës:

I sensed that Averroës, striving to imagine a drama without ever having suspected what a theatre was, was no more absurd than I, who strove to imagine Averroës with no material other than some fragments from Renan, Lane and Asín Palacios.

Thus Borges, the algebraist, works to a strict formula: Borges is to Averroës as Averroës is to Aristotle. But how serious is he being when he says that the story represents a defeat for both of them? Satire and panegyric can be taken as contradictory attitudes towards a given text, the first depending on a retreat from it, the second on an identification with it. Shortly before he at last feels that he has understood what Aristotle means by his terms, Averroës is recorded as defending in conversation the literary repetition of a poetic figure from earlier centuries, comparing Destiny with a blind camel. The repetition, as he maintains, establishes a relationship with four terms: it expresses the sadness of the man who repeats it as well as fusing his sadness with that of the poet who said it before him. A vast interval of time, full of unique and largely unrecorded circumstances, separates the first event from the second, but the repetition spans it with a formula of generic identity.

*   *   *

This Platonic (or Proustian) snub to the march of time is, for Borges, nothing more final than a literary device, and one whose acceptance, as he knows, is especially difficult now that we are all such convinced nominalists—the English he picks out as being even more nominalist than most. But if he is always turning back to Berkeley or Schopenhauer for support, this is only because their seamless idealism makes them the patron thinkers of the man who subtends a fictive world in print. Borges does not propose them as guides for living by, and is, indeed, given to quoting Hume's verdict, that Berkeley's position was irrefutable but unacceptable.

Measured against a thorough-going nominalism all literature tends more or less to the generic, so that, by tending much more vigorously than others in this direction, Borges is, as ever, performing helpful exercises in literary criticism. Indeed, he has written a story, 'Funes el memorioso', to exhibit the fate of the nominalist, since Funes is a young man unable to forget anything, so fact-bound that he cannot even achieve the humble level of generalization required to share humanity's system of numeration. Funes, who dies a dismally premature death, is suffocated by circumstances, whereas Borges planes so high above them that, in his terms, it is the circumstantial detail that makes his narrative *un*real.

Thus the whole process of literary invention (or discovery) is exposed—Plato again—as being one not of inclusion but of omission, modelled on a life that Borges has appraised as an 'education in forgetting'. The higher the writer hoists himself out of the empirical slough the more imposing are his allegories. Condensation and discontinuity, as in the Freudian 'dream-work', become instruments for achieving shock and intensity (Borges, who knows he has been influenced by the techniques of the cinema in this respect, has never managed to get his own scenarios produced).

The 'education in forgetting' goes through three stages: first there are events, then memories of events, then words representing the memories of events. In the end 'only words remain'. But if most of us

K

resent oblivion Borges sees it as a blessing. In a line of poetry that is unusually direct he has asked for the sort of eternal life which belongs to the animals, the life of the ever-punctual now: 'to be for ever, but never to have been'. Thus his stories, which deny this now so heartily, are really invocations of the Void, and the trivial circumstance that threatens them with conclusion a merciful release—it is striking how often the solution of a Borges mystery comes pat upon a shower of rain.

*   *   *

Because of the abnormal dissociation he has practised between the real world and the fictive one Borges asks to belong, like one of his heroes, Herbert Quain, 'not to art but to the history of art'. (Quain, a novelist with a rare line in the narrative uses of bifurcation, is granted an obituary in the *TLS*, a specially reinforced example of the detail that makes for unreality, since the *TLS* does not print obituaries!) Borges's writings are full of the idea of the world's literature as a cumulative adventure, as the slow but continuing conquest of chance by human laws, like in his fictional Babylon where the two finally become coextensive. And the function of the Babylonian scribes is interpolation, variation, omission. Obsessed with theology Borges may be, but not with its orthodox forms—he is the student of those who have extended or diverted theological tradition by their heresies. His firm assumption of his own place on the lengthening book-shelves of the human race, and his insistence that all books are one book, all writers one writer, are beliefs, moreover, which lay unusual store by the physical preservation of the literature of the past. There is, in Borges, no getting away from the preoccupations of the librarian.

The only one of his books to have appeared in this country before the *Personal Anthology* was *Fictions*, published by Weidenfeld and Nicolson in 1964. The result is that we now have some of his stories available twice, and the bulk of his writing still not available in English at all. The translations in this *Personal Anthology* read fluently enough, but Anthony Kerrigan's introduction is eccentric and the exchange of letters between him and a fellow-translator included at the end of the volume an unforgivable editorial liberty.

English readers have every reason to hope that the rest of Borges's fiction, and a selection at least of his essays, should appear over here. He had read, re-read and related to the present a whole mausoleum of English writers whom few of us today ever pick up at all, and some bumptious modernists might be startled and improved by coming across a sophisticated comment on the art of narrative illustrated from William Morris, G. K. Chesterton being quoted on the Death of the Novel, or what amounts to an equation between the practice of Robbe-Grillet and that of Joseph Addison.

II

THE BRECHT EXPLOSION

IT IS TWELVE YEARS since the work of Bertolt Brecht was first (and last) discussed on the front page of this journal. Though his *Threepenny Opera* had been running at the Royal Court Theatre for a month he was scarcely a familiar or particularly welcome name, let alone academically respectable. Yet in the course of 1956 he did manage to break through—in varying depth—to our theatre, to our critics, to the German departments of our universities and to the general public awareness. That was the year of the Berliner Ensemble's first visit to London. It was the year of *Look Back in Anger*, and the start of a radical renaissance in the English drama. It was the year of Budapest and Poznan and Suez and of the Twentieth Congress in the Soviet Union.

*　　*　　*

That August Brecht died at the age of fifty-eight, and his posthumous reputation has grown in the most amazing way. Plays which were regarded as controversial or even impossible in East Germany are now performed there; the West German boycott of his work which followed the Berlin Wall is now over; an exhibition of Brecht

BERTOLT BRECHT: *Gesammelte Werke*. General Editor Elisabeth Hauptmann. 'Stücke' and 'Gedichte' edited by Elisabeth Hauptmann and Rosemarie Hill; 'Prosa' edited by Herta Ramthun and Klaus Völker; 'Schriften' edited by Werner Hecht. Dünndruckausgabe: vols. 1–8. Werkausgabe: vols. 1–20. Frankfurt: Suhrkamp-Verlag. Respectively DM. 350 and DM. 120 the set.

KLAUS SCHUHMANN: *Der Lyriker Bertolt Brecht, 1913–1939*. (Neue Beiträge zur Literaturwissenschaft Band 20). 338 pp. East Berlin: Rütten and Loening. MDN. 13.50.

BERTOLT BRECHT: *Manual of Piety. Die Hauspostille*. A bilingual edition with English text by Eric Bentley and notes by Hugo Schmidt. 312 pp. New York: Grove Press. $10 (Not distributed in the United Kingdom and Commonwealth.)

BERTOLT BRECHT: *Über Lyrik*. Compiled by Elisabeth Hauptmann and Rosemarie Hill. 143 pp. Frankfurt: Suhrkamp-Verlag. DM. 3.

Brecht über Theater. Edited by Werner Hecht. 375 pp. Leipzig: Reclams Universal-Bibliothek. MDN. 2.50.

FRANCO FORTINI: *Verifica dei Potere*. Scritti di critica e di istituzioni letterarie. 345 pp. Milan: Il Saggiatore. L. 1500.

photographs is actually being toured in this country by the Bonn Government. Soviet theatres which were long chary of his formal methods have adopted him in the 1960s with enthusiasm and apparent success. The Latin countries have annexed and absorbed him as no other German writer. The Comédie Française's request to stage one of his plays may have come to nothing, but our own National Theatre has done *Mother Courage* and most recently his adaptation of *Edward II*. Books and academic theses on his work now come from all quarters of the globe; he is in the university syllabuses and the reference books. Above all, as his seventieth birthday celebrations (in both Germanies) showed earlier this year, his work is regarded as intensely actual in the developing countries and ex-colonies. This is because it is not only often militantly political but unusually accessible to the non-European theatre.

It has taken even more than this time for most of his writings to get into print, and the process has often seemed hedged with uncertainties. While the project for a vast East German scholarly edition was

BERTOLT BRECHT: *Der Jasager und Der Neinsager*, Vorlagen, Fassungen und Materialien. Edited by Peter Szondi. 112 pp. *Baal. Drei Fassungen.* Edited by Dieter Schmidt. 213 pp. *Baal. Der böse Baal der asoziale.* Texte, Varianten und Materialien. Edited by Dieter Schmidt. 234 pp. *Im Dickicht der Städte.* Erstfassung und Materialien. Edited by Gisela E. Bahr. 171 pp. *Leben Eduards des Zweiten von England.* Vorlage, Text and Materialien. Edited by Reinhold Grimm. 269 pp. *Materialien zu Brechts 'Der gute Mensch von Sezuan'.* Edited by Werner Hecht. 176 pp. Frankfurt: Suhrkamp-Verlag. DM. 3 each.

MAX SPALTER: *Brecht's Tradition.* Johns Hopkins Press. London: Oxford University Press. £2 16s.

FRITZ HENNENBERG: *Dessau-Brecht Musikalische Arbeiten.* 551 pp. East Berlin: Henschel-Verlag. MDN. 34.

Erinnerungen an Brecht. Compiled by Hubert Witt. 374 pp. Leipzig: Reclams Universal-Bibliothek. MDN. 2.50.

KÄTHE RÜLICKE-WEILER: *Die Dramaturgie Brechts.* Theater als Mittel der Veränderung. 286 pp. East Berlin: Henschel-Verlag. MDN. 17.50.

ANDRÉ MÜLLER: *Kreuzzug gegen Brecht.* Die Kampagne in der Bundesrepublik 1961/62. 126 pp. East Berlin: Aufbau-Verlag. MDN. 3.

AGNES HÜFNER: *Brecht in Frankreich 1930–1963.* Verbreitung, Aufnahme, Wirkung. 277 pp. Stuttgart: Metzler. DM. 32.

NORBERT KOHLHASE: *Dichtung und politische Moral.* Eine Gegenüberstellung von Brecht und Camus. 286 pp. Munich: Nymphenburger Verlagshandlung. Paperback. DM. 12.80.

The Drama Review, volume 12, no. 1 (T37). 176 pp. New York: New York University/Bantam Books. $2 or 12s. 6d.

ERNST SCHUMACHER: *Drama und Geschichte. Bertolt Brechts 'Leben des Galilei'* und andere Stücke. 523 pp. East Berlin: Henschel-Verlag. MDN. 19.50.

GERHARD SZCZESNY: *Das Leben des Galilei und der Fall Bertolt Brecht.* 211 pp. Frankfurt and Berlin: Ullstein. DM. 3.20.

sliding into limbo, his Frankfurt publishers extended their collected
edition from the original (1953) two volumes of 'early plays' to cover
virtually all the plays and adaptations; then, in a somewhat confused
arrangement, the poems; then the seven volumes of theatrical theory
reviewed in the *TLS* on December 3, 1964; then five of stories, novels
and aphorisms; concluding it with three volumes of notes and essays
on the other arts and one of political writings: a total of forty volumes, identifiable at once by their olive-green binding. Brecht was an
exceptional author in that he was by no means in a hurry to get much
of his work published, and the value of this edition lay in the fact
that most of the non-theatrical material had not previously been
collected and a good deal of it had never been printed at all. Value
for the Western reader that is. For although the standard East
German edition was identical, apart from its elegant red covers,
something seems to have stopped the appearance there of the last
four volumes of poetry (which include all the poems written in East
Germany itself) and the bulk of the stories and aphorisms. They have
not even been announced.

With the seventieth birthday as a pretext, Brecht's publishers in
the West and his editors in the East have now revised and replanned
the whole enterprise, this time with the East German publishers
abstaining. Not only have they eliminated those confusions and
duplications, even at times triplications, which marred the old olive-
green edition, but they have chosen an ingenious and economical
form of production. The pages were set in ten-point type for an
India-paper edition in eight large volumes (an edition of 7,000
selling at about £30), then photographed down to nine-point for a
web-offset semi-paperback edition in twenty volumes, selling originally at under £10. As a piece of publishing it has been brilliantly
successful. A first printing of 50,000 sets has already sold out, and
a further 25,000 are now in the shops. What this means for the
writer's work can be judged from the fact that fewer than 1,000
complete sets of the previous forty-volume edition were in existence
(the publishers having sold only 831 copies of volume 9 of the poems,
which is largely made up of unfinished work, some of it of great
interest). The complete set of the new edition can be bought for the
price of six or seven volumes of the old.

*   *   *

The advance publicity was optimistic in speaking of this as 'the whole of Brecht', because there still remain entire categories of material which have not been published at all. These are the diaries and notebooks, the letters, the film treatments and the transcriptions of interviews, discussions and rehearsals of previously published work. The *Herrnburger Bericht* has been tacitly omitted, as has some of the text of the *Modellbücher*. There are also some minor cuts. But here is the essential bulk of Brecht, decently indexed and set out in more or less rational order, and it allows us to revise and re-establish a picture of him which the endless books and articles on the subject are apt to confuse. For the corpus of his work is far larger than any-one knew twelve years ago; it is more varied; the proportions are different; it is full of surprises. At the same time, thanks to his endless habit of amendment and rejection, more of it lies under the surface. This is something which is not immediately apparent from the new edition but has been usefully illuminated by the best of the books and articles. The very idea of a Collected Works suggests something static and indisputable, such as was quite remote from Brecht's nature.

Brecht is usually thought of above all as a playwright, and secon-darily as a theoretician of the theatre. Within the general framework of his writing, which from the late 1920s on was political-philoso-phical, this is proper enough, but the other aspects of his work have been unduly overshadowed, partly because they were so largely inaccessible and partly because his living monument, and main guardian of his legacy, is a brilliant theatrical company. If the new edition is examined from the crudest quantitative point of view it can be seen that the poems, now set in chronological sequence and more than one to a page, take up over a thousand pages as against 3,000 for the plays (including adaptations) and 1,300 for the theoretical writings. The prose runs to 1,500 pages—there are far more short stories than might have been expected, some of them very ordinary—and the writings on literature, art and politics (which now follow those on theatrical theory) another 1,000. Qualitatively and also chronologically Brecht was a fitful prose writer who had difficulty in finishing any of his longer projects, but his poetry and critical-political concerns run like continual semi-private threads through his life and work. Though his last play *Turandot* is included, as well as one-acters and fragments and the unfinished rump of the *Tui-Roman*, it is in those two departments and the section of *Me-Ti* aphorisms that the most exciting additions to our picture of Brecht have oc-curred. In short, he has proved in recent years to be a finer and more

varied poet than even his admirers thought. His literary interests too
are wider and his independence of Stalinist orthodoxy more evident,
though it was seldom publicly expressed.

*   *   *

When the poems were last reviewed in the *TLS* some five years
ago roughly half of them had been published, covering most of
what Brecht had written before 1939. This embraced all the best-
known poems, though already there were surprises such as the
'Psalms' and the large number of unpublished poems reflecting 'the
crushing impact of cities'. Since then the editors have added (among
much else) the extraordinary prose poems called 'Visionen', the
coolly bitter verses written in and about Hollywood, the Lucretian
'Didactic Poem on the Nature of Man'—that vastly conceived fragment of which a versified Communist Manifesto was to form part—
and a mass of new poems on the theatre (including, beside additions
to the *Messingkauf* series, others bearing on Odets, Laughton,
Chaplin and Peter Lorre). The late (East German) Buckow Elegies
have been amplified, *inter alia* by the much-publicized poem about
dissolving the people and electing another, and emerge as a sequence
of beauty and considerable political-satirical force. Three outstanding
groups are dedicated to Brecht's collaborator Margarete Steffin, who
died of tuberculosis on the trip to America in 1941. There are love
poems, often in sonnet form; altogether the sonnets total about
forty. There is the introduction in the 1940s of the kind of *Domestikum*
(Brecht's own term) typified for him by 'On Watering the Garden'.
There is the containedly tragic 'Is the People Infallible?', written
when he heard that his friend Sergei Tretiakoff had been shot in the
Soviet purges.

The editors have now weeded out all the songs to Brecht's plays
and a number of poems whose elimination seemed called for, though
without always explaining why. Illustrations (surely essential to the
Kriegsfibel epigrams) and musical settings have been omitted, but
some translations by Brecht have been added (including four from
Kipling; the section 'Ideal eines Mannes in früheren Zeiten' in
Me-Ti is likewise a partial translation of 'If'), and the long-suppressed
'Song of the Red Army Soldier' is back in more or less its original
place. Sensibly, the songs and other poems included elsewhere in the
edition are indexed with the poetry proper, though it seems a mistake
to have lopped off the conclusion of the original 'Aus einem Lesebuch

für Städtebewohner' set simply because it is repeated in the (much later) *Me-Ti*.

It remains difficult to grasp the plan, if any, of the various groups of sonnets, partly, no doubt, because the early Augsburg Sonnets again appear only in part. Dr. Klaus Schuhmann's generally useful thesis on the pre-1933 poems is unfortunately of no help here. It is best on such points as the transition, already identifiable in Brecht's first book of poems *Die Hauspostille*, from the nature-sodden Augsburg poems to the earliest city-influenced works; or the reflections of 'Neue Sachlichkeit' in what immediately followed; or the start of Brecht's political poetry, which the author dates from the appearance in 1926–27 of '8000 arme Leute' and two other poems in *Der Knüppel*, an extreme left periodical not covered by the standard Brecht bibliography. Apparently Brecht deliberately left this poem out of *Hauspostille* for inclusion in a collection devoted to 'the new man'. The weaknesses of Dr. Schuhmann's book, apart from a slightly plodding analysis of individual poems, lie in the neglect of the purely musical (singing, performing) element in Brecht's verse and above all in the failure to index the poems discussed.

There is also some relevant information in the Grove Press bilingual edition of the *Hauspostille* itself, both in Dr. Hugo Schmidt's critical notes and in Eric Bentley's preface (which incidentally suggests that Faber turned down *The Threepenny Opera* on T. S. Eliot's advice). Professor Bentley's English translations, while welcome as covering the ground, are on no consistent pattern, sometimes respecting both metre and rhyme, sometimes neither, sometimes (and most successfully) metre alone. Brecht's own view on this point—which he himself naturally flouted—was that

perhaps all that should be translated is the poet's thoughts and attitude. In so far as the rhythm of the original is part of the writer's attitude an attempt should be made to translate it, but no further.

This is cited with many other revealing notes and essays in the small paperback *Über Lyrik* compiled by the editors of the poems. The value of this excellent collection lies not only in its handiness but in its inclusion of a high proportion of material not to be found in the *Schriften* section of the collected edition. E.g., precisely, Brecht's reflections on re-reading *Hauspostille* in 1940:

The bulk of the poems deal with *Untergang*, and the poetry follows society's decline right down to the bottom. Beauty founded on wreckage, delicacy from rags. Nobility is rolled in the dirt, meaninglessness is greeted as bringing liberation. The poet manifests no solidarity, not even with himself. Risus mortis. But it doesn't lack power.

* * *

The difficulty generally with Brecht's theoretical *Schriften* is that in his case no clear line can be drawn between 'theatre', 'literature and art' and 'politics and society'. In both old and new editions the editors have arbitrarily drawn one, with the result that radio, cinema and theatre criticism get discussed under 'literature and art', while the same heading covers a variety of mainly political writing, e.g. (to take the shortest, silliest and worst example), a note of about 1952 which says:

1. Poor people and artists are in favour of the Russians because the Russians are against poverty and in favour of art, while the Americans are against art and in favour of profits.
2. The Russians' mistakes are the mistakes of friends; the Americans' mistakes are the mistakes of enemies.

The first two of the three 'theatre' volumes of the new *Schriften* largely repeat the seven volumes of the previous edition, stripped of the sections on criticism and cinema, though the *Messingkauf* poems and practice scenes have been regrouped respectively with the poetry and the plays, while the *Katzgraben* notes have been rightly pruned. The third now groups together the notes to individual plays, which are no longer printed with the plays themselves. There are also one or two points in the 'literature and art' volumes that are very relevant to the theatrical theory, e.g., the opening note (of 1920) with its suggestion that 'humour is a sense of distance' (*Distanzgefühl*) or the paragraph 'To Jhering' which makes clear what he really meant by 'playing from memory'. It is worth noting too that the same editor has compiled a selection of the theatre writing for the Reclam edition, centring on the *Messingkauf*, the *Short Organum* and the *Katzgraben* notes.

Of Brecht's purely literary notes and essays, the most interesting part dates mainly from the 1920s. In those days he was exaggeratedly aggressive and out to shock his fellow-bourgeois—his attacks on Thomas Mann are a good example—but his judgments are often genuinely unexpected. Arnold Zweig's *The Case of Sergeant Grischa* is of no interest to him; Rilke's attitude to God is 'pansy'; Benn is 'aristocratic snot'; *Ulysses*, to which he makes several references, is the best book of 1928. Kafka, whom he later credits with practising *Verfremdung*, is 'a really serious phenomenon', not to be compared with the literary world around him. 'I don't read all that much', he says in 1926, but both then and later he writes at length about the detective story: initially with a certain bravado, then around the end of the 1930s as a rational, factual, intellectual form of art, showing men in action and meeting 'the requirements of the people of a scientific era better than the works of the avant-garde'. About the same time there is a series of thirty-two short paragraphs headed 'Funny' and summarizing the essential jokes of a number of classic and other works. Thus: 'It takes the devil's own aid for the scholar *Faust* to succeed in seducing a German girl.'

*   *   *

The real meat of the 'literature and art' volumes however is at once literary and political, because it deals (as in a sense do the Stanislavsky notes and studies in the theatrical volumes) with the communist world's long arguments about formalism and realism, first at the time of the Popular Front movement, then again after the end of the Second World War. From Brecht's point of view this began as a series of shots at Georg Lukács, whose aesthetically conservative concept of realism, unacceptable enough to him before 1933, had now become the dominant official line. The battle has been well analysed by Klaus Völker in *Kursbuch* (Frankfurt) no. 10, and there is a further valuable essay on it by László Illés, citing some of Lukács's writings in the 1930s Moscow Hungarian press, in the Hungarian Academy's symposium *Littérature et Réalité* of 1966. The joke in this case is that the two men have shifted positions in the cultural-political ranking, so that Lukács is now the outsider and Brecht the orthodoxly accepted figure. That does not make the essays now printed seem any the less sharply heretical; Brecht's defence of experimental art, even when uncongenial to him, his dismissal of what he calls 'a formalist theory of realism' and his dislike of a concept of 'popular' art with the word popular 'spoken as it were *de haut en bas*' are still very relevant in the communist world today.

On the other hand it makes it all the more regrettable that *none* of his broadsides ever found their way into print at the time, not even in *Das Wort*, the Moscow German-language magazine of which he was co-editor. Publicly at least, there was no battle at all. Last year when the *Schriften zur Literatur und Kunst* appeared in three volumes as

part of the old collected edition the editor excused this by saying that
Brecht withheld his side of the argument 'in order not to emphasize
differences of opinion between the anti-Fascist writers' at a time
when a common front seemed essential. This comment has been
dropped in the new edition, but if it really was Brecht's reason
history proved him wrong. At the same time he was, alas, prepared
to accept the rightness of the actual party slogans in cultural matters
—socialist realism good, formalism bad, cosmopolitanism bad, and
so on—by simply twisting them to mean what he himself wanted,
which was usually something quite different. Much the same kind of
equivocation and over-subtlety can be seen in his writings on political
issues proper, where he sometimes seems to have been arguing on
three levels: one for the public, one for his friends and one for himself. This was not just caution (he was not, after all, at that time
particularly dependent on the Party's good will) but one aspect of
his view of the relations between individual and community: 'We
may go astray and you may be right, so/Do not cut yourself off.'

The political writings proper, which make up the last volume of
the collected edition, are largely concerned with the theory of dialectical materialism or with short-term polemical writing against the
Nazis. Neither makes for specially attractive reading, though now
that we know more of Brecht's debt to Karl Korsch (subject of a
front-page article in the *TLS* of March 28, 1968, and of Wolfdietrich
Rasch's revealing study 'Brechts marxistischer Lehrer' in *Merkur*,
October, 1963), his undated note 'On my Teacher' is of particular
interest, e.g.: 'My teacher is a disappointed man. . . . He has a
sharp eye everywhere for the germs of developments that are going to
bring disappointment in the future . . .' Korsch, with Tretiakoff one
of the few men whom Brecht called by that title, was much with him
in Denmark in 1935 and 1936, and the incomplete *Me-Ti* aphorisms,
where Brecht voiced his acutest and most private criticisms of the
purges, of the corrupting effect of Stalinism on foreign communist
parties, of Stalin-worship and the perversion of Marx's own image,
of the shortcomings of communist functionaries and so on, bear
many marks of his influence. No doubt because they deal also with
other topics—including, irrelevantly and somewhat embarrassingly,
Brecht's chief love affair of the 1930s and 1940s—and are couched in
a fictionalized, orientalized form, they are to be found not among the
political writings but in the second volume of the Prose, along with
the newly published (but laboured and disappointing) fragments of

the *Tui-Roman,* a satirical and likewise mock-oriental satire on 'intellectuals' of a sociological bent, particularly such as flourished under the Weimar Republic.

*	*	*

Me-Ti (or the *Book of Changes,* as he also called it), in spite of some affectations, is among the most alive of Brecht's writings. Politically there is little in the *Schriften* that seems to go so far; his notes there on the Moscow trials, for instance, though written about the same time and partly (it seems) intended for so close a friend as Walter Benjamin, are much less outspoken: 'As for the trials, it would be quite wrong when discussing them to adopt an attitude hostile to their organizers, the Soviet government. . . .' There is, however, one really startling document among them which is grouped with the writings of the same period, the 'Preconditions for the Successful Leadership of a Movement Orientated towards Social Transformation'. Among the points which it puts forward are abolition of the leadership principle within the Party, a shift away from centralism, greater ethical emphasis (including the application of bourgeois morality), abstention from dishonest tactics, the substitution of proof for 'faith', finally no claims to primacy by the industrial workers, but the dictatorship of the proletariat to be seen as the simplest and quickest solution. Are these Brecht's own ideas? If so they certainly illustrate his inconsistency, though the last point also bears out Franco Fortini's very suggestive argument in his *Verifica dei Potere* that because of his feeling for the Far East and for country people Brecht tended to qualify 'the universalist-jacobin element in Marxism'—this being both a key to his differences with the 'Europocentric, indeed Germanocentric' Lukács and a reason for his appeal in the present climate of anti-colonialism and anti-racialism. Though Signor Fortini's essays in this collection range widely over other problems of present-day letters (he deals at some length with Lukács's influence in Italy, for instance), he also has an important chapter on the first anti-Fascist writers' congress in Paris in 1935 and the speech which Brecht made there. He is likewise illuminating on the reasons which made the German left wing so much a society within a society.

As for the plays, they are now much more compactly arranged—the new edition incidentally has running heads, which were irritatingly absent from the old—but nearly everything of importance was in print in one form or another ten years ago. *Turandot*, Brecht's last play, which was held back for some reason, is one of the least impressive to read, though it might perform amusingly. It too deals with the 'Tuis', or more or less progressive German intellectuals in Chinese costume, who are bullied by an Ui-type political gangster before the oppressed masses come bursting in, in one of Brecht's rare 'positive' (or happy) endings. The one-act plays, which were added to the old edition some eighteen months ago, prove to be short farces of a knockabout kind—in two cases with an ephemeral political point, like old Unity Theatre pantomimes—plus the oddly poetic *Der Bettler*. The fragments which follow them in the seventh 'plays' volume of the new edition have already partly appeared in various forms, but they are certainly the most interesting of the novelties, while *Der Brotladen* in particular is now seen as one of the missing keys to Brecht's work, thanks in part to its piecing-together and production by two of the younger directors of the Berliner Ensemble. It is only a pity that the text as published should give so slight an idea of the work that Brecht put into this play, which became partly diverted into *Happy End* (not regarded as Brecht's) and *St Joan of the Stockyards*. Only the three most coherent scenes are printed here, and half a dozen odd songs.

The problem of how to show the incessant evolution of Brecht's dramatic texts was at first going to be tackled by a vast 'historic-critical' (or Variorum) edition. It is now being resolved in a much less ambitious way by a series of paperback volumes in the 'Edition Suhrkamp', which is uniform in size with the new twenty-volume edition. This seems to have come about almost by accident, as the first of these booklets on individual plays contained nothing more helpful than critical articles and cast lists and already available notes by Brecht. The ice was broken in 1966 with *Der Jasager*, for which Peter Szondi collected the different versions of the text, plus Arthur Waley's *Taniko* on which it is based, and with the three unpublished versions of *Baal* presented by Dieter Schmidt. Four equally original volumes have now followed, giving further *Baal* material (including an incomplete version of about 1930), the 1921–22 text of *Im Dickicht der Städte*, the two early printed texts of *Edward II* (whose manuscripts have still to be found), and the German Marlowe translation from which Brecht worked; finally some ten years' worth of scenes, sketches and plans for *Der gute Mensch von Sezuan*. These books are invaluable for anyone at all closely concerned with the plays, and they often explain apparent awkwardnesses in the final text. They also say a lot about Brecht's method of working: his continual reconsiderations, his reluctance ever to be satisfied with what he wrote.

*   *   *

The latest critical studies of the playwright give (in one sense or the other) only partial views, apart from the general introduction provided in Dr. Frederic Ewen's *Bertolt Brecht*, which is not yet distributed in this country. Thus Dr. Spalter traces his slightly offbeat dramatic ancestry, from Lenz up to Karl Kraus, with analyses and examples which might help to extend our own theatrical repertoire; his final account of all Brecht's own plays is hardly necessary, and tries to cram in hopelessly much. Fritz Hennenberg's very fully documented book deals entirely with his collaboration with the composer Paul Dessau, making only the briefest reference to any other music for Brecht's works, but is incidentally worth studying for the light which it sheds on the texts, one of which, the anti-West-German 'Lehrstück' of 1951 called *Herrnburger Bericht*, is a notable omission from both collected editions. *Erinnerungen an Brecht* is an inexpensive collection of mainly biographical and critical material and obituary tributes of varying value. Käthe Rülicke-Weiler's *Die Dramaturgie Brechts* benefits spasmodically from her first-hand knowledge of the writer and some of his productions, and also from her notes of his remarks, but it bears the marks of its origin as a thesis for the SED Central Committee's institute for social studies. That is to say that it stresses the links between *Verfremdung* and dialectics; it works hard to reconcile Brecht with Aristotle and with Stanislavsky (whose writings he seems only to have known at second hand); it argues in too general terms that his dramaturgy was above all influenced by Soviet art, and sees Marx, Engels and Lenin as 'no less important than Shakespeare in Brecht's dramatic ancestry'. There are interesting details here for specialists—such as Brecht's project of 1956 for a critical production of *Waiting for Godot* and the suggestion that the 1951 production of *Señora Carrar* was intended 'to help recruiting for the People's Army'—but there are peculiarities too, not least the view that the 'principal contradiction' in Brecht's plays is that between the individual and society.

Brecht's reception in other countries has become almost a separate subject for study. André Müller's *Kreuzzug gegen Brecht* is admittedly a polemical work, dealing with the now fortunately outdated

West German boycott of the plays. Agnes Hüfner's account of his impact in France, however, is a pretty thorough piece of literary research, again undertaken presumably for a thesis; it presents a mass of material (which consists largely of quotations from French critics) without entirely digesting it, or ever going into such relevant questions as the extent of Brecht's own knowledge of and feeling for French literature, the suitability of that language for translation of his work, or—an intriguing side issue—his apparent failure to make any impression on that other outstanding communist poet, Louis Aragon. At the same time Norbert Kohlhase has made a competent if slightly artificial comparison between Brecht and Camus, originally a thesis in political science at Berlin Free University. There are also two very relevant articles in the special Fall 1967 issue of *The* (formerly the Tulane) *Drama Review*, where Henry Glade writes on the nine Brecht productions playing in Moscow last season and Lee Baxandall gives a first-rate account of Brecht's 1935 visit to the United States and of the Theatre Union production of *Mother*. Oddly enough nothing has yet been published on his special relationship with England, but there is new evidence of it throughout the writings on literature and art, right down to his affection for Edgar Wallace and his identification of the logical crime story with such English writers as Sayers, Freeman and Rhode. The Brecht-Archive in Berlin even contains his three-page scheme for an adaptation of *H.M.S. Pinafore*.

*   *   *

Is all this very confusing? Whether or not one likes Brecht it has to be admitted that there has been a steady widening of the visible range of his work, which overseas interest, academic concern and the actual volume of publications have all greatly increased. There has been something like a Brecht explosion, and this makes it a good deal more difficult than in 1956 to get a coherent picture of him or to write about his achievement anything like comprehensively. Perhaps the only answer for the moment lies in a more concentrated examination, in all its implications, of any single one of his works. This is the policy followed by Professor Ernst Schumacher, who in 1955 provided an all-round survey of the plays of the Weimar period, but now devotes an almost equally large study to *Galileo* alone. The very idea is suggestive. Not only is *Galileo* arguably the finest and/or the most important of Brecht's plays, but he took endless pains over it, writing three different versions over a period of seventeen years and eventually taking its production into his own hands; its theme too, besides relating to a well-documented historical story, derives from the central scientific-political concern of the 1940s and 1950s. By studying all the relevant material in depth the reader should be able to see how Brecht worked, how he used to modify and pursue his aims, how these in turn developed out of major contemporary issues and how far they helped to resolve them—something that naturally bears also on the rest of his writings.

Professor Schumacher shows this in great detail: his book too originates in a thesis (this time a high-level *Habilitationsschrift*) and it is a very much more serious piece of work than Dr. Gerhard Szczesny's polemical essay in Ullstein's 'Dichtung und Wirklichkeit' series, which uses some of the Schumacher material, and moreover prints the otherwise unpublished 1938–39 version of three crucial scenes, but gradually clogs up with arbitrary judgments and mis- or over-statements, to dismiss Brecht finally as snob, coward, victim of the Oedipus complex and second-rate playwright. In Schumacher's account with its broad background the reader sees how close Brecht's first version kept to the historical facts in order to show how, even in the then situation of the German scientific and technical intelligentsia, the truth can get out; he learns how it relates to Brecht's interest in the work of Niels Bohr and his group, and to the attitudes taken up by Dimitroff and Bukharin in their respective trials. According to Brecht this version was designed for an American production, though in fact it was staged in Zurich, and only once the tide of the Second World War had turned against the Germans. The German scientists were by then so committed to the war effort that the moral of the play seemed inappropriate.

When Brecht started revising it in the United States in 1944, in close collaboration with Charles Laughton, he twisted the historical story to stress the scientist's social betrayal, a message which, while now conflicting with the earlier one, became sharply relevant with the dropping of the first atomic bomb. At the same time, so Professor Schumacher suggests, he tried to bring out the class affiliations of the characters in what now seems a rather forced way. This was the version staged, with Laughton as Galileo, in Hollywood and New York in 1947; Orson Welles was originally to have been the director, but in the event it was Joseph Losey, whose own account seems to have escaped the author's notice. Brecht's hearing by the Un-American Activities committee fell that same autumn, and the Oppenheimer case followed (whose dramatized version is now in the repertoire of the Berliner Ensemble). It coincided with the final revision of the play, which introduced the concept of a Hippocratic oath for scientists, and led on to the idea of a play about Einstein, a possibility earlier considered (for an opera) by Paul Dessau.

Drama und Geschichte is an interesting study, and it is exceptional in giving a real impression of the depth of Brecht's work, though it could well have been somewhat condensed and Anglo-Saxon readers might find the preoccupation with 'dialectics' a bit laborious. There are one or two errors in the United States chapters—such as the suggestion that Professor George Rylands took the 'chief male part' in *The Duchess of Malfi* as adapted by Brecht—and the account of *Galileo*'s reception in the United States is unconvincing; it is as hard to believe in the alleged enthusiasm of the G.I. audience at a reading as in the bad conscience which is supposedly what led the staff of Mount Wilson observatory to object that Galileo was not really a social and intellectual traitor—as indeed he was not. Nor has the author looked far enough in his effort to prove that Brecht in 1945 originated the idea of a scientists' oath. In *Nature* for May 7, 1938, he could have found in a place of emphasis Lancelot Law Whyte's proposal that educational, cultural and technical institutions should ask their members to sign a declaration on Hippocratic lines, as a barrier to 'the advance of intolerance and the lie', i.e., in the first instance, Nazi abuse of the intellect. This was reported in other papers and discussed in a leader in the *New York Times*.

*   *   *

Plays change according to the circumstances in which they are performed, and it is difficult to see *Galileo* in East Germany without feeling that there is a close analogy between the rigid Aristotelian dogma enforced by the seventeenth-century theologians and Marxism-Leninism as the Stalinists understood it, and that the audience are well aware of the parallel. Though Professor Schumacher chooses not to discuss this, it is not untypical of the way in which Brecht's best works remain relevant to our preoccupations, even when his own conscious intentions were different. Perhaps then he would have rewritten *Galileo* yet again after 1956. It is not impossible,

because he was always anxious to retain control of his message and
never took anything as final. For

> Everything changes. A new beginning
> Can be made with your final breath.
> But what has happened has happened. And the water
> You once poured into the wine can't be
> Tipped out again.
>
> What has happened has happened. The water
> You once poured into the wine can't be
> Tipped out again, but
> Everything changes. A new beginning
> Can be made with your final breath.

So he wrote in America at the time of the collaboration with Laughton, and it is this concept of movement and renewal which so distinguishes him from other writers. It made him contradict himself; it made him ruthless in his judgment of his own writing, it made him uniquely indifferent to publication in his lifetime. Above all it gave him an intense restlessness which led him to nag and nag at apparently finished works, kneading every element of them, however separate, until the whole combination fitted the objectives of the moment. He sometimes failed, which is what helps give his writing its frequent ambiguity, but the very concentration of the effort makes for a similar concentration in his collected work, where language, structure, scenic methods, political analysis and theoretical exposition all hang together and interact. As he himself realized, the result has many imperfections and is often open to criticism. But unlike that of more polished authors it is worth exploring at any point.

NOTE

The translation of 'schwul', Brecht's term for Rilke's attitude to God on p. 146, has been amended following Michael Morley's letter to the Editor of the *TLS* on 4 November.

12

MEMOIRS AND ANTI-MEMOIRS

(a) ANDRÉ MALRAUX

THE NATURE of M. Malraux's *Antimémoires* is indicated by a Buddhist text which he puts at the beginning:

L'éléphant est le plus sage de tous les animaux, le seul qui se souvienne de ses vies antérieures; aussi se tient-il longtemps tranquille, méditant à leur sujet.

In his introduction he gives a fuller but rather unclear explanation of the title. Its real point is evidently to free him from the one-dimensional time-sequence of the memoir. His antimemoirs are three-dimensional. The primary axis is geographical, leading from Islam through India and Indochina to China, apparently following the route of a journey in 1965. At right-angles to this line he goes backward, when he sees fit, along the time-axis, without regard to place, inserting not merely contrasts between present and earlier impressions, but also episodes of more recent events, mostly of wartime experiences in France. Occasionally he deserts the space-time plane and darts along a third coordinate into fiction. Into the middle of all this, for greater confusion, he puts a section entitled, like the book, 'Antimémoires', which deals with some of his experiences after the liberation, including his relations with General de Gaulle. Throughout, cross-references abound between points defined in his three-dimensional space.

(*a*) ANDRÉ MALRAUX: *Antimémoires*. 605 pp. Paris: Gallimard. 28 fr. *Museum Without Walls*. Translated by Stuart Gilbert and Francis Price. 252 pp. Secker and Warburg. 25s. (Paperback, 12s. 6d.).

DAVID WILKINSON: *Malraux*. An Essay in Political Criticism. 224 pp. Harvard University Press. London: Oxford University Press. £2 8s.

(*b*) HAROLD NICOLSON: *Diaries and Letters, 1945–1962*. Edited by Nigel Nicolson. 448 pp. Collins. £2 5s.

(*c*) V. S. PRITCHETT: *A Cab at the Door*. An Autobiography: Early Years. 238 pp. Chatto and Windus. 30s.

(*d*) J. R. ACKERLEY: *My Father and Myself*. 219 pp. Bodley Head. 30s.

Before considering the book, it is well to remember what kind of
man M. Malraux is and how much we owe to him, particularly those
of us who grew up between the two wars. He was born in 1901. He
was trained as an orientalist, and in the 1920s he spent long, fruitful
and adventurous years in the East, taking part in revolutionary
activities in Annam and China. These gave rise to his best novels,
above all *La Condition humaine*, a novel of style, action and feeling
whose approach to life influenced a whole generation: the title
resounds in one's memory like a slogan. When the Spanish Civil War
broke out, he was quick into the battle, and made acquaintance with
the tough side of Stalinism. During the war he fought first in the
French army and, after the armistice, with great distinction in the
Resistance organization led by de Gaulle. He was Minister of Information from 1945 to 1946 in the first de Gaulle administration.
While de Gaulle was out of office he devoted himself to the analysis
of art. In 1958 he came back to office under the General and has been
long and actively the Minister for Cultural Affairs, a post which he
has held with great panache.

*   *   *

M. Malraux has more lives to look back on than most men, and
nearly all are creditable. He was early in fields which have since been
ploughed over and over again by others. He saw the nature and importance of Asian communism when it was almost unknown; he
foresaw the death of imperialism and wished to collaborate with the
future when most westerners in power hardly knew what the problems were; and, though on many occasions he collaborated with the
communists when by his fundamentally liberal criteria he thought
it the best thing to do, he was never a dupe nor an ideologist. In
spite of this active life, he never lost his interest in art. One looks
forward, therefore, with the greatest interest to his memoirs or
antimemoirs; and it is a pity to acknowledge that one is somewhat
disappointed.

*   *   *

This is an intensely personal book. In his mid-sixties, M. Malraux
can recollect emotion in something like the elephant's tranquillity.
From his point of view, writing it must have been a splendid experience. But from the reader's point of view it is imperfect. What are
probably to him the central and most significant points come over

least clearly—particularly the connexion between the different parts of the book. It looks as if it were designed to teach a lesson—but what lesson? That it is a study of the human condition is clear; but are there any general conclusions to be drawn? One of the key phrases, quoted from a priest, which appears in the first pages and again later on, is 'Et puis, le fond de tout, c'est *qu'il n'y a pas de grandes personnes* . . .' (the italics are M. Malraux's). But the theme is never developed. As one might expect, M. Malraux's world is one of highly adult, intelligent and dominant people: his next two quotations (he is not above a little demure name-dropping) are remarks made to him by Valéry about Gide and by Gorky about Tolstoy.

M. Malraux is more a man of action, imagination and sensibility than of clear analytic thought. When he generalizes, he is unnecessarily obscure and comes near to what Sir Peter Medawar (writing of a very different author) describes as 'that tipsy, euphoric prose-poetry which is one of the more tiresome manifestations of the French spirit'. When M. Malraux is in this mood one is tempted to think of a less spiritual explanation of the tranquil elephant. Intelligent and energetic as this animal is, it has a very inefficient digestive system. It takes a long time to deal with its massive intake and, while it does so, its stomach rumbles. Fortunately there is not much of this kind of writing, but the reader should be warned that the book starts on this note. He should persevere: action and sensibility get the upper hand, and M. Malraux's style is thixotropic. In slow movement and deep thought it is glutinous; but when it is stirred by action it runs as clearly as in his novels.

Fiction imposes its own discipline; so presumably do memoirs; but the antimemorial muse rides her subject with a light rein. There is far too little shape about the book; nearly one-tenth of the text is taken straight over from earlier works; and, except for the passages of action, it is too long. We are told that the work as a whole will only be published after the author's death (which, insha'llah, will be long deferred); some parts of this volume have been omitted for discretion's sake, and there will probably be three more. The publisher's note is ambiguous, and one does not know whether any further instalments will be published in M. Malraux's lifetime, though an asterisk on the title-page leads to vague anticipations. Thanks to the form of the book, one has no idea what will follow. Chronology is no guide, and he has plenty of material in hand: family history apart, there is little in this book which antecedes 1940, and nothing about his personal life (so far, Mme. Clara Malraux has nothing to hope or fear).

* * *

No single key to the construction of this incomplete book should be sought: it is better to regard it as an expression of the author's sensibility, noting his cross-references as far as one can. This gives certain clues. The first, of course, is his passionate interest in men under strain, a theme of all his novels. Therefore he is at his best when writing of the Resistance, in which he played a gallant and honourable part. It might be said that in the events of France at that time, history had created a subject for M. Malraux. This is enhanced by two particular factors. First, the experience of defeat, resistance and internal disputes among the resisters cleared his mind wonderfully: his loyalties became no less generous, but more concentrated; he was French before all. Second, his novels have always shown a horrified preoccupation with torture. In the Resistance, for the first time, he had direct experience of it. It was pure luck that he was not tortured himself—the very French luck of the wrong *dossier* having been sent to the Gestapo—but he came close to it, heard it and saw it. He did not suffer it, but his friends did. This, for him, was crucial. It is significant that the last section of the book, one of the best and the most moving, deals in the calm of retrospect with the horror of the German concentration camps and the problems of return to normal life: 'C'était le retour de Dante chez les distraits'.

The second main clue is to be found in M. Malraux's twin preoccupations with myths and with the absurd and the eccentric in life. There are keywords here which often recur in the book: *onirique* and *farfelu*. The former is obvious; the latter is well known to readers of M. Malraux, and consciously adopted: he reintroduced this strange word for the absurd into the French vocabulary.

Coincidences and conceivably significant juxtapositions mean a lot to him. *Onirique* or not, he is closer to Jung than to Freud. When the facts fail him, he bends them slightly, though he has a scholar's conscience. A trivial but not meaningless example shows the form. One of his favourite myths is that of Balkis, Queen of Sheba. He goes to Aden and twice refers to its greatest monuments, the 'citernes cyclopéennes attribuées à la reine Balkis'. The words *cyclopéennes* and *Balkis* evoke the mysterious past. But the word *attribuées* is no less significant: M. Malraux is an archaeologist and must know that for one hundred years these cisterns have been regarded as Roman work, whatever the museum attendant may have said. If you cannot find a myth, make one.

Myth imposes order: absurdity is disorder in life, against which the rational side of M. Malraux fights: 'L'arme la plus efficace de l'homme c'est d'avoir réduit au minimum sa part de comédie.' But myth is a slightly bogus form of order, and M. Malraux can never resist the fascination of the absurd and the mythical, particularly where they meet. The most noteworthy example is Clappique in *La Condition humaine*, wholly absurd, a play-actor and a perpetual creator of myths, to such an extent as to suppress all reality in his character. And yet, to M. Malraux, he was so fascinating that he threatened to run away with the novel, so that the surplus of Clappique had to be cut out and separately published.

The fictional parts of the book are high-spots of mystification. The first is a 'transposition' of *Les Noyers de l'Altenburg* (which already contained very brief transpositions from *La Voie royale*). Some rather unconvincing reasons are given for including it, which might have held water if it had been a serious rewriting of the original. It is not. He has cut it down by massive omissions but has hardly changed a word in the text of what remains. The introduction, the Turkish episode and the gas-attack have disappeared totally, but not without trace: some allusions to the Turkish episode have not been cleared up and render what remains less meaningful. The finale appears elsewhere, disconnected from the rest. The colloquy at the Altenburg has been stripped down to bare essentials, which is no bad thing, since a take-off of Pontigny means little in these late days. The suicide remains almost unaltered, and he tells us that in real death it is that of his father. One can conceive why M. Malraux got out his scissors (though the longer original makes far more sense), but not why he should have pasted the result into his *Antimémoires*.

*   *   *

The other piece of fiction is pure *farfelu*, and not a great success. In his recent voyage M. Malraux could not stop at Saigon for political reasons: so he pursues *La Voie royale* (which deals with the hill-tribes of Indochina) in a manner of pure mystification. Clappique (need one be surprised?) appears at a party at Singapore and recites a very long scenario of a film dealing with a French adventurer, David de Mayrena, who operated among these tribes in the 1880s and had himself briefly made king of one of them. Mayrena had already appeared as a long-dead character in *La Voie royale*. In this Chinese box of mystification one might guess that he was an invention too, but the reference books show that there was such a man, though (final touch of the conjurer) with a different Christian name. Mayrena is in part the original of Perken in *La Voie royale*, not one of M. Malraux's best bits of fiction; nor is this.

The rest of the book can be roughly divided, allowing for a good deal of overlap, into adventure, travelogue and political interviews. The adventures, as always with M. Malraux, are superb. A tank crew's first action in the war; M. Malraux's capture by the Germans, danger of torture and ultimate escape; near death in a light aeroplane caught in a storm and the strangeness of coming back to normal life after landing (a direct transposition, this, from *Le Temps du mépris*); swinging French Guiana round to the General: nothing could be better or more exciting—and moving as well. There is one aspect which makes one smile, without detracting from the merit of his stories. Our hero always comes out on top, at least in argument. He appears as a Modesty Blaise, using words as karate, and the enemy retires baffled. Probably they always did; but the total recall makes one wonder a little.

The travelogue is good, informed by his sense of the significance of works of art in their various surroundings, whether natural or confined in museums. He is best when shortest: a few pages on the interaction of pre-Columbian beliefs and Mexican Catholicism are far more impressive than longer, and sometimes more glutinous, dissertations on the cultures of Egypt and India.

The first political interview, just after the liberation, is with de Gaulle. The General himself says little, which is fair enough, since M. Malraux is still in office. M. Malraux says a lot. Once again, one is reminded of Modesty Blaise: like him, however effective, she needs a father-figure; behind her stands Sir Gerald, who says little but to whose wisdom she, the activist, bows. He starts off by a statement of his political position:

Je me suis engagé dans un combat pour, disons, la justice sociale. Peut-être, plus exactement: pour donner aux hommes leur chance. . . . Je suis allé me battre en Espagne. Pas dans les Brigades internationales, qui n'existaient pas encore, et auxquelles nous avons donné le temps d'exister: le parti communiste réfléchissait. . . . Puis, il y a eu la guerre, la vraie. Enfin est arrivée le défaite, et comme beaucoup d'autres, j'ai épousé la France.

Quand je suis revenu à Paris, Albert Camus m'a demandé: Devrons-nous choisir un jour entre la Russie et l'Amérique? Pour moi, ce n'est entre la Russie et l'Amérique, c'est entre la Russie et la France. Lorsqu' une France faible se trouve en face d'une puissante Russie, je ne crois plus un mot de ce que je croyais lorsqu'une France puissante se trouvait en face d'une faible Union Soviétique. Une Russie faible veut des fronts populaires, une Russie forte veut des démocraties populaires.

M. Malraux has said most of this already, but it is worth quoting, because it gives with great concision the expected answer to a question which never needed putting: why did M. Malraux desert the communists and join the General? Circumstances had changed; he had his own ideas and no illusions; he also had a taste for heroes. His path was laid out for him.

There is a fair amount more about the General over the years: all interesting, none illuminating, most of it touched by a spirit of virile hagiography.

The next series of interviews is with Nehru, an old friend whom he found highly sympathetic but with one reserve:

Il aimait l'originalité de la pensée, la saluait d'un sourire au passage, comme un amateur de peinture eût salué un bon tableau. Mais les intellectuels aiment cette originalité pour elle-même; je crois que Nehru ne l'aimait qu'agissante.

The long Indian passage which is wrapped round Nehru is rather disappointing. There is a sentimental admiration for Indian culture regarded strictly from outside, in an ideal form. The idea of a civilization bound to and by religion fascinates him from afar. One learns nothing very new; it is all a bit bookish (but good books—he can read Sanskrit) and he assumes a romantic view of the Indian peasant whom, as he says, he has never met, comparing him rather unfavourably with the French peasant whom he has just met as a fellow-soldier. The latter is brought into the picture by the conclusion of *Les Noyers de l'Altenburg*, lifted almost verbatim. Even on that slim basis of comparison, the Frenchman comes out rather well.

Finally, there is Mao. Here for the first time Modesty Blaise drops her karate. With de Gaulle and Nehru, M. Malraux did most of the talking. With Mao, where he was on official business, he listened, with a background of knowledge and sympathy which few westerners could achieve (the section starts with a brilliant short account of the Long March). But he remained a Frenchman and a Westerner, chipping in at the appropriate moment with a reminder that America was France's ally. One can assume that the long dialogue is accurately reported: notes were taken. It is one of the most interesting things in the book. Mao emerges as immensely impressive. This must have been shortly before the great cultural revolution, and shadows of it just show against the light of hindsight: the insistence that the young must work their passage. This chapter must be read as a whole, but one remark by Chairman Mao is worth quoting:

Vous savez que je proclame depuis longtemps: nous devons enseigner aux masses avec précision ce que nous avons reçu d'elles avec confusion. Qu'est-ce qui nous a attaché le plus de villages? Les exposés d'amertume.

The reader comes back to the final chapter on the concentration camps. It is a good reminder of what much of the book is about: the conversion of a man's field of action by the Resistance; not of his thought and feelings, which remained much the same throughout. In spite of a strong dose of the obscure and the *farfelu*, sanity and good will predominate whenever he has to act.

This complicated book relies on its cross-references. Need it be said that there is no index, even of names? When the next volume appears, before or after M. Malraux's death, and when more shortly the English translation of this volume appears (it is due from Hamish Hamilton later this year), one may hope that the publishers will have pity on the reader.

*   *   *

Twenty years ago M. Malraux launched that splendid phrase, *Le Musée imaginaire*, as the title of one part of *La Psychologie de l'Art*. His talented translator, Mr. Stuart Gilbert, found an equally splendid equivalent in *Museum Without Walls*. Each phrase has entered into its language, and has been used more than once in M. Malraux's titles. The book now published under that name is translated from a revised version, dated 1965, of the first part of *Les Voix du silence*. It is a study of significant juxtapositions such as M. Malraux loves. The main theme is the total change in our attitude towards works of art since first museums and then the development of good photographic reproductions have made works of art easily available and thus comparable across time and space; and the concurrent and connected tendency to regard paintings and sculptures not as idols or images but primarily as works of art. The book has the merits and defects of an improvisation by a talented pianist who has twice the normal stretch of hand: he does things which no one else could do, with a certain lack of discipline. But some of them vibrate in the memory.

The present edition is neat and well produced. The illustrations are necessarily reduced in scale from the earlier and more sumptuous version. It is not always easy to take the point made in the text, and occasionally a magnifying glass is needed. Almost everything has gone wrong with the list of illustrations, which should be totally rewritten for the next edition.

Mr. Wilkinson's *Malraux* is a useful contribution to the study of what is perhaps the least important aspect of M. Malraux's work: his thought. It is more than the essay in political criticism which the sub-title claims it to be: it covers most aspects of M. Malraux's development, and it is a pity that Mr. Wilkinson could not have read the *Antimémoires* before publishing his book. It is systematic and helpful in a difficult field. But M. Malraux is primarily an artist in action and sensibility, and his monuments are his novels and his works on the visual arts. He is infinitely and valuably suggestive, but he scarcely gains by detailed analysis in the cold light of Anglo-Saxon logic. He is an animal whom (if one may drop M. Malraux's own elephant metaphor) one would rather see burning bright than anatomized and laid out flat as a rug.

(b) HAROLD NICOLSON

IN 1962, V. SACKVILLE-WEST died. Nigel Nicolson has decided to end his father's diaries at this point too. 'His grief at her death can be imagined, but should not be laid bare.' He himself tells the story of his father's last years: the routine of work done with an empty heart, the third stroke, the retirement to Sissinghurst, the peaceful death in May of this year. Nigel Nicolson has made some use of his own diary in this third volume, and of letters to and from him and his wife and a few others; but as before the main constituents are Harold Nicolson's own diary and the letters that passed daily between him and V. Sackville-West.

Public affairs loom less than in the two earlier volumes, where Nicolson—with his great speech on Munich, his membership of the House of Commons through the war, his year of office in 1940–41—was playing a minor part in a grand international drama. In this volume he plays the lead in a domestic political farce. After 1945, when the electors of Leicester West rejected him, he was desperate to be back in Parliament, and if he could not be in the Commons he would make do with the Lords. It looked as if a peerage would be wafted his way. There would be drawbacks:

I dread Mrs. Staples [the cook at Sissinghurst] saying: 'His Lordship is weeding in the nuttery.' I am truly morbidly sensitive to ridicule, and I do not feel or look or think like a Lord.

But he liked the notion of being Lord Cranfield, a defunct Sackville title, having always thought of Nicolson as 'a common plebeian name', though in the same breath he noted in himself 'a fat grub of snobbishness'. Finally he brought himself to ask the Lord Chancellor, Jowitt, direct. There was a general air of benevolence towards the project, but nothing actually happened. He liked to think it was all lined up for the 1948 New Year Honours, but that his name was taken off the list at the last moment because—thanks to Attlee's admiration for *The Land*—V. Sackville-West became C.H. Two in a family would be excessive. So now, if into Parliament, it must be back to the hustings again, and he agreed to fight a by-election at Croydon North.

A few months earlier he had joined the Labour Party (it was as a *National* Labour supporter of the Conservative Government that he had been elected in 1935) from, as he admitted in his diary, a mixture of motives in which hankering for a peerage, admiration for Bevin's foreign policy, a feeling that 'the only angle from which to fight communism is the Labour angle', coexisted uneasily. His decision produced no public sensation, but family reaction was sharp. His mother said he had betrayed his country, his brother supposed he would resign from all his clubs, his wife did not like his associating with people who could not speak the King's English, but the hardest hit was his son Nigel. He had just been adopted as Conservative candidate for his father's old constituency, and was about to make his first speech there (Harold Nicolson had a gift for mistiming). To *his* diary he confided:

This decision will make me look a bit silly in Leicester—the father joins the young revolutionary party, the son the staid and stolid party. It is as if we appeared side by side, he dressed in running shorts, and I in a top-hat and tails. A Mr. Bultitude act.

Croydon North was lost, though quite honourably, but Nicolson's chance of another constituency was dished by an article he wrote in the *Spectator* on the election campaign: a light-hearted piece which indeed poked fun at himself, but also implied distaste and even contempt for his supporters. No hope of a peerage or a seat after that: the comedy was finished.

Yet in foreign affairs where his judgment was undisturbed by his own ambitions, his views were strong and clear. Suez he saw, as he had seen Munich, as mainly a moral issue:

It meant much to me that a Prime Minister who had made his reputation by his moral courage should out of exasperation have violated his principles and told his country a series of shameful lies.

(This time he and Nigel, who was to lose his seat at Bournemouth for his opposition to Eden, were squarely on the same side.) Arriving in South Africa in the course of a cruise in 1960, the fact of apartheid struck him with immediate horror:

You know how I hate Negroes and how Tory Vita is. But I do hate injustice more than I hate Negroes, and Vita screams with rage.

How could a man, so firm over such major issues, go so wildly astray over minor ones? His son suggests one reason: 'His conscience led him to express views which his upbringing rejected.' Certainly he did not like 'the masses in the flesh': but this record shows, too, the difficulty he found in making contact with anyone outside his familiar circles. He could find the right words for the great common experiences. Of his mother's death:

Well, my dear old Mummy is no more than a handful of dust. I dislike having ceased suddenly to be anybody's son. . . . There is nobody older than oneself.

Of his increasing deafness:

Oh dear! how age creeps up on one—slouch, slough, slop. Not like a winged chariot, but like an old pedlar in snowboots which are too big for him.

Yet he was always more sensitive to what separated him from other people than to what he had in common with them. He was uneasy, not only with the Labour Party workers in Croydon North, but also with a French farmer visiting Sissinghurst ('when told by Viti that I must come and speak to this man, I feel an extraordinary repugnance'—which he then dissects), with a literary American (some absurd generalizations about American professors), with a Chinese admirer of V. Sackville-West, with almost any casual encounter. Five years after becoming President of Morley College he was talking about students and staff entirely from the outside, and admiring the Queen Mother, who was opening a building there, for her 'gift of being sincerely interested in dull people and dull occasions'.

The strangest example of his aversion to stray contacts comes after a group of friends and admirers had presented him with a cheque for a cruise as a seventieth birthday present.

Going through the list of subscribers to my present, I find names that I don't know, or people whom I have scarcely met. There are only three or four of them, but my embarrassment at their having been asked is so intense that it poisons my pleasure at all the rest.

This strikes one as really horrid; but the opening words of the entry are 'I am an absurd person'. It is the presence of Harold Nicolson the observer, critic and castigator of Harold Nicolson the actor that gives the diary its continuing interest and redeems it, even when Nicolson is at his silliest, from the fatuity of, say, the Channon diaries.

'More and more do I cling', he writes in 1950, 'in almost desperate affection, to Viti, Ben, Nigel and my work and garden.' He piled work on himself: it was an economic necessity, but also a necessary habit. During one Sissinghurst weekend he wrote eight articles. This facility was a questionable gift: it made him undertake too much. He would find he was reviewing a book he did not like, but he could not afford not to review a book he had read with care, so there were compromises and insincerities: 'I suppose I am sinning against pure integrity.' The most substantial work, his anchor for four years, was the official biography of George V which he was invited to write soon after the Croydon debacle. It was really a history of the time with the King as central character—'I have no mystic feeling about the Monarchy, I regard it merely as a useful institution'—and he found it a congenial and absorbing task. It added substantially to his reputation and it brought him the K.C.V.O. Mixed feelings again:

... partly a conceited feeling that after all the work I have done in life, a knighthood is a pitiful business, putting me in the third eleven. I know that the K.C.V.O. is not supposed to be an assessment of my contribution to life, but rather a present from the Queen for a service rendered to the Monarchy. But other people do not realise that, and I feel as if I had got a fourth prize in Scripture when I should have liked the Newcastle. So one is more snobbish and vain than one imagines.

And childish too, with all these metaphors from school.

As for the other anchor, 'I suppose we are an eccentric family, although benevolent in most ways', and he tells his new daughter-in-law that

> there is one thing that I feel we lack as a family, and that is social gaiety. Vita is always thinking about Louis XIV, Ben is always thinking about Pollaiuolo, Nigel worries about coast erosion, and I am immersed in my reflections upon the nature of courtesy. The result is that we do not enjoy cocktail parties and make such an effort not to show our displeasure that we become taut, strained, dehydrated, absurd and unreal.

'It is an odd sort of life we have evolved for ourselves', writes V. Sackville-West from Sissinghurst,

> me here, and you in London, and then both of us in our real home over the ends of the week, so happy and quiet and busy. Few people would understand it, in fact people often think that we are on the verge of divorce.
>
> > How wrong they are.
> > How wrong!

No reader of this record will get it wrong: it speaks plainly of such strong and solid affections, yet even here there are gulfs of reserve and gaps in communication. V. Sackville-West is seen as deeply reserved, deeply feeling, passionate about being herself—poet, creator of Sissinghurst, V. Sackville-West, and never Mrs. Harold Nicolson—and passionate about Knole, which would have been hers had she been a boy. Much of this frustrated passion went to the making of Sissinghurst: after Nigel Nicolson had inherited it, and decided to give it to the National Trust, he discovered this entry in his mother's diary:

> Nigel can do what he likes when I am dead, but so long as I live, no National Trust or any other foreign body shall have my darling. No, no. . . . It is bad enough to have lost my Knole, but they shan't take Sissinghurst from me. That at least is my own.

Family affection could stand up to plain speaking. Husband and wife disagree on politics, on people, even at times on the garden ('She wants to put in stuff which "will give a lovely red colour in the autumn". I wish to put in stuff which will furnish shape to the perspective. In the end we part, not as friends.'). Sons censure their father's wavering policies, berate his literary style. Nothing seems to be glossed over out of kindness. A clear-sighted judgment and astringent humour mark the editing of this record: particularly evident in the sharp summaries at the beginning of each year's entries. More than anything, these qualities convince us of the truth of this double portrait that Nigel Nicolson has composed from his parents' words.

At the end their two lives, with all their tale of experience and achievement, narrow down to one point: she is fatally ill. All through a long cruise she keeps the knowledge from him: when the shock comes,

... it seems to sunder my life in two—the past being radiant with sunshine, and the present and future dark as night. Familiar objects (my pipe, my sponge, the book I have been reading) all seem like voices from the past. 'Last time I handled you, all was sunlit.'

The day she dies he writes his *Observer* review as usual; work is still an anchor. At his request, she is named at the funeral service simply as V. Sackville-West. Piecing together extracts from the last letters, the diaries and his own memories, Nigel Nicolson makes these last days deeply moving. The earlier volumes of this record extended our knowledge of politics, the war, the tides of opinion and the springs of action; this one adds to our knowledge of the endless strangeness and variety of the heart's affections.

(c) V. S. PRITCHETT

THIS IS ONE of the most skilfully composed and delightful volumes of autobiography for many years. It contains no remarkable events, no famous names, little even that is strikingly unusual. An impoverished but never positively hungry childhood spent in a variety of London districts and suburbs, a father whose financial failures necessitated frequent and sudden departures in the cab that attended at the door, a scrimping, practical yet slightly hysterical mother, occasional flights to Yorkshire relatives when London life became too difficult— out of such material, not intrinsically compelling or exciting, Mr. Pritchett has made a fascinating picture of the lush Edwardian world seen from a Kippsian viewpoint, and has also created or re-created one of the most considerable comic figures in recent literature.

Two of Mr. Pritchett's most marked characteristics as critic and short story writer are his faculty for striking off meaningful generalizations, and a tendency towards Dickensian comic exaggeration which is consciously kept under control by his hard common sense. Both are in evidence here, together with his feeling for cities as

M

living and changing entities. 'London was not a deeply known reality to him as it is to a real Londoner . . . to him it was a fantasy and encouraged fantasy in himself', he remarks of his father, and the last part of the book which describes the four years he spent in a firm of leather factors after leaving school at fifteen are full of his own love affair with London, a love affair conducted in the area round London Bridge and Tower Bridge on the unfashionable side of the river. Few people have captured the charm of railway stations better than it is caught here in the account of London Bridge, nobody has more carefully avoided the traps of belletrist sentimentality that yawn ahead of those attempting to express an absorption not with railway buffets, lines and stations, but with the dreams and visions they induce. And for a South Londoner there is a particular attraction in the accounts of life in Camberwell ('a street off Coldharbour Lane, in which the smell of vinegar from a pickle factory hung low'), Dulwich (a tall villa at the Norwood end, rent sixteen shillings a week), Bromley (a small semi-detached late Victorian villa facing open fields—' "the air was purer", Father said'). It is the world of some Wells stories and of Henry Williamson's first Phillip Maddison novels, the world described also a little earlier and more gloomily by Gissing, a semi-suburban, part genteel and part shabby area that was changing and vanishing even as the author grew up. The pictures of life in Yorkshire, when Mrs. Pritchett and some or all of the children were sent to stay with grandfather Pritchett in Repton, are equally vivid although less original. These periods of exile ended when their father, emerging from a disaster at Ipswich or a bankruptcy at Hammersmith, started up again in business.

There are many brilliant character sketches in the book, but undoubtedly it is dominated by the author's father, Walter Sawdon Pritchett. He is introduced on the second page suffering as a young man the Ipswich disaster, and bounces along throughout the narrative, often defeated by unkind fate but never finally put down, using his middle name to start as Sawdon Pritchett Ltd., Art Needlework Manufacturers, rashly buying grandfather clocks, pianos, quantities of heavy brocade, losing £800 in an action against a landlord, celebrating the move to Bromley by the purchase of five hundred rose bushes which Victor was required to catalogue and plant, turning to Christian Science and attributing everything to the Divine Will. Some of the episodes are uproariously comic, like the story of his misadventures with a Sunbeam car or the account of the day when

Victor and his brother were taken to enrol at Alleyn's, their first fee-paying school, wearing yellow and brown knickerbocker suits and banana-coloured shoes, instead of the required black jackets, striped trousers and black footwear. The interview between the headmaster, a retired Anglo-Indian Colonel given to long silences, and Pritchett père, who vainly employs all his commercial charm, and ends by saying that his time is money and that he has a train to catch, is purely farcical. It is typical of the book's tone that there are no reproaches and no account of the boys' feelings beyond the brisk phrase: 'Our first day at Alleyn's School in Dulwich began with the sort of shame we were used to.' Anything less tight-lipped would have made such scenes painful instead of comic reading, and that is not Mr. Pritchett's intention. They would also, no doubt, have disbalanced the portrait of his father.

Here one comes to the heart of the book, the fact that the portrait of Walter Sawdon Pritchett is not objectively true or false, but one made by his son in his own image. This is of course the way in which all intimate biographical portraits are composed, but Mr. Pritchett's affectionate yet firmly detached picture is so unassuming that the reader may not appreciate fully the art that must have gone into it, the rejection of one episode as too crude, the heightening of another as particularly illuminating. It would have been easy, on the facts shown here, to have made Walter Sawdon Pritchett an ogre, a mere cheat or a bumptious fool. His son's vision is different. Beneath the egoism, bullying, grandiose absurdity, he discerns a tenderness that was never openly expressed.

A clue was given to us, too late, after his death, by Miss H. (a partner in the Art Needlework firm) who had long ago broken with him, as people did. She knew our quarrels well. The central passion in his life, she said, was for his children. Yes—that, I now see, was true. He was in many ways far more female than he was male. He was one of those fathers who are really mothers; he had a mother's primitive, possessive and jealous love . . . He wished to preserve us for himself. He could not bear us to be out of his sight.

It does not matter whether this key really unlocks the door of a personality. Here as always the biographer is partly his own subject, and Walter Sawdon Pritchett is the masterly creation of the son who has written about him. Almost incidentally the self-portrait too emerges from these pages, that of a sensitive but basically tough, self-centred boy becoming a young man, still ignorant but with the intense curiosity of a critic. He emerges from the turbulence of family life magnificently well prepared to cancel out the long littleness of life by his gift for discovering in commonplace things and people something rich and strange. It seems unlikely that the volumes to come can be as good as this one, but the result will certainly be one of the half-dozen autobiographies of our time which are works of art.

(d) J. R. ACKERLEY

THE LATE J. R. ACKERLEY was a legend in his own lifetime: an achievement, one might say without malice, which usually owes more to art than to chance. His lifetime of writing produced only two works of fiction: a play in 1918 and a novel in 1964. The long interim included more than twenty years as literary editor of *The Listener* and two famous books of a semi-autobiographical kind, *Hindoo Holiday* and *My Dog Tulip*. Hence the legend: such gifted but (in a technical sense) unimaginative writers often put their talent into their work and their genius into their lives, and only forms of public introspection can bridge the gap.

Alternatively, one can try the materials nearest to hand: in nine cases out of ten, the immediate family. How many middle-class homes support a young Fifth Columnist, shredding the smug fabric from his study in the attic? The young Ackerley, like the young Isherwood, was one. After the trenches and Cambridge

I was toying with a new play . . . which required no research, being based upon the exasperatingly stupid and monotonous home life in Richmond from which I had again escaped. Little did I know then that beneath the surface of that dull domestic scene lay concealed a plot every whit as sensational and dramatic as anything I could devise.

Indeed the Richmond home had as many skeletons as cupboards. Its cigar-smoking, yarn-spinning paterfamilias, a banana importer of some substance, might outwardly have passed as a raffish acquaintance of the Forsytes. But his past was curious. He had been a trooper in the Royal Horse Guards, bought out by a gentleman friend with the preposterously suitable name of Count de Gallatin; had married —to predictable cries of jealous rage—a young Swiss lady whom he met in the Count's house; and when she died had remained unmarried for twenty-seven years, during which he contracted two 'stable unions' and begat six children. Mr. Ackerley's mother was the luckier of his two loves: in 1919 he married her, retrospectively legitimizing two surviving children. (Her eldest son died in the trenches in 1918.) The other household had to be content with sporadic visits from a gift-laden 'Uncle Bodger' who also roguishly called himself 'William Whiteley, the Universal Provider'. Only after his death, when letters were found containing (unsuccessful) instructions for further provision, did his son Joe know that the suffocating Richmond home was all of his life but only half his father's. Mrs. Ackerley died without knowing it at all.

Both filial tenderness and writer's block might drive one to 'make something' out of such a discovery. Mr. Ackerley tried it during the 1930s, put it on one side, and took it up again shortly before his death. The result is neither autobiography nor memoir; hopelessly short of material on its alleged subject, perpetually straying into self-exposure (some lodged asymmetrically in an appendix), it is nevertheless satisfying, moving, even formal. It combines a thoughtful high-handedness with time and memory which would not disgrace the *nouveau roman* with a primly skittish style worthy of Bertrand Russell. When used for the homosexual confession box—which is quite often—the effect is startling.

Early in the decade I travelled up to Liverpool with my father to visit his sisters. In the restaurant car where we were having lunch a good-looking young waiter was instantly recognized by me as a 'queer'. While my father studied the menu I exchanged smiles and winks with this youth. Towards the end of the meal, when the business of serving it was over, he passed me with a meaning look and backward glance and disappeared down the corridor. Excusing myself to my father for a natural need I followed him. He was waiting for me by the door of the toilet. We entered together, quickly unbuttoned and pleasured each other. Then I returned to finish my coffee. I had scribbled down my address for this amusing youth, but never heard from him again.

Such passages seem to give the book a purposeful core: an attempt to relate two generations of secret sexuality. At one point the author's life involved much prowling of pubs and streets in search of guardsmen, with whom he fulfilled what must almost certainly have been Count de Gallatin's desires. But the centre will not hold. There is no evidence that the Count ever got what he wanted, and precious little that the father's fecund duplicity had much to do with the son's promiscuous furtiveness—which ended, incidentally, like a discarded hobby, when the famous Tulip entered his life. The book's dedication to her is therefore probably just, if not to all tastes.

But better such unfulfilled purposes than no purpose at all. The quest breeds concision. There is far more straightforward portraiture in Mr. Ackerley's 200 pages than in most slabs of plain narrative. It is a real work of art; and works of art should contain puzzles rather than solve them. Even after Mr. Ackerley has stripped himself to the buff, we know mainly how little—particularly how sexually little—we know. His own secret is as safe as his father's; both posthumous blabbers remain—the phrase is at least good for a giggle—impenetrable. Ah, but the pleasure of trying. . . .

13

FICTION OF 1968

(g) C. P. SNOW

The Sleep of Reason

THE YEAR IS 1963, Sir Lewis Eliot is in his late fifties and has retired at least temporarily from the battles of politics. In the Midlands town where he grew up the College of Art and Technology at which his old friend George Passant once lectured (see *Strangers and Brothers*) is now one of the new universities, and he has been elected to act as Students' Representative on the University Court. Two couples, men and women, have been found frolicking naked in a sitting room and Arnold Shaw, the Vice-Chancellor, wants them sent down for good. When their appeal is heard Eliot persuades the Court to agree to a compromise by which a decision is left over for two months so that attempts can be made to place the students elsewhere.

Such an opening may suggest that this is a novel about the student revolt, but that would be misleading. Only one of the students, Dick Pateman, plays any further part in the book, and the incident is designed to lead into the main theme, which is concerned with a sadistic murder. Pateman's sister and her lesbian room-mate, Cora Ross, torture and kill an eight-year-old boy. Cora is a niece of George Passant, and when the girls are arrested Eliot is drawn into the case out of loyalty to him. Or to the ghost of Passant, for time has converted his eloquence to garrulousness, and has turned his search for the good life of total freedom into a mere quest for young girls. The ravages of time are seen also in other figures from the past,

---

(g) *The Sleep of Reason.* 406 pp. Macmillan. 35s.
(h) *A Very Private Life.* 192 pp. Collins. 21s.
(i) *Couples.* 458 pp. André Deutsch. 30s.
(j) *The Military Philosophers.* 243 pp. Heinemann. 25s.
(k) *I Want It Now.* 255 pp. Cape. 22s. 6d.
(l) *The Vale of Laughter.* 352 pp. Gollancz. 30s.
(m) *High.* 347 pp. Hodder and Stoughton. 35s.

like Eliot's father whose happiness is destroyed by the decision of the
male voice choir to which he is secretary that in his eighties he is too
old for the job. The treatment of old Mr. Eliot is typical of the book
in this aspect. He appears in the first chapter cheerfully providing and
helping to eat a lavish schoolboys' tea for his grandson Charles, is
glimpsed again later when the catastrophe of dismissal from the
choir has struck him, and provides a coda to the story by his off-stage
death and funeral.

But still this is not the basic subject, nor is the book deeply concerned with the progress through life of Martin Eliot, Francis
Getliffe and other familiar characters from earlier novels who move
on the periphery of the story. Taking the Moors Murders as a basis,
and perhaps blending with the case of the New Zealand schoolgirls,
Pauline Parker and Juliet Hulme, who coolly made and crudely
carried out plans for murdering Pauline's mother, Snow has tried to
analyse the basis of the sadistic violence that marks the 1960s. His
title comes from Goya: 'The sleep of reason brings forth monsters'.
Why does reason sleep, where do the monsters come from? The
answer given here leads back to George Passant's belief in ultimate
and complete freedom, the ideas to which the youthful Eliot listened
although he never fully shared them. 'Those declarations were full
of hope', he now reflects. 'George's great cries had nothing Nietzschean about them. They were innocent when they proclaimed that
there was a fundamental "I" which could do anything in its freedom.'
But when his brother Martin suggests that starting from this point
you can go further, to any length, to the point of torturing a child to
death because you 'want to teach it to behave' in the girls' words,
Lewis Eliot has no certain answer. His creed and his hope are
perhaps put into the mouth of a minor character who refuses to
believe in absolute evil. 'We've seen horrible happenings here. But,
you know, in the future people are going to do better than we have
done.' The sleep of reason will be only temporary.

The message is cheering but at the moment it does not seem very
plausible; and what is more important, nor does such an approach
make a satisfactory novel. What reason can do to analyse the bases
of such behaviour is done here at great length. Much of the last half
of the book is taken up by the trial. There are counsel's speeches,
judge's summing up, psychiatrist's evidence about degrees of
responsibility, long and intelligent discussions about the ultimate
issue in some of which the counsel concerned take part to a degree

which seems rather unlikely during the course of a trial: but the theme is one unsuited to C. P. Snow's great talents. At one or two points Eliot suggests that he can enter into the feelings of the murderers. Recollecting films of Auschwitz he thinks that along with horror at watching them he felt shameful pleasure, a pleasure 'almost without emotion . . . titillating, trivial and seepingly corrupt', and reflects that the same pleasure had been present in the court room. Yet in truth Eliot does not seem to be sharing a feeling but stating an attitude. Like his creator he is too fully convinced of the power of reason to be able to reveal a catharsis of pity and terror in such actions. The interpretative sympathy of a Dostoevsky is needed here, and the descriptive skill of a Trollope is no kind of substitute. To understand the actions of Cora Ross and Kitty Pateman it would be necessary imaginatively to conceive them, and a writer who regarded them as titillating and trivial (in these words it seems fair to identify Eliot with his creator) could never do that.

The murder also appears to involve, and the book to leave untouched, questions about the whole nature of society. If the girls are not mere freaks, if they have some responsibility for their actions (this is the decision of the Court and it is one which the author seems to share), do these actions not reflect in some degree upon the nature of Western society and the whole life that Lewis Eliot has led? Is not this ghastly exercise of absolute authority nearer reality, nearer what life is like for many millions of people in the world, than Eliot's discussions, speculations, small personal gratifications and griefs, unending walks down the corridors of power? Such questions do not occur to Eliot, but they are likely to be in the minds of many readers of this book. It would be wrong not to feel grateful to C. P. Snow for his courage in dealing with a subject which is at the heart of our present society: yet it has to be said also that it is one which he cannot deal with adequately precisely because of his virtues as a realistic novelist and as a rational human being.

(*h*) MICHAEL FRAYN

A Very Private Life

THE TROUBLE WITH MR. FRAYN is that there is a whole queue of gifts and talents and other virtues inside him jostling to get out and hit the typewriter. This made him an ideal columnist; all he had to do was let them out in turn for short, invigorating bouts of exercise on the machine. Harnessing them to make a single coherent work is much more difficult, and up to now in his novels Mr. Frayn has not always achieved it. *The Tin Men* gave a splendid outing to his genius for technological-cum-social satire; it was imaginative and funny, but the characters were hopelessly flat. *The Russian Interpreter* was in its unexpectedly conventional way perfect: memorable characters, beautifully constructed story, first-rate writing. But the similarly conventional *Towards the End of the Morning* which followed was in places stereotyped and a bit dull, suggesting that the story must have unusual force and its setting and climate a particular grip on him if the form is to concentrate his talents rather than to squeeze some of them out. This was confirmed by his television play *Jamie on a Flying Visit* (produced earlier this year): his one really disappointing work to date.

A Very Private Life goes straight to the top; it is an outstanding short book which nobody else could have written, and it ought to be put into the classic modern repertoire alongside *Animal Farm*. Unlike its two predecessors it is not naturalistic; 'Once upon a time there will be . . .', it starts, thus succinctly indicating the fusion of fable and science fiction story which have gone to make it up. It is divided into brief sections of a few paragraphs or a few pages, each formally balanced—the writing is as good as that in *The Russian Interpreter*—and set under an exact and telling cross-head. It can be (and indeed demands to be) read at a sitting. It can be re-read and re-re-read. It can be read aloud.

In it Mr. Frayn returns to the kind of social and technological speculations which underlay his first novel, though now in a more detached and altogether more organized way. He supposes that drugs and electronic communications and the control of personality and the emotions develop along already visible lines until it is possible for a large section of humanity never to move outside its houses or to enter into direct contact with other people at all. Everything, from a cup of coffee to the three-dimensional materialization of one's aged relatives in a holovision chamber, is then on tap or can be dialled. Conversation, education, sexual pleasure, reproduction: all are provided by a tangle of pipes and wires, and the happy, infinitely well-adjusted recipient need only lie back on his hovercraft-like aircushion and ask for what he wants or

simply switch off. This very private life, of the title, is for the so-
called Inside People, who take the decisions and give the orders,
getting their information electronically from all over the world and
communicating in turn with the thinking and doing machines. It is,
as the heroine's father tells her, 'the perfect freedom which men
have always dreamt of'. For

> what crippled and cut short all men's earlier experiments in freedom is that
> they were public; and the public freedom of one man must necessarily
> impinge upon the public freedom of others; so that public freedoms inevit-
> ably limit and destroy each other. But our modern *private* freedoms
> impinge upon no one and nothing. And no one and nothing can impinge
> upon them.

'What's it like outside, Mummy?', she asks when she is about four. It
is this fatal curiosity which is the theme of the story. Partly the question is a philosophical one; nearly everything experienced during her
childhood—lessons, parties, unforgettable seaside holidays—comes
to her through the holovision chamber in her windowless, air-
conditioned, evenly-heated room, and if she wants to laugh or cry or
calm down or imagine beautiful landscapes all she need do is take
the right pill. What then is real, and what is beyond? At the same
time it is a social question—almost indeed a racial question—for
outside live the Outside People, who '*have* to travel around—they
have to transport their bodies to wherever their hands are needed'—
and live among things like bicycles and bread and stew, something
that strikes her, when she first confronts it on a plate, as 'like
a piece of paranoiac imagery on one of the violence channels'. So
the story itself is a quite simple one of Uncumber's disastrous
explorations in an outside world which proves to be grey, dusty,
and clogging up with sludge under a thickening detritosphere
hundreds of miles up.

It is in fact a love story, as she sets out for 515–214–442–305–217, a
location somewhere the other side of the globe among the great sea
vegetation farms, to find the bald, hairy, middle-aged man whom she
got by accident one day on the holovision. And the handling of love
is by no means the least entertaining aspect of this profoundly
entertaining book. There is love via the holovision chamber, where
the barrier of transparent walls can be overcome by judicious use of
drugs like Libidin and Orgasmin; there are babies by delivery tube
('Daddy and I sent off the things to make him with'); there are also
the earthy couplings of the world outside, the complex domestic life

of the bald man, the near-slapstick of Uncumber's eventual seduction—and her ultimate disillusionment as he too reaches for his pills and she finds that for all his attention to business he is only 'an anthropoid stoking machine. . .'. It is all the more effective because the Inside People's artificial pleasures are not always guyed, some of their climaxes being conveyed by vivid imaginative writing, with no element of stylistic parody.

Animal Farm was about the October Revolution and the perversions which it underwent under Stalin. *A Very Private Life* is about things which now or in the near future seem likely to concern us more closely: drugs both medical and hallucinogenic, longevity, the treatment of personality, penology ('We don't think in terms of *guilt* and *innocence*. We just ask: are you happy, or are you unhappy . . .?'), mass communications, dropping-out, the reduction of so many aspects of life to numbers or to strips of magnetic tape, the problems of food and waste, and ultimately of perception and of life itself. Only its last two paragraphs seem slightly feeble. Not that it has a happy ending in any accepted sense. It would indeed be a deeply depressing book if it were not for the skill with which the author handles his material and the sanity with which he looks at it. To see difficult subjects so straight and describe them so well is a rare achievement.

(*i*) JOHN UPDIKE

Couples

MUCH HAS BEEN MADE of the frankness with which Mr. Updike details the sexual behaviour of the New England community in which his fifth, and most substantial, novel is set—as though he had attempted a kind of Kinsey Report which burrowed deeper than any case-history can. It should therefore be said that nothing in *Couples* is any less serious, or more pornographic, than the jacket, taken from a Blake drawing of Adam and Eve, and that the success of this novel in America is more probably due to the prevailing guilt feelings of a society in which the ad-man's dream—and Mr. Updike himself is not above falling for some of that starry-eyed phraseology—turns out to induce not contentment but boredom. Worse, the boredom, which is generally recognized among educated people, will so easily be relieved by temporary sensations of sexual excitement and scandal, or by the ethic of permissive liberalism, that the dangerous emotions which shake a society—or a marriage—are best kept submerged. The survival of those who, admittedly by accident, fail to conform to this pattern and defy every taboo of their friends and community is what Mr. Updike is trying to assert. Since sexual taboos are those which most Americans are thought to be liberated from, it is necessary for these in particular to be exploded, although Mr. Updike is not exactly optimistic about the chances of any kind of raw understanding of the sexual relationship lasting very long in the society he writes about.

Tarbox is the all-American dreamtown; rustic, full of community feeling and local pride, expanding enough to be thinking about inter-racial committees, yet safe and small enough for everyone to bump into everyone else buying do-it-yourself equipment at the weekend; parties, at which even the longest-married couples dance affectionately and the children are sleepily lifted home from strange beds in the small hours, provide the ten superior couples of Tarbox with a sense of security and a subject of conversation. The book opens with Piet and Angela Hanema, ready for sleep after one such evening, remarking the arrival of a new couple, Ken and Foxy Whitman, who will bring fresh blood to Tarbox society. Piet, whom the stolider members regard as 'neurotic', is a Dutch puritan, and as such the random element, not quite as securely to be categorized by his fellow hus-bands as the noisy and vulgar Freddy Thorne, always making passes but known to be a cuckold. Piet has made his way with the Tarbox women, and the statuesque and serenely unattainable Angela has chosen to ignore his lapses. Piet and Foxy, who is pregnant, have an affair which begins by sounding very like most other Tarbox affairs—a matter of propinquity, because Piet is in charge of renovating the Whitmans' house. But, unlike the cheerful manoeuvring that goes on between some of the other couples—one surreptitious session in the afternoon becomes, because it seems easier that way, a mildly embarrassed and drunken swap agreed on by both parties to absolve any feelings of remorse—Piet and Foxy are slow and painful in their approach to bed, and when Foxy finds she is pregnant by Piet he has no scruples about the necessity for an abortion. So desolate does Piet's life become when Angela and Ken both reject their adulterous partners, that Foxy's return to his barren room looks like the final irony; he no longer wants anything but his wife and daughters, all

Foxy offers is staled and sad and finished—'they had been let into
God's playroom, and been happy together on the floor all afternoon,
but the time had come to return the toys to their boxes, and put the
chairs back against the wall.'

It is as an outcast that Piet tentatively welcomes Foxy back, and it
is by 'an exploration of a sadness so deep people must go in pairs, one
cannot go alone' that both discover a kind of lovemaking which has
nothing to do with Tarbox ritual. How much this has to do with their
defiance of the approved sexual code—it is 'when the mouth condes-
cends' that 'mind and body marry', Piet decides—and how much
simply to do with a need which extends further than desire or pleasure
or solace, the need to recognize something primitive, chaotic, and as
awesome as the fire burning the Tarbox church—this Mr. Updike is
not prepared to say. He drops many hints both by symbols and by
moralistic comment—'Man is the sexiest of the animals and the only
one that foresees death', 'We are all exiles who need to bathe in the
irrational'. It is clear that we are intended to judge both Piet and
Foxy and the Tarbox couples in the constant awareness of the
'charnel odor, breathed through Death's jaws': the flesh, defying its
own destruction, may offer solace to both jaded citizens and desperate
lovers, but it is all part of the 'screen of couples and houses and
days' behind which a Calvinist God imposes his arbitrary will.

Where the seriousness of Mr. Updike's intention is allowed to
obtrude—when he indulges his well-known taste for purple passages
of description, and the precious, transient quality of a moment is
caught—this is a superb explosion of talent, and most moving.
Tarbox itself, the basketball afternoons, the bathroom flurry, the
children on the beach and the Sunday morning sermon—all such
scenes are so much better done than in any other domestic American
fiction that it seems doubly sad to admit that the central situation, of
Piet and Foxy, falls flatter than any American pancake. The words of
lovers are incurably ludicrous in print; the difference between one
orgasm and another impossible to convey in words. The result is that
despite all the tenderness, and the delightful cruel humour with
which some participants are portrayed, this communal orgiastic
dance inevitably begins to look gratuitous, to look precisely like the
titillating relief from bored complacency which Mr. Updike is so
fiercely contemptuous of. Perhaps he was too ambitious, perhaps
Piet became more of a symbolic scapegoat and less of a suffering man
as his destiny took shape. It is not he, nor Tarbox behaviour, nor

even the malaise of American society, which makes *Couples* much more than a commentary on sexual habits; it is the earnest idealism with which Mr. Updike, contemplating the pathetic struggles of civilized man, offers glimpses of what is behind the 'screen' of daily life—an acceptance of fate where everyone is 'beyond all blaming'.

(j) ANTHONY POWELL

The Military Philosophers

QUITE EARLY in this addition to his sequence, in one of those characteristic episodes of crucial surprise so familiar from all the previous volumes of *The Music of Time*, Nicholas Jenkins suddenly realizes that he knows the young A.T.S. driver taking him across wartime London on an Intelligence mission. This attractive and miserably sullen girl is, in fact, Charles Stringham's niece, Pamela Flitton, daughter of Stringham's sister Flavia by her first marriage; as a six-year-old bridesmaid at the Stringhams' wedding, she was sick in the font. Here, Jenkins's reflections follow in the expected form: Pamela's significance for the future is hinted at, past associations are evoked, and a quietly meaningful observation about time and human character is slipped in.

In this instance Jenkins's observation on Flavia's predilection for drunken husbands—'the sequence of inevitable sameness that pursues individual progression through life'—serves as an unobtrusive clue to Mr. Powell's approach in *The Military Philosophers* and, to some extent, the last two novels in his series, where a modification of style has also been apparent. The formality and the repetitions inherent in the 'intricate measure' of the human dance (as described at the beginning of the first book, *A Question of Upbringing*) have given way to something slightly less patterned and methodical. In the tension that has existed throughout *The Music of Time* between the patterns suggested by the requirements of fiction and the more chaotic nature of human fact, the untidiness of real life has recently been winning out. 'Sequence' and 'progression' in human affairs are now more important than the repetitions in 'the steps of the dance' going on around Jenkins. It is a small, but very subtle and definite, shift of emphasis in Mr. Powell's grand design.

The compromise between fiction and life now arrived at partly

accounts for, but is more probably *explained* by, the vast accumula-
tion of detail which must make the plot and the point of the later
novels incomprehensible to anyone who has not started with Volume
One. In *The Military Philosophers* we find Jenkins assigned, in 1942,
to that section of the War Office responsible for liaison with other
Allied forces—engaged first in contacts with the Poles, then with the
Belgians and Czechs. As in *The Valley of Bones* and *The Soldier's
Art*, we follow all the well-known characters (and, at a rough count,
some thirty new ones) through the chances of war, this time glimps-
ing them through a smokescreen of military bureaucracy. Widmerpool continues to play his power games, now at the Cabinet Office.
Sunny Farebrother executes colourful intrigues with the old charm and
resource. Prince Theodoric is outflanked by his left wing. Stringham
and Templer—distantly, and with terrible casualness—are killed.

No one important is left out. But many names are introduced, it
seems, only to keep the reader up with them: there are so many
characters by now that such scraps of news about old acquaintances
invariably take up much of the author's space. Gone are the extended
comedy sequences of the earlier novels (the old school dinner in *The
Acceptance World*, the visit to Thrubworth in *At Lady Molly's*).
They are replaced by the anecdotes (not *always* very striking or
relevant) of the military raconteur, some short comic episodes, and
a lot of very brief character sketches, notably of the foreign military
attachés. A number of highly promising new figures, like the obstruc-
tive bureaucrat Blackhead, are introduced only to be quickly
dropped. The formal dance has apparently almost broken up under
the pressures of war.

And yet there is a groundswell of purpose under the surface of
these confused waters. *The Military Philosophers*, bafflingly detailed
and superficially bewildering, shows considerable fineness of observation, and firm control of a scheme: the demonstration of the
essential continuity in human character, 'the sequence of inevitable
sameness'. The old characters decline and die, or assert themselves
and survive, whichever is appropriate. For Widmerpool, not surprisingly, war is simply the continuation of personal aggrandisement
by other means. Very interestingly, neither Widmerpool nor Mr.
Powell's major new creation, the appalling Pamela Flitton, is treated
humorously here: grave issues of motive and responsibility are
raised by Widmerpool's indirect implication in the deaths of both
Stringham, whose money he ironically inherits, and Templer, with

whom Pamela has been involved. This is a theme of unaccustomed grimness which Mr. Powell explores with a brilliantly suggestive obliqueness. The ludicrous gyrations of Jenkins's acquaintances have turned (as they always might have done) into more sober and lifelike movements. Comedy seems only an incidental. In this sense, after eight volumes of his sequence, Mr. Powell's is still a developing talent. The judgment does, however, require qualification. In spite of this partial withdrawal from the solipsistic, Mr. Powell's characters and settings are still fundamentally subject to Jenkins's own quirky vision, which celebrates the sheer diversity and oddness of human existence in a markedly personal way. Events, even harrowing war-time events, must adjust to his personal view to be grasped at all: the horrors of the battlefield on which Field Marshal Montgomery's hands move on the map (a fascinating scene) have to be exorcized with literary and historical associations. As the series enlarges it becomes increasingly curious that Mr. Powell should ever have been regarded as an impartially penetrating social observer on a broad scale. His talent is still entirely for the nuances of what is currently known as 'interpersonal behaviour'—whether worked out in the manners of the dances and parties of *A Buyer's Market* or in the minute military protocol of the later books. The fabric of social behaviour, not the fabric of society itself, is his theme; and there is little 'inwardness' with his characters, even Widmerpool himself. The increasing maturity of view, the resistance of easy comic opportunities, is a matter of growing knowledge of men in their outward social roles; this is the extent of the development.

At the very end of *The Military Philosophers* Jenkins encounters Archie Gilbert, the sartorial perfectionist of all those society balls in the 1920s. The war is just over, and the two of them meet accidentally while choosing demob suits from the great array offered them free at Olympia. The new clothes, like the army greatcoat Jenkins affects at the beginning of *The Soldier's Art*, are masks for a new role in life and in peacetime society, players' costumes. Archie ponders.

'. . . Have you decided what you're going to take from the stuff here? It might be much worse. I think everything myself.'
'Except the underclothes.'

Jenkins's reply, the very last words of the novel, suggest an exceptionally self-aware symbol, at once defining and accepting the limits of Mr. Powell's art.

N

(k) KINGSLEY AMIS

I Want It Now

Mr. Amis's new novel is a kind of anti-striptease. Its chief character, Ronnie Appleyard, a highly successful television interviewer with a programme of his own, throws off various trappings of greed, insincerity, cold lust, indifference to injustice and so on at precisely marked points in the story, and stands at the end without a stitch except his decency, kindliness, sincerity and so on. The agent of this change is a girl he meets at a party, Simon Quick. Simon, narrow-hipped, sallow, with 'kind of lion's-mane-coloured straight hair', is so rapidly eager to go to bed with him, it appears, that she simply asks her hostess for a room for herself and Ronnie, and gets them both thrown out. But she proves to be terrifyingly frigid, as well as liable to do embarrassing things, and Ronnie is just about to ditch her when he discovers that she is the daughter of a very rich woman. Money is one of the things Ronnie very much wants now; and from then on he suffers plenty of humiliations both at the hands of her mother's set and at the body of Simon. But moral regeneration is proceeding:

Putting his faith in the fragmentary code of amatory ethics he had known her to act on once or twice, he said abruptly: 'You must. I love you, Simon.' Saying it made him feel a bit of a shit, another recurring hazard of the present operation, but perceptibly less of one than he had expected. Good show.

And later:

His brain was in turmoil. He was experiencing an emotion, a desire, a thought—whatever it was, it was altogether new to him, remote, unpredictable by any intuition or technique, as if it had suddenly dawned upon him that what he had always most wanted to do was induce a naked girl—or possibly a girl naked but for a transparent mackintosh—to stand before him while he pelted her with cream buns. All at once he knew what this sensation was. It was pure, authentic, violent sentiment of a liberal or progressive tendency.

Finally Ronnie discovers that Simon is not going to inherit after all; but by now it is too late. He wants to marry her and teach her to make love happily, he rescues her from her mother on the eve of her being married off to an impotent American and they go out of the book 'in a diagonal shuffle, arms about shoulders'.

As a study of character-development, this is all quite banal. But Mr. Amis knows that, and does not really mind. He is not interested in subtle stirrings of the spirit, Sarrautean *tropismes*: changes of feeling—especially changes for the better—are to be described, rather, in the way an uneasy but witty man would explain them to his still cynical friends, and left at that. Moreover the plot in *I Want It Now* is as much a peg to hang other things on as offered for its own moralizing sake; and many of the other things are very good indeed.

The degenerate *mœurs* of the television studios are brilliantly portrayed, from the opening of the book, where Ronnie floors an interviewee with a false fact he has invented on the spur of the moment, knowing that next week his apology for the error will only compound his success with the viewers, to the farcical scene at the end where for the first time in his life Ronnie forgets he is on the screen and flails into Simon's mother during a discussion pro- gramme on 'The Rich' (McBean the producer meanwhile adroitly scooping up all the most unflattering shots of everybody). But the rich, even more than the televisually successful, are the real interest of *I Want It Now*. Lady Baldock, Simon's mother, who at Ronnie's first sight of her is wearing 'a kilogram or so of jewelry and a heavy dry white silk dress, the bodice of which had evidently been sprayed with glue and then fiercely bombarded with diamonds', is the chief object of study. She is a merciless buyer-up of people: she invites Ronnie out to Greece to keep Simon peaceful while her marriage is being fixed up, then sends him packing at short notice when he dares to contradict her in public. She is a past-mistress at battles of meanness—'Stilton-paring'—with the other rich she almost exclu- sively hobnobs with (*The Meanness of the Rich* might have been an alternative, anti-Snovian, title for the book). After the Greek trouble, she nevertheless gets in touch with Ronnie again—partly to enlist his support in getting her on television, which she wants to do to impress a rich Greek, and partly to invite him over to America to show him how completely he has lost Simon to his American rival. (She is finally betrayed—and Simon rescued—by her much-dis- regarded husband, 'Chummy'.)

Other steadily recurrent pleasures in *I Want It Now* are that comedy of discomfort Mr. Amis has always had an unfailing eye for—drink in Greece tasting 'like cricket-bat juice—rubber grip and springs thrown in along with blade and handle', or a slippery glass of very chilled orange juice sliding out of Ronnie's hand onto a Turkish rug in America; the same sharp, disbelieving eye turned on the purely ludicrous—a 'copse of dyed pampas grass' in a London drawing room, cemeteries in America where the tombstones are laid flush with the ground to make it easier for the motor-mowers; and a sheer concern for accuracy of notation where convention normally rules, such as the observation that people do not say 'Eh?' so much as 'Ng?'

But the very pleasures of the book help to undermine its story. It is hard, in fact, to know who is making all these sprightly observations. One never quite believes it can be Ronnie—or if it is Ronnie, one can never quite believe he is the harassed, brutal, ambitious success the story requires him to be. *I Want It Now* demands more than the usual ration of suspension of disbelief, as Ronnie—if it is Ronnie—might be inclined to put it. But given that ration, it is always excellent reading.

(*l*) PETER DE VRIES

The Vale of Laughter

THE TITLE OF PETER DE VRIES's new novel, *The Vale of Laughter*, is an example of the kind of inversion of the expected that is perhaps his most frequent comic device. One thinks of incidents like that in *Let Me Count the Ways* where Tom Waltz undergoes a Pauline conversion as the result of a miraculous sickness acquired on a visit to Lourdes, or that at the end of *Reuben, Reuben* where Geneva breaks up the family in order to start a school for children from broken homes.

At the same time the title is an indication of the religious preoccupations that have increasingly been the subject of de Vries's work. Life for him is not a vale of tears: if it is cruel, the cruelty is that of a practical joker. De Vries's God, like Hardy's, sports with man, but the result is not—as in Hardy—tragedy, but divine comedy.

In that extraordinarily painful novel, *The Blood of the Lamb*, de Vries explored the relationship between religion and comedy. Towards the end of the book Wanderhope visits his young daughter in hospital, where she is suffering from leukaemia, taking with him a cake as a present. He arrives to find that she is dying, and there is a horrifyingly detailed description of the obscene effects of the disease on the body of a beautiful child. Later that night Wanderhope, grief-stricken and somewhat drunk, finds himself in front of a statue of Christ: remembering the cake he is still carrying he hurls it in the face of the statue. It seems to be a gesture of complete rejection of religion, but at the same time it is literally the action of custard-pie comedy. The point is given further meaning by a conversation earlier in the novel where Wanderhope and his daughter are talking about slapstick films and the 'sacred subject of the thrown pie': 'And have you ever noticed, Daddy . . . that after the one guy throws his pie and it's the other guy's turn, the first guy doesn't resist or make any effort to defend himself? *He just stands there and takes it*.' (de Vries's italics.)

The argument in *The Blood of the Lamb* about the relationship between religion, suffering and comedy is a complicated one, of which this account only suggests the outline. The reason for mentioning it here is that the new novel deals with the same subject, only this time with the emphasis (as the title suggests) on laughter rather than religion. Joe Sandwich is a compulsive clown and practical joker. After one of his father's many coronaries he visits him in hospital: ' "My God", I said, grinning into the oxygen tent, "you must have a strong heart to stand all this." ' (His father's main worry is about uttering worthy last words. In the event, a sudden thunder-clap causes him to exclaim 'Jesus H. Christ', with which he expires.)

Joe's clowning makes for a novel that, if less well organized than some of de Vries's previous works, is as consistently funny as anything he has written. But as well as provoking laughter the book comments on the nature of laughter. Why, de Vries's critics have sometimes asked, does he turn everything to a joke? He turns the question, by asking it of Joe Sandwich. 'These practical jokes. Isn't there an element of cruelty behind them?' Joe's wife asks him, to which characteristically he replies, 'It's the tale that dogs the wag.' His psychologist cousin makes the same point: ' "You're the clown of the family," he said, frowning studiously. "Humour is mysterious. Where does it come from? Whence does it arise? What is the impulse to crack a joke about everything?" ' One answer is that of Wally Hines, a psychologist who is humourlessly researching into the nature of laughter. Joe, he says, is 'one of those people who cannot take reality neat, whether out of anxiety or its second cousin, self-consciousness, and who therefore must knead it continually into nonsense shapes'.

Joe's own answer is subtler. He avoids the question, as perhaps de Vries himself does, by denying (or at least confusing) the distinction between comedy and tragedy:

> Tragedy and comedy are basically the same ... Shelley regarded *King Lear* as a comedy. So did Yeats. He said *Lear* was gay. Coleridge said *Hamlet* verges on the ludicrous. ... A man got killed on the Thruway the other day in an accident he got into trying to fasten his safety belt. Is that sad or funny? When Benny was in high school he organized that mass meeting to protest student apathy, and four people showed up. Sad or funny?

Joe Sandwich's own exit proves the point. He who lives by the joke, dies by the joke.

(*m*) THOMAS HINDE

High

High is hard to summarize without putting readers off. *Another* English professor discovering the blessings of adultery on a mid-Western campus? And realizing finally that this strange world is not a complete liberation, but too strange for him? And, perhaps worse, a professor called Maurice Peterson writing an expatriate's novel about a professor called Peter Morrison, who in turn is writing a novel about the campus, which bears a striking similarity to a novel which Peterson is reading about the campus ... shades of Kinbote, fruits of Sarraute, and generally a recipe for disaster, down to the narcissistic agnosticism (who is writing whom, then?) of the end.

But *High* is, in the teeth of such forebodings, an excellent novel. Mr. Hinde has paid his conventional dues thoroughly enough, in most of his previous nine novels, to be given the benefit of the doubt: his Pirandelloish tricks are likely to be there to augment invention, not to disguise its lack. And the conventional virtues of this ultra-conventional genre are strongly present, when one is not too busy playing with Chinese boxes.

> They ate at a plastic Tudor steak-house, the best in town, attached to a bowling alley. There were black plastic hay racks on the walls, seashell-pink plastic cornucopia of lilies above the tables and golden plastic

carthorse brasses over the constantly flaming natural-gas log fire. Three-inch-diameter candles from the Danish shop stood in oval mauve candle glasses from the Swedish shop and the whole was lit by a concealed pink ceiling glow to ancient-passage dimness—till a table of six dark-suited, crew-cut, baby-clean executives complained of the glare and it was turned down to the brightness of an outdoor starlit night.

We have been here before (*Stepping Westward, One Fat English-man, Night and Silence Who Comes Here*, let alone the home-grown varieties from Lurie to Malamud). At least one respectable academic tome on the campus novel is already burdening a few bookshelves. But Mr. Hinde can do a little more than convincing backcloths or sad reflections on 'the true American inability to underdo anything'. Peterson is welcomed with a fatuous announcement about the possibility of tape-recording and replaying his lectures ('facilities available to have you do a real first-class job on your classroom instructional techniques'). His reaction goes beyond sneering. 'It was a speech no Englishman could have made, so totally free from apology, doubt, protective alignment with the doubt of others.' In the same way, he suffers both embarrassment and surprise from an evening with the archetypal pushful student and his girl. Through European eyes, the couple hardly seem to know each other, let alone like each other. But their troubles cannot be written off as the pimples of unsophistication. The girl consults him, later, when the boy's random aggressiveness really worries her.

She had a quality which he couldn't easily name. Braveness was too simple. Just of staying with things that happened to her. It was less that she seemed to refuse easy escapes than that she knew already at seventeen that there weren't any.

There aren't any for Peterson, either, stuck with a wife and four daughters who treat him with a chill mixture of dependence and contempt. A few glorious lays, an acid trip which sends him scurrying home to them (even though he returns later), and then only the fantasy consolations of Peter Morrison's different way of doing things. Morrison has a red beard and a red Triumph, a breezy way with the picaresque, all the straightforwardness that Peterson longs for. He takes speed pills rather than acid trips, goes to New Orleans with his co-ed and buys a gun to punish her dismissal of him. He has better highs. He is a true *alter ego*, an expression of Peterson's moment of anxiety after a confrontation with a somewhat too conventional figure, the local refugee psychiatrist and mystery man.

'Suddenly he was desperate and frightened. Would he ever again know anything for certain without at the same moment knowing *and* believing its exact opposite?'

Thus Peterson's Morrison problem becomes Morrison's Peterson problem; even our fantasies have fantasies, which may look remarkably like ourselves. It would be a mistake to take either version of *High* as definitive, the true account of a breakdown to which the other half is the key—though Mr. Hinde's earlier books have bordered on the clinical. The ambiguity is more fundamental—and potentially more tiresome. What saves it from mere chaos is the neatness, plainness—even the familiarity—of the basic materials which are shaken into such kaleidoscopic patterns. Contemporary mystifiers, from Godard to McLuhan, might learn something from this elegant, cerebral, quiet-voiced achievement.

14

WALTER BENJAMIN

TOWARDS A PHILOSOPHY OF
LANGUAGE

BAD LUCK, now posthumous, dogs Walter Benjamin (1892–1940).
During his lifetime this most original, most delicately perceptive yet
incisive of German, one would surely say of European, literary and
cultural critics (*Kulturkritiker*) was known to only a handful of
friends or uneasy colleagues. He completed little of what he planned
and eked out a precarious, splintered existence. Ideas he initiated,
theories he argued in an elusive compact vein, have been taken up
and noisily exploited since. Malraux's *musée sans murs* and view of
the metamorphoses of art through photography and montage stem
from Benjamin's 'Das Kunstwerk im Zeitalter seiner technischen
Reproduzierbarkeit'. McLuhan's brilliantly orchestrated capriccios
on print and causality, on messages and media, on dramatic image
and social forms are anticipated, with a scruple and subtlety of
proposal foreign to McLuhan's purpose, in Benjamin's masterpiece,
the *Ursprung des deutschen Trauerspiels* of 1928 and in such short
papers as 'Traumkitsch' or 'Kleine Geschichte der Photographie'.
Much of what has been written about Brecht in recent years is
grossly inflated or thrown off balance by pro or anti-Stalinist bias.
Benjamin's 'Was ist das epische Theater?', his 'Kommentare' on
Brecht's poems, his decisive paper 'Der Autor als Produzent' and
his conversations with Brecht now seem more and more sane and
prophetic (all these texts are gathered in *Versuche über Brecht*.
Suhrkamp Verlag, 1966). When Kenneth Burke or George Steiner,
working almost as idiosyncratically, as alone as Benjamin did, seek
to make of poetics, of literary criticism, elements of a coherent

WALTER BENJAMIN: *Angelus Novus*. Ausgewählte Schriften 2. 546 pp. 34s. 6d.
Briefe. Edited with commentary by Gershom Scholem and Theodor W. Adorno.
Band I, 484 pp. Band II, pp. 485–855. £6 (Paperback, 37s.). *Über Walter Benjamin*.
173 pp. 7s. Frankfurt: Suhrkamp. London: Barmerlea Book Sales.

'philosophy of language' (*Sprachphilosophie*), they are developing instigations found throughout Benjamin's essays and fragments, in his famous study of Goethe's *Elective Affinities*, written in 1922 or in the early 'Über die Sprache überhaupt und über die Sprache der Menschen'. Benjamin's 'Probleme der Sprachsoziologie' of 1935 not only prefigure the currently so fashionable approaches of Richard Hoggart and Raymond Williams; added to the torso of Benjamin's work on Baudelaire and *Paris, die Hauptstadt des XIX Jahrhunderts* (the ever renewed, never completed magnum opus), they show, as Hoggart and Williams have not, what a genuine 'sociology of literature', a sociology grounded in philosophy and poetics, can be. But the sadness lies not in the exploitation or development of Benjamin's ideas by other or lesser men; it lies in the vulgarization of those ideas, in the insensitive, sloppy use of them one finds, for example, in the glossy recipes of Miss Susan Sontag. And it lies also in the attempts, now strident, to make political capital of Benjamin's harried latter years and death (a suicide on the French-Spanish frontier on September 26, 1940, as unnecessary, or as much compounded of nobility and gaucherie as were so many events in Benjamin's career).

*   *   *

Put in a simplified way (and simplification may be a virtue in view of the arcane dust being raised over the matter in East Germany, in West Germany and in émigré circles in New York) the quarrel rages over the primary political focus of Benjamin's later and incomplete work and over the policies pursued, both textually and in respect of interpretative gloss, by Benjamin's editors. Some of the Byzantine intricacies of polemic may be seen in Werner Kraft's and Helmut Heissenbüttel's articles in the *Merkur* for March, 1967, in the Walter Benjamin issues of *alternative* (October-December, 1967, and April-June, 1968) and in the three-part essay on Benjamin by Hannah Arendt published in the *Merkur* (January-April, 1968). A swarm of statements and counter-statements, of acrimonious glosses and personal reminiscences have arisen in the wake of the main combatants. During Benjamin's lifetime, the main of his work met silence; now it meets personal vanity and political rhetoric.

So far as they can be disentangled, the données of the affair are these. From 1915 on Gershom Scholem was a dominant presence in Benjamin's psychological and intellectual life. *Major Trends in*

Jewish Mysticism, Scholem's classic book, is dedicated to the memory of Walter Benjamin and it is clear that the author saw in his younger friend a being uniquely equipped to meld the critical tradition of German philosophy and European humanism with the renascent national sensibility of Judaism. After 1930 it seemed as if Benjamin might follow Scholem to Jerusalem. Scholem had helped provide a stipend to support Benjamin's intended study of Hebrew and there are numerous points in the correspondence of the two men in which Benjamin declares himself on the point of departure. But he did not go and a crucial exchange in March-April, 1931, shows that Scholem regarded Benjamin's deepening involvement with Marxism as sterile and self-betraying. Benjamin was to be a successor to Spinoza, Hamann and Humboldt. Instead he was falling under the influence of Lukács, whose *History and Class Consciousness* had been a revelation, and under the personal sway of Brecht. Benjamin's involvement with Adorno began in 1923; here was, manifestly, one of the few contemporaries or near-contemporaries whose conception of philosophical criticism and post-Marxist sociology was relevant to his own and comparable, at least in seriousness and intellectual drive. Max Horkheimer's and Adorno's Institut für Sozialforschung, from late 1935 on, sponsored most of Benjamin's writings and sought to give him some measure of financial security.

The Institute emigrated to America and invited Benjamin to follow. Benjamin had an American visa, obtained for him by Horkheimer, in his pocket when he committed suicide at Port Bou, a few miles from safety. Adorno, together with his wife Dr. Gretel Adorno, became the champions of Benjamin's legacy. With Friedrich Podszus they gathered and edited the two-volume edition of Benjamin's *Schriften* (1955). The Adornos, supported by Hannah Arendt, fought for Benjamin in New York and Frankfurt where Adorno had returned in 1949. Scholem kept the remembrance of his rare, luminous friend fresh in Jerusalem and gathered a small Benjamin archive. Adorno and Scholem combined forces to produce a two-volume edition of Benjamin's letters. This was published by Suhrkamp, who have themselves done much for Benjamin's survival in 1966. So much for the seemingly straightforward facts.

But are they straightforward? Or does all this loyalty to Benjamin's memory and prodigious editorial labour in fact represent a distortion of the true Benjamin, an attempt related, as may be the

Institute in Frankfurt, to cold-war ideology and a characteristic émigré anti-Marxism parading under neutral colours? Does Rolf Tiedemann's *Studien zur Philosophie Walter Benjamins*, published under Adorno's aegis in 1965, constitute a deliberate falsification of Benjamin's actual intellectual development and methodological position? So say Rosemarie Heise, Piet Gruchot, Helmut Lethen and others. Schematically, their case is this. In Capri, in the summer of 1924, Benjamin meets Asja Lacis on holiday from her work as a film director in Moscow. Under the impact of this meeting and of his reading of Lukács, Benjamin declares himself a thoroughgoing Marxist. It is this commitment that lies at the true basis of his refusal to go to Israel and which explains his repeated intention of collaborating with, indeed of joining, the K.P.D. Benjamin is in Moscow in the winter of 1926-27 and writes the article 'Goethe' for the great Soviet Encyclopedia.

*   *   *

From 1930 onward, Brecht crystallizes Benjamin's Marxism and leads him to develop the key notion of the 'writer as a producer of commodities'. This notion, applied to Baudelaire and French art and industry in the nineteenth century, was to inform Benjamin's magnum opus. Had Benjamin lived to complete his *Pariser Passagen*, dialectical materialism would have produced its long-awaited masterpiece, a profoundly imaginative application of Marxist methodology to the history of art and society in bourgeois France. But it was not only poverty, solitude of spirit and the gnawing greyness of exile which prevented Benjamin from hammering out his great work. It was the subversive role played by the very men who have, since 1955, professed to be Benjamin's champions and faithful legatees. The key moment occurs in November, 1938, with Adorno's rejection of the 'Paris des second empire bei Baudelaire' which Benjamin had submitted to the *Zeitschrift für Sozialforschung* in New York. This rejection not only lamed Benjamin at a vital point in his evolving work but conveyed to him the strong inference that further advances toward a full-fledged Marxism would not be tolerated. As Horkheimer and Adorno were guaranteeing what meagre means of existence Benjamin had in his Paris exile, such an inference carried obvious weight. Nor is Gershom Scholem's role what it might appear. Benjamin's attraction to Judaism was never as intense as Scholem would make out; the 'mystical' strain evident in some of

Benjamin's early work and in the 1922-23 project for a literary journal, *Angelus Novus*, was soon overcome. By reprinting his admonitory letter of March, 1931, in the *Briefe*, Scholem is seeking to assume a prophetic, justifying stance. He is making it appear as if he foresaw the collapse of the K.P.D., as if he could have saved Benjamin from frustration and death had Benjamin turned away from Marxism and returned to some imaginary fold of religious-humanistic idealism. Scholem's authority has gone to suggest that Marxism crippled Benjamin's natural development whereas it, in fact, liberated his energies and gave his scattered, often amateurish essays a commanding focus.

*　　*　　*

What is the evidence for all this attack and revaluation? A collection of manuscripts, drafts for letters, notes, etc., designated as *Benjamin-Nachlass* in the Deutschen Zentralarchiv in Potsdam (the existence of this archive was revealed, seemingly casually, in a footnote to Tiedemann's bibliography, *Studien*, p. 212). According to Hildegard Brenner's interview with Rosemarie Heise, published in *alternative* 56/57, this archive contains clear proof of Benjamin's deep involvement in Marxist texts and in Marxist approaches to nineteenth-century art and literature. Marx's *Eighteenth Brumaire* and articles in the *Neue Rheinische Zeitung* were the object of Benjamin's constant study; his analysis of Baudelaire was to be developed in the context of a study of Blanqui and of the 'Entwicklung der Boulevardpresse' in the light of Balzac and Marx's uses of Balzac. The archive, moreover, shows that the draft for Benjamin's important answer to Adorno's critique in December, 1938, differs from the text given in the *Briefe*. Similar divergences concealing the extent of Benjamin's Marxist commitment may be found between Benjamin texts as released by Adorno in Frankfurt and as published in Marxist journals or as stated in the material of the Potsdam dossier. A letter from Asja Lacis to Miss Brenner, dated Riga, November 14, '67, and reproduced in facsimile in *alternative*, confirms Benjamin's resolute involvement in Marxism and rejects the 'reactionary' testimony of Werner Krauss and the 'risible' assertions of Tiedemann. Reviews of Fyodor Gladkov's novel *Cement*, of Lenin's *Letters to Gorki*, etc., written by Benjamin in 1926-27, show the force of his Marxist-Leninist inclinations. Benjamin is an example—perhaps the most instructive example in modern intellectual history—of the evolution from bourgeois idealism to Hegelian-Marxist-Leninist materialism. His works, fragmentary and imperfectly articulated as they are, must be rescued from those who sought to undermine them during Benjamin's life and would appropriate them to their cold-war purposes now. American-financed sociology and Jewish mysticism have no right to claim Walter Benjamin for their own.

*   *   *

Where in all this is the truth? First one must discount the tone of argument on both sides. The exacerbation of Jewish sensibilities taking up the ashes of an unbearable past is fully understandable; but there is an uncomely contrast between the chivalric lucidity of Benjamin himself and the sybilline *lourdeurs* with which Miss Hannah Arendt, so prompt to regard any criticism of her own work as *lèse-majesté*, turns on Adorno and Tiedemann (*Merkur*, 1968, 1/2, pp. 56–7). The other side is no better: the proponents of a Marxist Benjamin 'falsified by Adorno and his clique' commonly express themselves in that post-Stalinist and sub-Brechtian prose still practised in Weimar and by Western imitators. *Umfunktionierung*, the new cant word, begins to sound very much like *Gleichschaltung*. Much of the polemic is tawdry dust, activated by a resolute but mendacious refusal to accept obvious psychological probabilities. *Of course* Gershom Scholem is right when he affirms that Benjamin was deeply interested in Jewish history, and thought often and seriously of emigrating to Israel (witness, among many, the letter of April 25, 1930). *Of course* it is true also that Benjamin did *not* share any ready Zionism, that he felt emotionally and intellectually rooted in classic and West-European humanism (a brilliantly perceptive letter of November 8, 1923, shows how early Benjamin envisaged the tragic interweaving of German and Jewish destinies and his own unique role therein). To the very last, and when he must have known it was too late, Benjamin felt that emigration to either Jerusalem or New York signified an abandonment of irreplaceable values. There is nothing sinister about this ambivalence, there is no question of evidence being falsified. There is scarcely a feeling, thinking European Jew in this century who has not at some time, in complete sincerity, regarded emigration to Israel as the only sane course; yet who has, even in extremity, found himself trapped in his own needs of spirit, in his own unwillingness to exchange the legacy of Spinoza,

Heine and Freud for that of Herzel. But *pace* the insistence of the Potsdam contingent on Benjamin's materialism, Benjamin's Judaism went very deep. It permeates his specific 'humane philology', his hermeneutics and life-long meditation on the mystery, in the full sense, of the word.

His view of the poetic act and of the commentary solicited by that act closely reflects interests in the cabbala, in the Talmudic techniques of analysis and interpretation, which he shared with Scholem. (It is precisely to Scholem, in a letter of January 13, 1920, that Benjamin announces his *leit-motif*, 'eine Untersuchung, welche in den grossen Problemkreis Wort und Begriff (Sprache und Logos) fällt.') Like that of Wittgenstein, like that of Kafka—who more than any other contemporary seemed to him to embody the 'metaphysical scandal', the numinous paradox of poetic creation—Benjamin's Jewishness is a question of a peculiarly acute, peculiarly vulnerable relation to the mystery of language. Scholem's memoir of Benjamin in the new Suhrkamp booklet *Über Walter Benjamin* is the fullest, finest statement of this aspect of Benjamin's work.

* * *

The matter of Walter Benjamin's Marxism is much more complex. Here again, however, naivety and sheer bad faith fog the issue. Repeatedly Benjamin stated that he wished to be 'the first real German literary critic', the first to devote all his gifts and energies to the philosophical-philological elucidation of German literature. His studies of German baroque tragedy and of Goethe's *Wahlverwandtschaften* fully justify Benjamin's hopes of primacy; they have no immediate precedent or rival in German literary criticism. Nevertheless, the scope and professional pursuit of literary criticism (books on books in interminable mirroring) seemed obviously inadequate to Benjamin. He was, from the very outset, looking for 'something larger'. He did not find it in Gustav Wyneken and the latter's youth movement, the Freie Schulgemeinde. He did not find it in Scholem's vision of the new Jerusalem. Marxism or, more exactly, the Kantian-Hegelian 'para-Marxism' of the early Lukács seemed to offer what so many of Benjamin's Jewish and intellectual contemporaries were seeking, a *Weg ins Freie* (Schnitzler's title), a 'de-trivialization' of the life of the mind in a late bourgeois era.

Marxism with its promise of a rational poetic of history, of a verifiable mythology of social relations, did not exclude or diminish the métier of the literary critic; on the contrary it gave to that métier a new urgency and dignity, a place among the historical sciences. As the letter to Scholem of September 16, 1924, makes plain, moreover, Benjamin saw in Marxism, and indeed in the human involvement and praxis of communism, a counter to that sombre, introspective bias in himself which he called 'mein Nihilismus'.

But Moscow proved no utopia and Benjamin returned from his brief sojourn with mixed feelings (he had had to re-do his 'Goethe' article to satisfy the exigencies of Soviet culture). From 1930 on, Benjamin's dilemma was an all too-familiar one: he saw in the K.P.D. a force, very probably the sole effective force, against Nazism. But he had few illusions about Stalinism or its exploitation of a harried, self-demeaning middle-class intelligentsia. A key statement occurs in Benjamin's letter to Max Rychner dated March 7, 1931. Benjamin believes that there is a modulation possible—'albeit a tense and problematic one' from his 'very particular language-philosophical stance' (*sprachphilosophischen Standort*) to the 'manner of seeing' of dialectical materialism. There is no such relation or mediation to the *Saturiertheit* (saturation? sterile, complacent plenitude?) of 'bourgeois *Wissenschaft*'. Intent on directing his thoughts towards those matters in 'which truth is most densely present', Benjamin finds himself looking to Franz Mehring (a direction which obviously links him to Lukács) rather than to 'circumlocutionary profundities' originating in the school of Heidegger. But in that very letter, only a few sentences later, comes a statement that makes nonsense of the gross simplifications argued by Herr Gruchot *et al*: 'If I may express myself in one word: I have never been able to inquire and think otherwise than, if I may so put it, in a theological sense—namely in conformity with the Talmudic prescription regarding the forty-nine levels of meaning in every passage of the Torah.' It is because even the 'stalest communist platitude' has more such levels of meaning *today*—in Berlin in March, 1931—than 'bourgeois profundity', that Benjamin is seeking a working entente with Marxism.

He found such an entente manifest in Brecht and, at certain points, in his own relationship to Brecht. Brecht seemed to Benjamin not only a master of language and of dramatic form but a human being who had been able to reconcile obvious artistic integrity with an urgent, concrete political focus. Brecht's subversive-didactic relations to his audience seemed to prefigure the heuristic yet necessarily ironic or provocative functions of art under a future socialism. But here again, the motives involved were by no means partisan or programmatic. Tiedemann (whose pretentious jargon and obeisances to Adorno make most of his work on Benjamin unusable) is surely right when he points out that Benjamin felt drawn to Brecht's 'simplicity'. Benjamin's style and cast of feeling were convoluted, almost antiquarian, and always subject to the temptations of preciousness. Brecht's marvellous astringency, the sinew and cleansing vulgarity of his discourse were a fascinating corrective. Benjamin clearly felt them as such. Yet even where the fascination was most vivid—during the time spent together at Svendborg in the summer of 1934—Benjamin kept his own, deeply personal, position intact. The topic for discussion is Kafka and it is precisely here that Benjamin observes the limitations of Brecht's sensibility and the necessary irrelevancies of the Marxist categories. Brecht's commentary is often acute, but it leaves out the core, that manifold of parable and allegory, of language used to defeat language in a dialectic far nearer to Kierkegaard than to Marx, which Benjamin feels himself uniquely equipped, indeed summoned (*berufen*) to elucidate. Reading these exchanges, and the notes dated June-August, 1938, one is struck, moreover, by an ironic paradox. When Hildegard Brenner and Asja Lacis would refer us to Brecht's great influence on Benjamin, they had better refer us also to the fact that it was from Brecht's disenchanted, laconically clairvoyant asides and allusions that Benjamin received confirmation of his own fears and instincts about Soviet Russia. Brecht would have been the last to advise his friend to take refuge there.

*   *   *

No concise summary will do. Benjamin's Marxism, like Ernst Bloch's or Lévi-Strauss's (to which it leads) is a formidably complicated, personalized, shifting and, indeed, at times self-contradictory phenomenon. It is compounded of psychological need and political helplessness, of intellectual excitement and an emotional thrust toward simplicity, of the Judaic obsession with messianic justice and of bitterness toward the academic mandarinate of the bourgeoisie. If Marx's political writings drew Benjamin toward Paris and the exemplary role of French society in the making of the modern, so did Proust (whom Benjamin endeavoured to translate), Valéry and

o

Gide. What Benjamin does owe to Marxism, though it is a realiza-
tion incipient in Taine, is the understanding of art, of the work of
literature, as a *product* specific to the modes of production in a given
society. To Brecht and Benjamin, Marxism brought confirmation of
the notion (a notion they had both arrived at personally and *before*
they studied Marx) that the modern city is the defining locus of
imaginative life, that the industrial city—*la ville tentaculaire*—has
literally re-structured our inner landscape and the habitat of our
dreams. That notion, with specific reference to Baudelaire as the
'first modern poet', was to be worked out in *Pariser Passagen*.

* * *

Rather than quarrel, in terms as gross as they are obsolete, over
Benjamin's attitude to the K.P.D. or alleged Cold War support for
Adorno's Institute, one must seek to understand the prophetic,
'structuralist' character of Benjamin's uses of Marx. The work of
art and the industrial city interact in a close mesh of economic,
social, linguistic structures. The poem and the paper on which it is
printed, Baudelaire's particular 'coding' of experience and the gait
and sociology of the Paris *flâneur*, interrelate to form a syntax, a
significant entity which the *Kulturkritiker* must 'read' precisely as
the mathematician reads a set or the geologist a stratified landscape.
It is because he fails to grasp Benjamin's 'structuralism' *avant la
lettre*, because he sees in it only arcane philology and wants a more
palpable sociological method, that Adorno rejects the Baudelaire
fragment. Not because he and Horkheimer detect some sinister
Marxist coloration. (This, of course, does not make the rejection
any the less obtuse; it probably makes it *more* so.) Benjamin's
Passagen fragments and work on Baudelaire, the concepts of linguistic structure and society embryonic in the *Ursprung des deutschen
Trauerspiels*, the aim of 'total re-creative interpretation' which he
set the critic, make of him one of the two forerunners of *structural-
isme*. The other is Hermann Broch in his monograph on *Hofmannsthal und seine Zeit*, notably in the section 'Die Kunst und ihr Un-Stil
am Ende des 19 Jahrhunderts'. When Broch analyses the 'sociology
of *décor* and bad taste', when Benjamin sees nineteenth-century Paris
and a Baudelaire sonnet as related elements in the anatomy and
myth of capitalism, they anticipate much of what is now in vogue.
The Marxism of Benjamin, like that of Lévi-Strauss's *Mytho-
logiques*, is a recognition of vital reciprocity between matter and

feeling, between human experience and the available expressive syntax.

* * *

But why bother with these arcane echoes of the past, why wade into this morass of exegesis? Is it worth insisting on certain obvious truths (i.e., that Scholem and Adorno—however pure their motives, however disinterested their editorial labour to which, after all, much of Benjamin's achievement and presence owes its survival—tend to patronize their unfortunate, dead friend, that the growth of his stature in relation to *theirs* poses psychological traps? Or that a man writing letters to friends far away, to backers whose emotional and material support he urgently requires, may omit from a finished version acerbities or provocations he will put in a rough draft?). The answer is that Walter Benjamin is worth getting right, that his example can today be, more than ever, beneficial. His understanding of philology and evaluative commentary as creatively akin, his conviction that literary criticism must exhibit a delicacy of form, an imaginative *élan* strictly comparable to that of the work it discusses— true criticism is a vital *mimesis* of the poet's act—these are badly needed correctives to the pompous moralizing and parochial gossip now prevalent in English academic and 'journalistic-critical' stuff. For Benjamin, commentary and exegesis are a manoeuvre of love, a penetration by way of scrupulous delight. (This precisely is the ontological, the religious aspect of his 'philology'.)

Any homunculus in and around the fens can learn to show his teeth and make of literary criticism an exercise in closing books. To *open* books for others is the true and lasting function of criticism. Benjamin's work on baroque tragedy, on Goethe, on Baudelaire, on Hofmannsthal, on Hebel or on Gide shows how authentic judgment is internalized, how the real critic, analogous in this respect to an actor, works from inside the life-form of the object he animates (to which, literally, he 'gives a second soul'). We need Benjamin's focus, again almost religious, on the specific miracle of human speech, his intuition, directly prefiguring Chomsky's theory of universals and generative grammar, of a 'lost' unified language (cf. 'Die Aufgabe des Übersetzers', an astonishing piece dating back to 1923). It is in Benjamin that much may be seen of that necessary conjunction between modern linguistics and the study of literature, without which such study will continue its present decline into self-satisfied triviality. Benjamin's 'difficulty'—and he is a severely demanding writer—is no gratuitous embellishment: it stems from his persistent grasp of the fact that language is the most complex of human phenomena and that no approach to literature innocent of a sense of that complexity can be other than banal and academic. Benjamin will never write his *Urgeschichte des XIX Jahrhunderts* (whose very title exactly anticipates Lévi-Strauss's theory of 'sociological-archaeology') but the direction of spirit is plain for others to follow.

* * *

What we require now are not rebarbative polemics but usable translations of Benjamin into English. This is a fiercely difficult task. His German prose has a playful concision, a self-qualifying dialectical pattern partly personal, partly influenced by expressionism and the cabbala. It is even more difficult to translate than that of Ernst Bloch to which it bears certain resemblances. There may be a case here—admittedly a case rare in critical prose—for a parallel text, the original on one side, an English version, necessarily literal and even clumsy, on the other (will the National Translation Center in Texas, with its exciting plans for a Loeb Library of living languages, please note). Whatever the method available, we need to have Benjamin's monographs on tragedy and on Goethe, his principal Baudelaire fragments, his paper on translation, his 'Problem der Sprachsoziologie' and something of his commentary on Kafka and Brecht accessible in English. (A volume containing some of these works has just been announced by Harcourt Brace in New York.) The letters are of secondary importance and the choice of some 300 made for publication by Adorno and Scholem may, in fact, have been excessive; too much here is dead, unrecapturable hope. When the main of the work is available to a wider circle of readers Walter Benjamin will emerge as one of the most penetrating philosophical critics, as one of the sensibilities most 'sweetly strong' (in the sense of *soave forza*), that European culture has produced since Coleridge.

15

HEALING WORDS

(a) DOCTOR LACAN'S STRUCTURALISM

FORTY YEARS AFTER news of its existence began to reach the special numbers of fashionable reviews, psychoanalysis is getting its second wind in France. Judging by the spate of books published and announced, it is in for a marathon run, reminiscent of the effort which made that country illustrious as a centre for psychiatric research at the end of the nineteenth century. Technical publications have of course enjoyed a subterranean existence all along, but never have popularizations been so eagerly bought; and the novelty lies in the appearance of many works which testify to an overwhelming desire for radical reassessment. This takes the form of epistemological essays, like J.-B. Pontalis's *Après Freud* or Paul Ricoeur's *De l'Interprétation, Essai sur Freud*, of a *Vocabulaire de la Psychanalyse* (by J. Laplanche and J.-B. Pontalis, and already out of print), but chiefly of translations or reprints of most major contributions to the field. In the past few years there have appeared books by Anna Freud, Karl Abraham, Geza Roheim, Ernest Jones, Melanie Klein, Karen Horney, Sandor Ferenczi, and the main French psychoanalysts, as well as new translations of works by Freud himself, the third volume of his biography by Ernest Jones, his letters to various correspondents, the inevitable essay on Woodrow Wilson, written jointly with William Bullitt. Last in every sense of the term, though hardly least, a translation of his complete works, which is intended to be the French equivalent of the Imago *Gesammelte Werke*, or the English *Standard Edition*, is now under way.

*　　*　　*

This revival of interest may be due to some democratization of psychoanalysis; but since there was already a demand for popular

---

(a) JACQUES LACAN: *Ecrits*. 924 pp. Paris: Le Seuil. 50 fr.
(b) GAY WILSON ALLEN: *William James*. 556 pp. Rupert Hart-Davis. £4 4s.

205

information, it is more likely that the change has come from the top, and that the public asks for more books on the subject because, after fifty years of quasi-unanimous rejection by its leading thinkers and writers, the French intelligentsia is now philosophically ready for the psychoanalytical message. Freud has recounted, in his *Psychopathology of Everyday Life*, how he 'forgot' a colleague's suggestion about the fundamental bisexuality of man until, his theory having matured in the meantime, he could 'discover' this indispensable notion himself. Such a maturing process has been taking place in the past twenty years and is at present culminating in a profound epistemological unrest; this in turn makes the disquieting implications of psychoanalysis easier to accept, even if it is, paradoxically, to use them to buttress hopes which may prove extravagant.

It is fair that one of the chief beneficiaries of such dialectics should be a theorist who has played an outstanding part in rethinking many key notions. Not the least astonishing example of this hunger for information is the speed with which an exceptionally large first edition of *Ecrits*, by Dr. Jacques Lacan, a massive tome of over 900 pages and of now legendary difficulty, went out of print. True, this was to some extent a *succès de curiosité*; although the book is very convenient, since it is a collection of texts first published in periodicals which are now often inaccessible. Lacan's fame had been spreading steadily since 1951, when he began, first private teaching, then seminars at the psychiatric hospital of Saint-Anne and lately at the Ecole Normale Supérieure. These eventually attracted such a mixed public that a year ago, when the badge craze spread to France, a prominent weekly could suggest several for highbrows, among them, specifically 'pour femme du monde', *I like Lacan*.

*　　　*　　　*

If there is a public demand, therefore, Lacan can be said to have created it to a considerable extent. There had in fact been a proto-renaissance after a split among French psychoanalysts in 1953 resulted in the foundation of the Société Française de Psychanalyse (of which Lacan was a leading member), and especially after the appearance, in 1956, of the journal *La Psychanalyse*, in which the ambition to define the field of psychoanalysis and connect it to other lines of research was conspicuous. Maurice Merleau-Ponty and Georges Bataille had often urged Lacan to publish the text of his seminars; the influence of his teaching can be observed in works by Maurice Blanchot and Michel Foucault, in René Girard's *Mensonge romantique et vérité romanesque*, in Edmond Ortigues's *Le Discours et le symbole*, in Roland Barthes's studies on semiology and Louis Althusser's 'reading' of Marx.

But it can be felt still more basically. The current revival of interest in psychoanalysis is distinctly historical in feeling; it is marked by the desire for a return to origins which is a common factor in so many avenues of modern thought. Now a 'return to Freud' is a leitmotiv of Lacan's writings. The latest split in French psychoanalysis has produced a group centred on him, the Ecole Freudienne; *Ecrits* has appeared in a new collection, 'Le Champ freudien', which he directs. The methodological import of such an attitude appears clearly in Paul Ricoeur's essay, as defined by its title, or in the *Vocabulaire de la psychanalyse*, in which there is an attempt to recapture the sharp outlines of early concepts and research, often contrasted by Lacan with the complacent and sclerotic orthodoxy in much of today's psychoanalytical establishment. An embryo of such a dictionary can be found in *Ecrits*, in the shape of a list of Freudian notions in the original German.

*   *   *

Lacan's insistence on the Freudian letter springs from an admiration which his own work shows to be well-grounded, but also, no doubt, from common intuitions (and perhaps, sometimes, prejudices); it can occasionally look like megalomania, as in the aphoristic blurb, where 'Freud's discovery' is lengthened to 'Freud's discovery by Jacques Lacan'. But if the memory of Freud can hardly be said to have ever been lost, the same, perhaps, does not apply to the significance of his teaching. For, Lacan says, the return to Freud is a return to 'Freud's meaning'. And Freud's meaning is structural.

The timing of *Ecrits* could not have been better, coming as it did on the crest of the structuralist wave. Structuralism as the 'new philosophy' has many features in common with the 'new novel', notably that of being to some extent due to a negative convergence, in which thinkers separated by reasons both personal and ideological are united in what they reject. Yet the cartoonist who showed Lévi-Strauss, Foucault, Barthes and Lacan (only forgetting Althusser) as savages concocting in one melting-pot the philosophy of our time was not entirely wrong, especially since structuralism, which elsewhere has remained close to its linguistic origins, has won acceptance in France through its application to ethnology. This technique, inasmuch as it assumes as a working hypothesis the existence of organized wholes, transcendent to the individuals who are their elements or agents and working unconsciously in them, could hardly avoid being set up as a philosophy, which has found its most extreme form in Foucault's *Les Mots et les choses*. It has resulted in the fall from grace of humanism, and even of man—certainly of the 'human sciences', a term since then written only in inverted commas. Lacan is aware of this when he defines the unifying thread of his book as 'the debate of the Enlightenment'.

* * *

Sartre has attacked the whole new movement as being the last-ditch defence of bourgeois ideology. The two axes he had assigned to a modern anthropology, psychoanalysis and Marxism, are replaced in Foucault by psychoanalysis and an ethnology of which Lévi-Strauss is the high priest. But whereas in the latter structuralism often seems to amount to a denial of history, Lacan's main tenet, that the structure of the Unconscious is the very structure of language, guarantees the respect of history, or perhaps—a less loaded word—that of the diachronic. But his insistence on structure comes from the equally great emphasis which had been put on the historical aspect in the individual.

Structuralism has given rise to some unexpected alliances which look like wartime coalition governments, and Sartre now finds himself fighting side by side with the personalists. Lacan, who shows great scorn for the loose thinking which is sometimes associated with that trend, agrees with Foucault's findings, in *La Naissance de la clinique* and *Histoire de la folie à l'âge classique*, about the alienating effect of some types of humane treatment. Any therapist must, if he is to be successful, feel a genuine respect for the other's person; but although psychoanalysis was born of psychotherapy, it cannot be reduced to it. It must, instead, achieve scientific status, and might well provide the central position from which the social sciences can achieve theirs. Epistemology is therefore central to Lacan's preoccupations, and is said by him to be possible only on the basis of a profound change in the conception of man as the subject of science. Here his teaching sharply diverges from the main western tradition, which identifies subject and consciousness, and sees in the

Cartesian Cogito the typical experience of knowledge. Instead Lacan offers formulas like 'I think where I am not, I am where I do not think'. The position from which one speaks is an essential part of the text, as he stated again recently, in a briskly ironic interview granted to some philosophy students, and he constantly insists on the fact that his theories spring from the unique experience of analysis.

Sartre, in *L'Imaginaire*, divided the field of knowledge into 'the certain' (which comes from phenomenological insight) and 'the probable' (which comes from scientific experiment and induction); but Lacan, while admiring Sartre's analyses of sadomasochism in *Being and Nothingness*, for instance, points out that, although brilliant and convincing in the manner of a work of fiction, they are not accurate. And he defends Freud's *scientisme* as the only atmosphere which could allow his theories to be conceived. Science, of course, is in one sense not facts but theory; but, according to Lacan, the notion of structure allows us to surmount the dilemma between a description and a theoretical model. Its status, in relation to earlier concepts, is that of topology compared to geometry—this difficult subject is dealt with in, among other texts, 'Remarque sur le rapport de Daniel Lagache'. The unrest currently affecting the social sciences is in some ways similar to the crisis about the foundations of mathematics at the turn of the century—a parallel which is not irrelevant if one considers the importance that logical and mathematical symbolism are now taking in the theory and method of the social sciences. This is a cause of considerable difficulty in *Ecrits* since Lacan, a convinced exponent of the two cultures, would include in the training of future analysts all the latest intellectual aids. Psychoanalysis must pass from a sterile formalism to a genuine formalization, he says, adding: 'We are attempting an algebra.'

* * *

These remarks may suffice to indicate the exceptional importance of this work. All these points are discussed in specialized articles— slightly rewritten papers for congresses, or texts of seminars. The connecting essays are of particular interest since they bring the collection up to date and strongly reiterate Lacan's aims and position. Yet the very conception of the book raises doubts. Gide expressed admiration for Joyce, who confronts posterity with his most forbidding work, the sheer cliff of *Finnegans Wake*. Much the same could be said about *Ecrits*—though it will not, we hope, be Dr. Lacan's last work! Many autobiographical and polemical footnotes hint that difficulties put in his way by adversaries, and a primary concern with his teaching, have delayed publication until there was, he says, a danger of unwelcome exploitation. Yet this 'new reader', to whom the book is addressed, if he has hopes of having been given Lacan's *summa analytica*, will to some extent be disappointed, for many features of the book seem almost calculated to frustrate and baffle him. True, there is a statement to the effect that it is not an introduction, but a discussion, of Lacan's system, and that the reader is expected 'to come from some fairly firm (intellectual) position', whether inside or outside psychoanalysis.

But this discussion cannot be entered into fruitfully without some rudiments of such revolutionary and closely connected ideas. The summaries of some of Lacan's seminars, in the *Bulletin de Psychologie*, are hard to find; he uses graphs, symbols and terminology which are not sufficiently explained, and the *Cahiers pour l'Analyse*, written by his later disciples at the Cercle d'Epistémologie of the Ecole Normale Supérieure, do not make matters any clearer. Much was also assumed to be known in the polemics which followed the appearance of the book.

Of the three sorts of order conceivable in this type of work, the most convenient would be the didactic, in which the contents are arranged according to the effect they are to have on the reader; this is missing here (the text of the seminar on Edgar Allan Poe's *Purloined Letter*, placed first so as to provide 'a stepping stone to [Lacan's] style', will be by-passed by the wise beginner until he has reached the necessary proficiency). Or the order could be logical, and this is represented here by an 'Index raisonné des concepts majeurs' by a disciple—but it refers only to involved passages where these concepts are made use of. Or finally, it could be the chronological order of conception, and this is the one Lacan has chosen. One can understand an author's reluctance to recast texts spanning thirty years, many of which are already famous; but the 'position of immanence' which results from this, although structuralism should enable us to cope with it, is much more of an obstacle even than the difficulty of the style, although the latter—which wants a section to itself—offers many possibilities of error when one tries to deduce connexions.

Worse, the 'new reader' is made to feel that he is on the outside looking in, that many jokes and passwords, amounting to a veritable mythology, can be understood only by the elect, and in case this should escape him, Lacan tells him so. This is forgivable among people who must often feel like old comrades from wartime but, to borrow a simile from psychoanalysis, it is not certain that such a 'position of deprivation' will work as well with a reader as it does with a patient. Here Lacan seems to have inherited the Symbolist and Surrealist tradition of dealing haughtily with the public; in spite of some similarity of political choice, we are far from Sartre's statements about the duty to popularize ideas. The biographical apparatus is almost pedantically complete, whereas references to other authors are often absent or imprecise. The index is very different from the type normally found in such publications. It reflects Lacan's wide reading, and his insistence on a thorough cultural grounding for budding analysts; but there are some oddities. Ludwig Binswanger, although mentioned in the text (in an important connexion), is not to be seen in the index; on the other hand, St. Matthew is, but merely because Lacan borrows a turn of phrase from him. St. Benoît Labre is there also, because he is cited by Klossowski, himself cited by Lacan. As for Campanella and Machiavelli, it turns out that these are highbrow names cited once by Poe's hero Dupin, and this is, according to Lacan, 'just so much eyewash'.

Now, Lacan's style. The title of the book is to be taken literally: these texts bear the marks of *written* style, and Lacan has justified the peculiarities of his own (for which 'Mallarméan' and 'Gongorist' are accepted descriptions) in two different ways, while oddly neglecting a third which a psychiatrist might have been expected to offer. One is that he thereby wants to avoid the exploitation of his doctrine for 'hermeneutic' ends; to which can be answered that while the normal public may well be bewildered, such stylistic difficulties will present no obstacle whatever to the type of reader he has in mind. Another is that these texts were at first directed at doctors, who were not used to thinking on symbolic lines, and that such an elliptic, allusive style has therefore a pedagogic purpose. While this claim has been strongly denied by some critics, it is a fact that Lacan's style is catching; this first appears more obviously in his admirers, but also insidiously in his detractors, who often cannot resist a sly pastiche. It is evident, in any case, that it springs from a taste and a need in him. His style hardly recalls Freud's, but both admire writers for their poetic insight and their finicky search for *le mot juste*: Gide is in this regard favourably compared with Pierre Janet, and Lacan's own concern for the nuances of Freud's vocabulary has borne fruit in modern psychoanalytical theory.

* * *

Some of his texts are clear and vigorous; others are a florid weave of puns, alliterations, quibbles, neologisms, *précieux* vocabulary and syntax, and sudden drops into coarseness, with an extensive use of cultural references, from the most abstruse to the most slangy. It may not be to everyone's taste, but it can be quite funny. Syncretism and its practitioners are stigmatized as 'flousophie' and 'faufilosophes', who speak 'franglaire'. One's command of French colloquialisms will be further tested by allusions to the 'forêt de Bondy' and the place 'où les Athéniens s'atteignirent'. Quotable instances of humour include the passage about the introduction to the seminar on the *Purloined Letter*, which Lacan had advised readers to tackle *after* the main text; this advice was mostly disregarded, since, he remarks, 'a taste for obstacles is the ornament of Being's perseveration' (we do not claim this as the best translation for a sentence which, incidentally, neatly epitomizes Lacan's doctrine). It can be memorably poetic, in the manner of Michel Leiris's *Bagatelles végétales*. Even when it fails, it is mentally exciting.

And this is where the strongest justification of such a manner of writing could lie. What has chiefly affronted critics is not Lacan's style as such, which would be nothing new in a literary text; it is its incongruousness in a work purporting to be scientific. But actually, why not? Stylistic brilliance does not necessarily exclude scientific rigour. Communication is not in danger: except here and there, when he is misled by treacherous genitives, Lacan is comprehensible. It is a well-known property of style that once it is made allusive it becomes oracular; this is not a negligible side-effect, since mystery and ambiguity in the object are thus conveyed with a unique efficacy. Some have 'translated' roughly Lacan's periphrases; as in the case of the *kenningar*, those curious Scandinavian metaphors described by J.-L. Borges, not only the effect but the meaning is lost, which makes the efficacy of such treatment questionable.

As many modern critics have pointed out, clarity is not a universal attribute of good style; it is only the style of persuasion. But poetic riddles take time; our hectic *civilisation des loisirs* has none left to unravel them. Emile Benveniste, in the first number of *La Psych-*

analyse, contrasted the wealth of signifiers in the language of the Unconscious with their relative scarcity in ordinary language. But this is so, to a great extent, because a spontaneous exuberance, which comes out in slang and which modern literature has helped us to tolerate, is constantly repressed by society, for reasons of efficiency, or, alas, respectability. Lacan counters the reproach of over-intellectualization by alluding to the sophistication of mental processes in the least imaginative of people; this applies not only to content but also to expression. His first work was on paranoia, and the verbal fireworks in some types of psychoses are evocatively and movingly described in his book. As one reads him and feels, metaphorically, one's muscles growing first extended, then stiff, then more agile, one realizes the impoverishment we have all undergone.

Other readers may be put off by numerous personal attacks which, especially when couched in a style of violent abuse, are the least accepted form of polemics. These sometimes spring from resentment, but more often from a passionate concern for intellectual ethics. Lacan characterizes several examples of doctrinal slovenliness as 'abject' and derides some facile descriptions of 'genital love' as 'Miss Lonelyhearts style'. His *vis comica* is undeniable in this connexion. But whatever side we take—if we must—let us remember, if seeing an adversary called 'laughing cowdung' makes us wince, that when Molière treated the same subject he used the language of farce because it alone could do justice to a Diafoirus or a Purgon.

*   *   *

Such features can make the whole work seem almost self-defeating. Yet it would be a great pity if the reader, instead of being thankful for this *gai savoir*, was finally deterred by aspects which, though often aggravating, are nevertheless superficial. To those who, having read Lacan's articles over the years, now reread them in bulk, what comes through forcibly is the good sense of so many of his attitudes, the depth of his insights, and the impressive coherence of his doctrine.

The main objects of his attacks are those who, installed in the comfortable posture of rigid orthodoxy, denigrate any theoretical effort, without seeing that therapy itself suffers thereby. He also denounces the social exploitation which must follow when the criteria of the cure are defined as an adaptation to society or an identification with the analyst—whose own motives for adaptation may be all too evident. Freud said to Jung about Americans: 'They don't know that we are bringing them the plague'; but Lacan thinks that Americans did far worse to Freud. The wrong turning taken by psychoanalysis starts, according to him, with the place taken by the Ego in modern theory. This can amount to a rejection of Freud's main discovery, the Unconscious. The Ego is, on the contrary, for Lacan, the locus of alienating identifications. His first article, reprinted here, was devoted to the 'phase of the mirror', which prepared the way for such a conception. Unlike the young animal, the human child, which is born in a state of prematurity and suffers from motor incoordination and a fragmentary apprehension of his own body, rejoices in watching a unified and well-controlled image; this experience crystallizes his desires, and lays the foundations of narcissism. Lacan therefore bases his theory on a careful differentiation between three regions of being: the real, the imaginary, and the symbolical. His conception of the imaginary is in some ways similar to Sartre's, for it is a construct of the self, but what Sartre explains by means of freedom is explained by Lacan thanks to a notion born of his application of structuralism to psychoanalysis, that of the primacy of the symbolical. The whole conception can, however, be profitably compared with Sartre's first work, an essay on the *Transcendence of the Ego*.

Lacan's main preoccupation has been to supply, not new material, but a new framework in which 'the classical sub-structures of psychoanalysis can be integrated'. His work is in this very similar to that of Lévi-Strauss. The texts he starts from are chiefly Freud's, but he also makes use of later contributions. On one occasion, in a review article on *La Jeunesse d'André Gide*, we get Lacan on Delay on Gide on Gide—a fascinating palimpsest! Thus he gives fresh accounts, for instance, of fantasies, of perversions, of the child's feeling of omnipotence, of transference, of the libidinal stages, and gives elegant solutions to some hitherto unsolved problems. But such theoretical considerations have their repercussions on practice, and sometimes lead to a radical reorientation of treatment.

*   *   *

The main similarity with Lévi-Strauss, however, comes from the application to a new field of the principles of structural linguistics— an application which, though later in date, is less unexpected than it was in Lévi-Strauss, for psychoanalysis is, as Freud always insisted, a 'talking cure'. And it is through paying attention to the apparently most trivial phenomena, and his interest in language, that he was rewarded by his great discovery: that of the Unconscious, which was, properly speaking, the discovery of its mechanisms. But the most momentous aspect of it was that such mechanisms applied equally to slips of the tongue, to dreams, to witticisms, to symptoms, to forgetting; all were determined by a meaning, but only through being conditioned by the laws of language. But, as Lacan puts it, 'Geneva 1910, Petrograd 1920' explains that Freud could not yet have at his disposal the proper conceptual tools, those of structural linguistics, as elaborated by Ferdinand de Saussure and the Russian formalists. Among the latter, Roman Jakobson showed the way in his *Fundamentals of Language* when he compared two types of aphasia to metaphor and metonymy, and related these two poles of rhetoric, assimilated to resemblance and contiguity, to the Freudian mechanisms of condensation and displacement.

This idea is taken up by Lacan. 'Language' means, of course, for him any relational form, and exists long before the acquisition of motor and auditive techniques, as soon as the baby can articulate two couples of opposites, which is the simplest example of a process of symbolization. In showing the development which follows from such beginnings, Lacan is led to differentiate between *need, desire* and *demand*. Undifferentiated need must submit to the laws of language, the essential character of which is that it is made of signifiers which endlessly refer to one another without ever being pinned down to any given signified; it is thus fragmented into separate elements, which can then be commuted, a fact which allows us to understand how communication, the study of behaviour, and, of course, psychoanalytical treatment, are possible.

Taking up Freud's famous case-history of Little Hans, Lacan shows that the myths successively invented by the child cannot be explained except by considering them all together and 'reading' them both vertically and horizontally, as one would read an orchestral score, that is to say, by considering their structural necessity. Thus can be established a syntax of transformations; the fixations at various libidinal stages can be interpreted as the use of obsolete signifiers. Analysis is then teaching the patient to 'speak' in a new code, which necessitates a fundamental recentering:

The subject begins the analysis by speaking about himself without speaking to you, or by speaking to you without speaking about himself. When he is able to speak to you about himself, the analysis will be finished.

Language, the order of the symbolical, is taken here as pre-existing, and Lacan does not try to explain its origin, any more than would a linguist, except to say that this origin cannot be genetic. This last point may be a metaphysical option, and has prompted accusations of idealism; but Lacan has been defended on the grounds that in idealism the chain of signifiers must rest on some notion of the ultimate good, which is not the case here.

Need can be satisfied by a specific object; desire, on the other hand, is impossible to satisfy, for it is a desire for a sign, for a gift, which is the other's desire. A lot is spoken today about object-relations; but Freud stressed rather nostalgia and longing. In spite of the wishful thinking of some philosophers, there is no pre-established harmony between desire and any object. There seems to be, therefore, as Freud had surmised, a basic flaw in human sexuality; and the asymmetrical development of the sexes privileges neither. In both, maturity is conquered at the cost of symbolical castration. *Totem and Taboo* shows the relation between castration, law and death, symbolically if not historically: and *Beyond the Pleasure Principle* shows death as the absolute master in the Hegelian game of master and slave. The tactful neglect with which the notion of a death-instinct is treated today epitomizes, for Lacan, the shallowness of our time, with its optimistic ideologies.

Such theories (of which only the barest outlines can be given here) will displease many: culturalists, organicists, phenomenologists, logical positivists, adherents of various philosophical and religious doctrines, and all other schools of psychoanalysis inasmuch as their conclusions are acknowledged but modified. Behaviourists might abstain, since their field (that of the *sign*, which works on a stimulus-response basis, as opposed to the *symptom*, which is essentially over-determined) is specifically left aside; but of course they will probably reject the system *in toto*. We can see why, when Lacan describes truth, at the end of 'La Chose freudienne', as

essentially complex, humble in its functions and a stranger to reality, independent of the choice of sex, akin to death, and, on the whole, rather inhuman, Diana, perhaps . . .

he imagines the analyst in the part of the unfortunate Acteon. Lacan's work has many facets, which may not all convince to the same degree; but one hopes that the dialogue which such challenging ideas call for will take place.

A few words should be added on the subject of psychoanalysis and society. One would not expect a psychoanalyst to be starry-eyed about all the fine ideas on man and his 'rights' which modern liberals have inherited from the Enlightenment, and Dr. Lacan is not. The Index of Concepts rightly acknowledges that there is, scattered in the book, a theory of ideology, and that it consists of a critique of 'the ideology of freedom' and 'the ideology of free-enterprise'. There is in 'L'Agressivité en psychanalyse' a bitter picture of Western society, which has shown its true colours in Victorian capitalism and colonialism. The ideology of freedom is criticized, not because of a lack of foundations, but because (as appears in 'Fonction de la psychanalyse en criminologie') it merges in fact with the other ideology, which uses it as an alibi.

This is where the chink in the theoretical armour might be. Do the facts warrant such an interpretation? According to the index, there would not seem to be any positive suggestions in the book. But there are: only, they are passed off not as values but as science. Lacan's theory, which stresses intersubjectivity, leads him to see salvation from 'civilization and its discontents' in a society whose structures, from the family upwards, are strong. Hence some yearning glances towards societies which are now fast disappearing (an attitude also found in Lévi-Strauss). On the other hand, humanism is excused by him if the context is naive enough: this is admittedly a sentimental reaction; but in 'La Science et la vérité' he acknowledges an effort to insert his theory of language into historical materialism. This corroborates Althusser's attitude towards Marxism, an attitude of which Lacan approves, but which has spread some alarm among socialists.

The impression one derives from *Ecrits* is that of a profoundly conservative, not to say reactionary, attitude, which does not seem to follow from the scientific theory. It is curious, in this connexion, to find Lacan unexpectedly in the camp of the culturalists. For since, as he agrees, the personalities of the real parents play a major part in the development of the child, inasmuch as they confirm or contradict the great Oedipus schema, the fate of humanity seems to depend, to a large extent, on what Karen Horney called 'the neurotic personality of our time'. But we can question Lacan's diagnosis when he writes as a *sociologist*, and wonder whether all modern ills really spring from causes which exclude progress, or whether, on the contrary, present changes, which have been described as a mutation,

P

will not lead to another equilibrium, about which it would be idle to prophesy.

(b) WILLIAM JAMES'S MELANCHOLIA

'GREAT WITS ARE sure to madness near alli'd.' The relation between insanity and genius is a loosely stated topic that people have been arguing about for centuries. The issues have become more definite since Dryden's day, and are more methodically handled than by Lombroso; but the central question remains unanswered: how far do certain kinds of psychological abnormality favour outstanding achievement? There are two main approaches, the statistical and the 'pathographic'. Analysis of numerical data by Terman and his colleagues disproved the common belief that the exceptionally gifted are more prone to instability than the general run of mankind; and individual pathographies have been scrutinized with clinical minuteness, to see whether the abnormal mental state of each genius studied was a necessary condition for his exceptional performance, and synchronized with it. Such exercises in medical biography require a psychiatrist to interpret the data; notable men—Moebius, Maudsley, Jaspers, Delay, Reiter and a good many more—have essayed the task. Some have concentrated on the effects of outright mental illness, others have looked at the apparent fruits of a deviant personality rooted in the subject's constitution. Often illness has been clearly the outcome of hereditary predisposition, or it has accentuated personality traits affecting daily life, and, in the higher levels, affecting also literary, artistic or scientific creation.

*　　*　　*

Studies which focused on fluctuations of mood—cyclothymia, manic-depressive psychosis—have been among the most convincing. Lange-Eichbaum cited a number of men of genius who were at the mercy of their emotional ups and downs: extended to men of talent it would be a very lengthy list. Goethe, Cowper, Haydon, Robert Mayer, Luther are famous examples. Among psychologists, Fechner and William James stand out.

Fechner's dramatic story is well known: at the age of thirty-nine he had a severe depressive breakdown which obliged him to give up his chair of physics at Leipzig. After his long-delayed recovery—

which he regarded as literally miraculous—his religious convictions were intensified and led to a stream of philosophical publications on such themes as the mental life of plants, the pervasive nature of consciousness, the foundations of belief. They included his *Zend-Avesta*, containing the programme of psycho-physics for which he is now chiefly remembered.

*   *   *

At first blush there seems little in common between James, the extrovert Harvard professor, the exponent of pragmatism, and Fechner, the determined champion of a pan-psychic gospel, with psycho-physics as a by-product of his philosophic concern with the relation of mind and matter. But (although James said of him that 'it would be terrible if even such a dear old man as this could saddle our Science forever with his patient whimsies, and in a world so full of more nutritious objects of attention compel all future students to plough through the difficulties, not only of his own works but of the still drier ones written in his refutation') they did in fact have a good deal in common—not least in the influence of depressive illness upon their thought and interest as philosophers. The sequence of James's emotional swings and the way they determined or coloured some of the salient features of his life and teaching can be traced through Professor Allen's sensitive biography. They disclose what a heavy burden James had to carry.

*   *   *

When he was nineteen and a promising student of painting, he developed indigestion and trouble with his eyesight which appeared to be nervous. It put a stop to his painting. He became an undergraduate in the Chemistry Department at Harvard, but within a year he was having more trouble with his eyes, as well as headache, backache (like his brother, Henry), and anxiety. Because of this he withdrew from the university for a time and read at home.

He was undecided about his choice of profession, but was attracted to medicine, and particularly to psychiatry: 'Of all departments of medicine that to which Dr. Prince [the medical superintendent of a mental hospital] devotes himself is, I should think, the most interesting.' In the New Year he entered the medical school, though without illusions. 'My first impressions are that there is much humbug therein, and that, with the exception of surgery, in which something positive is sometimes accomplished, a doctor does more by the moral effect of his presence on the patient and family, than by anything else.' While making these candid observations, he seemed outwardly happy, but he said that all through the winter of 1866–67 he was on the verge of suicide.

In the following year, when he was studying in Germany, he had a great deal of pain in his back for which no physical cause was found, and was tense and tremulous. To his friend, Wendell Holmes, he wrote in September, 1867, that he was a mere wreck, given to tedious egotism: his deadness of spirit must be felt to be appreciated; and to his father he confided that 'thoughts of the pistol, the dagger and the bowl began to usurp an unduly large part of my attention'. Although he was reading very widely and wrote a great deal, he felt his life was empty and he was apathetic and restless. In his diary he made an entry in May, 1868, that he felt an 'unspeakable disgust for the dead drifting of my life' and bemoaned the erotic longings which he could not satisfy: the theme recurs from time to time, and there is no reason to dispute Professor Allen's conclusion that until James was thirty-four (when he met his future wife) he had never had a real love affair. In 1869 he obtained his medical degree, but his back was again giving trouble, and he was very introspective. The death from tuberculosis of his cousin, Minny Temple, shook him profoundly in 1870 and it was then that he had a severe mental shock. He described it in detail (as the experience of a young Frenchman) in *The Varieties of Religious Experience*.

Whilst in this state of philosophic pessimism and general depression of spirits about my prospects, I went one evening into a dressing room in the twilight . . . when suddenly there fell upon me without warning, just as if it came out of the darkness, a horrible fear of my own existence. . . . It was as if something hitherto solid within my breast gave way entirely, and I became a mass of quivering fear. After this the universe was changed for me altogether. I awoke morning after morning with a horrible dread at the pit of my stomach, and with a sense of the insecurity of life that I never knew before, and that I have never felt since. . . . I have always thought that this experience of melancholia of mine had a religious bearing. . . . The fear was so invasive and powerful that if I had not clung to Scripture texts like 'The eternal God is my refuge'. . . I think I should have grown really insane.

James's father (as he indicates in a footnote) had had a closely similar experience which resulted in his becoming a Swedenborgian.

*　　　*　　　*

An appointment as instructor in physiology in 1870 made a great difference to James: as he said to his father, 'What a difference there is between me now and me last spring: then so hypochondriacal and now feeling my mind so cleared up and restored to sanity. It is the difference between death and life'. The language was somewhat exaggerated; as his mother said, he had to express every fluctuation of feeling and especially every unfavourable symptom; but at the time he had little of this kind to report, to justify his mother's comment that he had a morbidly hopeless temperament, with which he had to contend all the time. His brother Henry similarly could not get rid of the feeling that William 'takes himself, his nerves, and his physical condition too hard and too consciously . . . I wish he had a little more of this quiet British stoutness'.

In October, 1882, he was much distressed by insomnia, and his mind seemed to him a stagnant pool. In the following year he had a change of mood, which deserved to be called hypomanic:

Yesterday I was parturient of psychological truth, being in one of my fevered states you wot of, when ideas are shooting together and I can think of no finite things. I wrote a lot at headlong speed.

But he was soon complaining again of insomnia, though he looked vigorous and vital 'like a nervous thoroughbred'. A perceptive friend discerned 'in spite of his playfulness, a deep sadness. You felt he had just stepped out of this sadness in order to meet you, and was to go back into it the moment you left him.' He complained much about tiredness—'the fagged state that drove me abroad the last two times' and 'my miserable nervous system'.

What had become a fairly chronic dissatisfaction and gloom was intermittently deplored. In 1893 he wrote to a man who had lately been his student:

After our year of gentlemanly irresponsibility I seem to have forgotten everything, especially psychology, and the subjects themselves have become so paltry and insignificant seeming that each lecture has seemed a ghastly farce.

Some of his friends robustly adjured him to stop dwelling on his decay. F. W. H. Myers, vexed at James's refusal, because of his health, to become President of the Society for Psychical Research, wrote:

Your mental and physical disorganization and decay is never by any chance perceptible to anyone but yourself, and, moreover, when you are actually in the presence of friends you are able to make an effort . . . which presents you to them as a source of wisdom and delight.

Myers evidently did not recognize the self-depreciation as a typical depressive symptom, as James himself did at this time: 'I have been rather melancholy all summer . . . I shrank to nothing, psychology shrank to nothing. It passed away, however, and now not a trace left.' In 1898 his old symptoms—insomnia and fatigue—returned, and he had much worry through the alcoholism of his brother and political developments which he felt obliged to combat. His heart gave ominous signs of the trouble which was to kill him twelve years later. He became increasingly irritable, prone to self-pity and fits of despair, but still presenting a very different front to the world. His brother Henry noted in 1904:

Whenever one is with William one receives such an immense accession of suggestion and impression that the memory of the episode remains bathed for one in the very liquidity of his extraordinary play of mind; and I seem to recollect, thus, how he gave life and light, as it were, to the truth, the interest, of the change wrought all about there.

This contrast between what he felt and how he seemed to others is, like many other features of his melancholy, set down in his description of the Sick Soul, in *The Varieties of Religious Experience*. He quotes the passage in which Tolstoy recalled his suicidal despair while he seemed outwardly healthy, and physically and mentally vigorous. There can be no doubt that, in writing these chapters in his Gifford Lectures, James was dispassionately reviewing some of the forms of his own malady. At times it is not done so dispassionately.

The world now looks remote, strange, sinister, uncanny. Its colour is gone, its breath is cold. . . . When disillusionment has gone as far as this, there is seldom a *restitutio ad integrum*. One has tasted of the fruit of the tree, and the happiness of Eden never comes again.

James's attitude towards mental illness was, inevitably, complex.

Borderland insanity, crankiness, insane temperament, loss of mental balance, psychopathic degeneration . . . has certain peculiarities and liabilities which, when combined with a superior quality of intellect in an individual, make it more probable that he will make his mark and affect his age, than if his temperament were less neurotic. . . . The psychopathic temperament, whatever be the intellect with which it finds itself paired, often brings with it ardor and excitability of character. The cranky person has extraordinary emotional susceptibility. . . . His conceptions tend to pass immediately into belief and action; and when he gets a new idea, he has no rest till he proclaims it, or in some way works it off.

In a sentence which testifies to his insight into his own strength and weakness, he emphasized that:

few of us are not in some way infirm, or even diseased; and our very infirmities help us unexpectedly. In the psychopathic temperament we have the emotionality which is the sine qua non of moral perception; we have the intensity and tendency to emphasis which are the essence of practical moral vigour; and we have the love of metaphysics and mysticism which carry one's interests beyond the surface of the sensible world.

And he goes on to ridicule 'your robust Philistine type of nervous system, forever offering its biceps to be felt, thumping its breast, and thanking Heaven that it hasn't a single morbid fibre in its composition'. His opinion was that for inspiration, or the transmission of a cosmic consciousness, the neurotic temperament furnished the chief receptive condition. There is a touch of Lombroso in these ideas, but his basic concern may be recognized in his letter to Clifford Beers in 1905: 'I have long thought that if I were a millionaire with money to leave for public purposes, I should endow "Insanity" exclusively.'

*   *   *

For orthodox medicine James had very little respect, and for the orthodox practice of psychiatry none at all. He was, however, ready to try unorthodox treatment, and to champion it, on occasion. In 1887 he paid ten or eleven visits to a 'mind-cure' practitioner,

a sterling creature. . . . I sit down beside her and presently drop asleep, whilst she disentangles the snarls out of my mind. . . . I am now, unconsciously to myself, much better than when I first went &c. . . . What boots it to be made unconsciously better, yet all the while consciously to lie awake o'nights, as I still do.

In 1893 he again went to a 'mind-curer', and concluded that

it is barely possible that the recovery may be due to a mind-curer with whom I tried eighteen sittings. . . . I should like to get this woman into a lunatic asylum for two months, and have every case of chronic delusional insanity in the house tried by her. . . . I may possibly bring it about yet!

And, just as he had arranged hypnotic treatment for his sister Alice when she was in the last painful stage of cancer, he took Christian Science treatments in 1909 when he was having severe attacks of angina pectoris and felt very tense.

His insistence that 'mind-cure' was primarily a religious movement, with Christian Science as its most radical exponent, led him to some rash assertions about the essential nature and prospects of 'mind-cure':

Seeing its rapid growth in influence and its therapeutic triumphs, one is tempted to ask whether it may not be destined (probably by very reason of the crudity and extravagance of many of its manifestations) to play a part almost as great in the evolution of the popular religion of the future as did those earlier movements (Lutheran and Wesleyan) in their day.

James wanted it to be a religion of optimism, and as Pierre Janet dryly noted, 'Tout cela est bien Américain, c'est un traitement de la dépression par l'affirmation constante de l'énergie'.

*   *   *

James had a penchant for spiritualism and other occult studies, which caused him to attend many séances (with Mrs. Piper as the medium) and to confess his inability, after twenty-five years of psychic research, to find evidence for his intuitive belief that our lives are like trees in the forest which commingle their roots in the darkness underground, in 'the continuum of cosmic consciousness'. Ernest Jones's explanation of Freud's interest in telepathy and other occult phenomena fits James equally well: there was in both men an oscillation between credulity and scepticism, a tug of war in which respect for evidence struggled against the wish to believe, or at any rate (as James put it in his Presidential Address to the Society for Psychical Research) the wish to accumulate all possible records of what seem to be supernatural phenomena. Freud, in an unguarded moment, wrote to Hereward Carrington that if he had his life to live over again he would devote himself to psychical research rather than to psycho-analysis. James, in the year before his death, wrote a popular article, 'Final Impressions of a Psychical Researcher', in which he admitted that he had been studying the matter closely for twenty-five years but was no further than he was at the beginning and that he was 'tempted to believe that the Creator has eternally intended this department of nature to remain baffling'.

Advocacy of the mind-healers' cause entailed a painful clash with the medical profession in Boston. The doctors had promoted a Bill which would have made it impossible for anyone who had not a medical degree to practise psychotherapy; the main target was Christian Science. James saw this as a threat to the mental treatment of 'a class of diseases with which my occupation has made me somewhat conversant', as he wrote to the *Boston Evening Transcript*; this obstruction to free study of psychological treatment would be a public calamity. Eventually he was asked to give evidence before the Legislative Committee of Massachusetts; he told them their duty:

You are not to ask yourselves whether these mind-curers do really achieve the successes that are claimed. It is enough for you as legislators to ascertain that a large number of our citizens . . . are persuaded that a valuable new department of medical experience is by them opening up.

His popularity among the doctors and his reputation among the scientists suffered, as he foresaw. It is noteworthy that in spite of his great distinction and his friendship with men like James J. Putnam and Morton Prince, there was during his lifetime no reference to him or his writings in either of the two medical journals concerned with mental disorder—the *American Journal of Insanity* and the *Journal of Nervous and Mental Diseases*, though other psychological works, both normal and morbid, were adequately noticed. But James's pluralism played a large part in moulding Adolf Meyer's thinking and teaching, and so indirectly influenced American medicine.

He is still remembered for an eponymous theory of emotion, a philosophical doctrine, and an interpretation of religious experience. The James-Lange theory postulated that emotion as a subjective experience is the perception of visceral and other bodily changes brought about by exposure to a specific situation; neurophysiological advances have made the theory quite untenable. His doctrine of radical empiricism can be regarded as a philosophical antecedent of logical empiricism, trammelled by its association with a pragmatic criterion of truth. His Gifford Lectures, written *con amore* ('religion is the great interest of my life') bore witness to the influence of his father as well as to James's preoccupation with the happiness of the individual, to be effected through the will to believe: religious experience, he thought, consists in connecting with that 'subliminal consciousness', the 'discovery' of which by F. W. H. Myers was in James's eyes epoch-making:

I cannot but think that the most important step forward that has occurred in psychology since I have been a student of that science is the discovery, first made in 1886, that in certain subjects at least, there is not only the consciousness of the ordinary field . . . but . . . a consciousness existing beyond the field [which] casts light on many phenomena of religious biography.

This was not the happiest of James's judgments. He was too ready to believe that hysterical and hypnotic phenomena reveal 'whole systems of underground life' through which spiritual forces could be brought to bear on human beings.

But it is not his philosophic or psychological tenets that now ensure for James contemporary attention; it is the vividness and clarity of his writing, the frankness and balance of his exposition, his humour, and the aptness of his metaphors and images. An example of his unbuttoned style is afforded by the letters to his wife describing the audience at his Chautauqua Lectures:

Minds so earnest and helpless that it takes them half-an-hour to get from one idea to its immediately adjacent next neighbour, and then they lie down on it . . . like a cow on a doormat, so that you can get neither in nor out with them.

And, of his brother at de Vere Gardens:

Harry is as nice and simple and amiable as he can be. He has covered himself, like some marine crustacean, with all sorts of material growths, rich seaweeds and rigid barnacles and things, and lives hidden in the midst of his strange heavy alien manners and customs; but these are all but 'protective resemblances'.

A few letters later he wrote that he had been to the Brighton Aquarium and seen 'four cuttle-fish (octupus). I wish we had one of them for a child—such flexible intensity of life in a form so inaccessible to our sympathy.' There is no doubt that he had an extraordinarily attractive personality; many people echo Logan Pearsall Smith's verdict—'the most charming man I ever met'.

Professor Allen has been able to include much information from letters and diaries which was not available to James's previous biographer, Ralph Barton Perry. He has produced an absorbing and faithful account of a many-sided man's character and achievements. It is gracefully written, and enables us to see why William James's standing as the foremost American psychologist is so constantly attributed to his personality—warm, humorous, tolerant, lovable—his clarity of vision, and his gift of vivid and felicitous expression. The mental crises that punctuated his life could not dim his vitality: it suffuses his letters and shines out of what others wrote about him.

INDEX

This index, in addition to referring to articles and reviews in the present volume, also shows other major reviews of the year which have appeared in the *T.L.S.*
Date references and page numbers *in italic* are to articles and reviews in the *T.L.S.* not reprinted in this volume. Page numbers in parentheses are given only where the reference is not immediately obvious from the article.